BUILDING SOCIAL CAPITAL IN THAILAND
Fibers, Finance, and Infrastructure

Between 1984 and 1994 Thailand had the most rapid economic expansion in the world. This book offers an explanation of this successful record of economic growth in Thailand, and in Southeast Asia more generally. In a highly original argument, the book explains why Thai leaders adopted a market-driven strategy from the late 1950s, and also shows how the overseas Chinese in Thailand built on their community's social capital to overcome the market failures common to all developing countries. Unger takes an interdisciplinary approach, building on the literatures of social capital and embedded autonomy. He considers the unique organization of Thai society, and the impact this has had on the country's institutions, and their political and economic outcomes. The book includes detailed analysis of the financial and textile sectors, as well as the development of heavy industries and transportation infrastructure.

Danny Unger is Professor of Government at Georgetown University. He has published widely and was editor of *Japan's Emerging Global Role* (1993) and co-author, with Alasdair Bowie, of *The Politics of Open Economies*, published by Cambridge University Press in 1997. He has spent considerable time in both Thailand and Japan.

CAMBRIDGE ASIA-PACIFIC STUDIES

Cambridge Asia-Pacific Studies aims to provide a focus and forum for scholarly work on the Asia-Pacific region as a whole, and its component sub-regions, namely Northeast Asia, Southeast Asia and the Pacific Islands. The series is produced in association with the Research School of Pacific and Asian Studies at the Australian National University and the Australian Institute of International Affairs.

Editor: John Ravenhill

R. Gerard Ward and Elizabeth Kingdon (eds) *Land, Custom and Practice in the South Pacific* 0 521 47289 X hardback
Stephanie Lawson *Tradition Versus Democracy in the South Pacific* 0 521 49638 1 hardback
Walter Hatch and Kozo Yamamura *Asia in Japan's Embrace* 0 521 56176 0 hardback   0 521 56515 4 paperback
Alasdair Bowie and Daniel Unger *The Politics of Open Economies* 0 521 58343 hardback   0 521 586836 paperback
David Kelly and Anthony Reid (eds) *Asian Freedoms* 0 521 62035 X hardback   0 521 63757 0 paperback

To my parents, who gave me life and liberty.
And all the others without whom
I might have finished sooner
but been much less happy.

BUILDING SOCIAL CAPITAL
IN THAILAND

Fibers, Finance, and Infrastructure

DANNY UNGER

CAMBRIDGE
UNIVERSITY PRESS

PUBLISHED BY THE PRESS SYNDICATE OF THE UNIVERSITY OF CAMBRIDGE
The Pitt Building, Trumpington Street, Cambridge, United Kingdom

CAMBRIDGE UNIVERSITY PRESS
The Edinburgh Building, Cambridge CB2 2RU, UK   http://www.cup.cam.ac.uk
40 West 20th Street, New York, NY 10011–4211, USA   http://www.cup.org
10 Stamford Road, Oakleigh, Melbourne 3166, Australia

First published 1998

Printed in China by L. Rex Printing Company Ltd

Typeset in Baskerville 10/12 pt

A catalogue record for this book is available from the British Library

Library of Congress Cataloguing in Publication data
Unger, Danny, 1955–
Building social capital in Thailand: fibers, finance, and infrastructure/Danny Unger.
p.   cm. – (Cambridge Asia-Pacific studies)
Includes bibliographical references and index.
ISBN 0-521-63058-4 (alk. paper). – ISBN 0-521-63931-X (pbk. : alk. paper)
1. Thailand – Economic policy. 2. Thailand – Social policy.
3. Thailand – Foreign economic relations. 4. Thailand – Politics and government.
5. Industrial policy – Thailand. 6. Finance – Thailand. 7. Infrastructure (Economics) –
Thailand. I Title. II. Series.
HC445.U54   1998
338.9593–dc21   98–6508

ISBN 0 521 63058 4 hardback
ISBN 0 521 63931 X paperback

Contents

PART THREE

Acknowledgements

Over the years – let me not count them – I have accumulated an imposing baggage of debts to the many people who helped me complete this book.

Professors, the staff, and perhaps most of all other graduate students of the Department of Political Science at the University of California, Berkeley, made the experience a valuable one for me. I am particularly grateful to Professors Karl Jackson, Chalmers Johnson, Marty Landau, Herbert Phillips, and Robert Scalapino, as well as the teachers of Japanese and Thai, including Bill Kuo, at Berkeley. My fellow graduate students took on the ongoing task of socializing me into the profession. Clark Neher at Northern Illinois University also provided consistent encouragement over the years. Among those who made the most immediate contributions to this project by reading drafts of work first written long ago are Leslie Elliott Armijo, Karl Fields, Jim Mahon, Jim McGuire, and Liz Norville.

In Tokyo I received help from the members of the International House–based *kenkyukai*. In addition I benefited a great deal from comments on early drafts of this work from Rick Doner, Susan Pharr, and Clark Neher, and from Alisdair Bowie's comments on later drafts. At Georgetown University I received a great deal of encouragement from Jim Reardon-Anderson, David Steinberg and George Viksnins. In the course of the publication process I benefited enormously from comments and criticism from anonymous reviewers, as well as John Ravenhill, the series editor. My copyeditor Venetia Somerset helped me a great deal in making the book read more smoothly and the argument more accessible.

My thanks also go to the Departments of Education and Defense for the Foreign Language and Areas Studies fellowships that helped me through graduate school. The fellowship office at Berkeley was very helpful in guiding me through the process of getting a Fulbright-Hays Doctoral Dissertation Research Abroad fellowship. The Department of Education and the Fulbright office in Tokyo helped as well. Thanks to Susan Pharr, I was able to do further research as a post-doctoral fellow at Harvard University's program on US–Japan relations. And Charlie Pirtle at Georgetown University's School of Foreign Service helped me to get funding for a summer's follow-up research in Thailand.

My debts sprawl most widely when I turn to the many people in Japan and Thailand who helped me with various parts of the research that went into writing this book. There simply are too many people for me to try to name, but I remain very grateful to all those who took time to try to answer my questions. In Japan, particular thanks are due to Tanami Tatsuya of the the International House who really got me started, the late Karu Hiroshi of Keizai Doyukai, and Suehiro Akira, now of Tokyo University. Extraordinary assistance also came from Iwasaki Shinichi of Wacoal, Wada-san of Asahi Glass, Inoue Hisashi of Hitachi, Sonoda Shigeki of Ajinomoto, Tashiro Shigeo of Dupont-Toray, and Yoshikawa-san of Toray. In Thailand, I received especially great help from Chirayu Issarangkul Na Ayudhya of the Crown Property Bureau, Anand Panyarachun, then with Saha-Union, MR Chatumongkol Sonakul of the Ministry of Finance, Mehdi Krongkaew of Thammasat University, Boonchu Rojansathien, then of the Social Action Party, Snoh Unakul of the NESDB, Pramode Vidtayasuk of the Ministry of Industry, Chakramon Phasukavanich and Savit Bhothiwihok, then of the NESDB, Kusuma Sanitwongse, Chai-anan Samudavanija, and MR Sukhumbhand Paribatra of Chulalongkorn University, Tsubaki Teruo of Marubeni, Robert Muscat at the Department of Technical and Economic Cooperation, Janjai Ingkavet of the Metro Group, Peter Train of Coopers & Lybrand, and Buc Coleman of the National Fertilizer Corporation, Tarrin Nimmanahaeminda of the Siam Commercial Bank, Vichit Suraphongchai of the Bangkok Bank, Aswin Kongsiri of the Industrial Finance Corporation of Thailand, Virabongsa Ramangkura, then adviser to the prime minister, Atchaka Sibunruang of the BoI, Hattori-san of Thai Toray Textile Mills, Roger Montgomery of United States Aid for International Development, Paul Handley, then of the *Far Eastern Economic Review*, Motoda Tokio with the BoI, Anuporn Kasemsart of the Crown Property Bureau, Peter Beal of Development Services Ltd, Ehara Norihoshi of the Japan External Trade Organization, David Lyman of the American Chamber of Commerce, and for help in getting me started, Sirin Nimmanhaeminda of the PTT, Peter Mytri Ungpakorn of *The Nation*, Parichat Chotiya, then at Massachusetts Institute of Technology, Thanadee Sophonsiri of

D. S. Land Corp., and Chamnong and Khunying Supacharee Bhirom Bhakdi and their family. In Thailand, the tolerance of the National Research Council enabled me to secure a visa to conduct my research.

Finally, at Georgetown I received help from graduate students, including Mari Horne and Balbina Hwang.

DANNY UNGER
Georgetown University

Abbreviations

AFTA	ASEAN Free Trade Area
APEC	Asia-Pacific Economic Cooperation
ASEAN	Association of South-East Asian Nations
BECL	Bangkok Expressway Co. Ltd
BMA	Bangkok Metropolitan Administration
BoI	Board of Investment
BoT	Bank of Thailand
BTSC	Bangkok Transit System Corporation
ESB	Eastern Seaboard
ESDC	Eastern Seaboard Development Committee
ETA	Expressways and Rapid Transit Authority
GATS	General Agreement on Trade in Services
GATT	General Agreement on Tariffs and Trade
GDP	gross domestic product
IFCT	Industrial Finance Corporation of Thailand
IMF	International Monetary Fund
JETRO	Japan External Trade Organization
JICA	Japanese International Cooperation Agency
LTMO	Land Transport System Management Office
MoF	Ministry of Finance
MRTA	Metropolitan Rapid Transit Authority
NAP	New Aspiration Party
NEDB	National Economic Development Board
NEDCOL	National Economic Development Corporation Ltd
NESDB	National Economic and Social Development Board
NFC	National Fertilizer Corporation
NGO	non-government organization

NIE	newly industrializing economy
NPC	National Petrochemical Corporation
OECD	Organization for Economic Cooperation and Development
OECF	Overseas Economic Cooperation Fund (Japan)
PDP	Palang Dharma Party
PTA	Port Authority of Thailand
PTT	Petroleum Authority of Thailand
SEC	Securities and Exchange Commission
SET	Stock Exchange of Thailand
SRT	State Railways of Thailand
TTMA	Thai Textile Manufacturers' Association
UNIDO	United Nations Industrial Development Organization

A Note on Japanese and Thai Names

Japanese names in the text are surnames. For bibliographic references, their surnames appear first and, in those cases where their English language publications use Japanese name order (surname first), no comma appears between surname and given name. In referring to Thais in the text I use surnames to refer to authors on whose work I am drawing, but given names to refer to prominent Thais likely to be familiar to many readers.

Introduction

In a report on Thai public sector developmental roles, the World Bank argued in the late 1950s that Thai government agencies worked without a guiding vision, and that as a result state initiatives were uncoordinated and ineffective. The administrative apparatus was hobbled by tradition, hamstrung by status concerns, and short on personnel with technical skills; it lacked cooperation across departments and suffered from diffuse authority and responsibility. The Ministry of Agriculture, for example, provided few extension services and the Department of Industry did little for its clients. The obstacles to highway construction and maintenance included poor planning and *ad hoc* budgeting. And repeatedly the report's authors bemoaned the absence of information and Thai officials' lack of appreciation for the value of data.[1]

Thirty-five years later the World Bank was reporting that Thailand (known as Siam until 1939) had registered the most rapid economic expansion in the world between 1984 and 1994.[2] What happened? Had Thai public administration transformed itself over the 1960s and 1970s? Did growth take place despite a hapless public sector? Was Thailand's economic growth all the work of the Chinese-dominated private sector? Or of foreign capital? Was the economy's collapse in 1997 evidence of the ephemeral nature of its earlier success?

There is something in each of these. The abilities of Thai public officials and the performance of Thai state institutions, for example, did improve during the 1960s and thereafter. Nonetheless, the more important story in Thailand is the willingness and ability of Thai state officials, beginning in the late 1950s, to encourage private investment. Officials asserted only minimal control over the allocation of that investment; they left the Chinese, with the help of foreign capital, to transform Thailand's economy.

1

Thai state officials have presided over a market-driven strategy since the late 1950s. One publication ranked Thailand eighth in the world in economic freedom between 1993 and 1995.[3] If Thailand's economic success resulted from market forces, perhaps a Ministry of Finance (MoF) official had it right when he said of the government of Prime Minister Prem Tinsulanonda in the 1980s that its claim to fame was to have done nothing, to have sat back and let things happen.[4] State authorities and politicians, however, were not above trying to use available policy instruments to shape markets and favor friends. Various state agencies intervened extensively in markets to try to shape incentives facing private firms and to help them accumulate and reinvest profits. Officials used formal policy as well as "back door" interventions.[5]

But no overall strategy guided public sector initiatives. As in the East Asian newly industrializing economies (NIEs), Thai officials formulated five-year development plans. In Thailand, however, plans served only very loosely as predictors of actual policies. Even in the area of macroeconomic management, where the record of Thai officials was particularly strong until the mid-1990s, Ammar Siamwalla insisted on using the phrase "behavior pattern" in describing officials' selection of public policies: "Please note the use of the term 'behavior pattern' rather than the more purposive 'policy.' To use the latter term would be altogether too flattering."[6]

This book's central argument is that the relative absence of cohesive groups within the Thai polity worked against policy deliberations, consensus formation, and the mobilization of broad political support. Cohesive groups within which individuals can reach compromises and foster shared understandings of common problems constitute what social scientists call "social capital." The paucity of social capital in Thailand had the effect of weakening efforts by Thais to cooperate in pursuit of shared goals.

This book studies the impact that institutions have on politics and economics. It treats institutions as independent variables and notes their effects (or those of their absence) on politics and economics. It tries to explain the character of specific Thai institutions not only in terms of Thai political conflicts or the strategies leaders adopt to achieve their goals, but as products of broadly shared social habits and norms. This perspective suggests that institutions are not entirely products of apolitical institutional engineers concerned only to enhance economic efficiency. Neither can we explain them fully as creations of politicians sensitive to ways in which institutions distribute power, status, and wealth among various social groups. An adequate understanding of institutions requires that we recognize also that inherited ideas and norms about what is desirable and possible shape the ways in which institutions develop. Like enduring institutions, ideas and norms are shaped by "path dependence" – the shadow cast by the past. In short, broad cultural understandings have institutional consequences.[7]

For a full century following Thailand's[8] absorption into the world market economy, dating from the middle of the nineteenth century, Thais experienced little or no per capita income growth.[9] Beginning in the latter 1950s, however, the Thai economy began setting a remarkable record of stable and steady growth. The baht was one of the world's steadiest currencies, and Thailand was the only oil-importing developing country that managed economic growth in every year following the oil price hikes of the 1970s.[10]

This book offers a particular way of understanding Thailand's rapidly growing prosperity of the last forty years. We need to start by explaining how Thailand's politics became conducive to the adoption of a wealth-producing (market) economic framework. We also need ways of understanding the very favorable economic results that followed commitment to that framework. While we often conflate these two issues, it is necessary to separate them here. The first concerns conditions that facilitate adoption of an effective market strategy (Why did Thai leaders opt for a market strategy? Why were they able, politically, to implement one?); the second involves the ways in which individuals and firms respond to a framework of incentives once it is in place (Why did business perform so well?). In attempting to shed light on both these questions, this book argues that the political framework that gave rise to broadly market policies emerged from specific characteristics of Thai social organization, in particular the dearth of social capital. The nature of this social organization did not make leaders' adoption of market policies inevitable, but neither did leaders operate entirely independently of their political and socioeconomic context – one which constrained their policy choices. Broad social patterns of organization, the specific preferences of national leaders, and the administrative capacities of state agencies alone did not determine policies. Together, however, limited social capital, conjunctural factors inducing Thai leaders to favor market policies, and the previous failures of state agencies in implementing interventionist strategies predisposed policymakers to adopt a market strategy.

Development strategies that worked elsewhere by attracting political support and supplying political resources did not work in Thailand. In South Korea and Japan, for example, for decades active state intervention in the economy was successful in both economic and political terms. Of course other countries, in addition to Thailand, discovered that dirigiste strategies failed to yield economic growth or to attract adequate political support. In Thailand, however, the political elite was not sufficiently unified in the 1950s to sustain the failed strategy after it nearly bankrupted the treasury. Competition within a small circle of political leaders encouraged them to reach out to groups able to lend potent political resources – the military's arms and the Chinese business community's cash. As elsewhere, Thai leaders discovered the structural power of capital. Unless they provided investors with adequate guarantees against arbitrary seizure of their property or imposition of punitive regulatory controls, investors would fail to invest and the economy to grow. The structural power of capital therefore constrained Thai leaders. The influence of the United States and international financial institutions also shaped the leaders' policy choices. Ultimately, however, a particular conjuncture of political forces rooted in broad patterns of social organization determined the nature of the political coalition supporting market policies that Thai leaders forged in the late 1950s. This brief outline provides us with our initial, abstract answer to the first of the two questions posed above: why did a market strategy become attractive to Thai leaders? We turn now to the second issue.

A fairly serious commitment to the market helps to achieve sustained and rapid economic growth in any social setting. But market policies and even smoothly functioning markets may not always result in similar rates of economic performance – the vigor of the response to market economic policies varies. Different levels of "civic market competence" among groups across and within societies mean that even with similar macroeconomic policies and regulatory frameworks, economic effects diverge.[11] By adjusting prices and other incentives, increasing information or otherwise diminishing risk, state officials may be able to unleash investors' "animal spirits"[12] and stimulate a strong response to a broadly market-ruled economic framework. Public policies and institutions alone, however, may not entirely explain variation in responses to common economic conditions across countries. Where market failures persist, private actors will have to devise their own means of overcoming those impediments. Individuals and firms' capacity to bypass market failures depends in part on their ability to cooperate with one another, a skill that varies over time and across populations.

The nature of a nation's social organization helps to explain why some economies grow more rapidly than others. Market policies in some settings induce more ebullient responses than they do in others. Something like this claim is probably what people have in mind, for example, if they suggest that sluggish economic performance in the United Kingdom during much of the twentieth century resulted not only from bad economic policies but also from the rigidity of its social classes.[13] These classes, this claim implies, conditioned the ways in which individuals and firms responded to frameworks of material incentives. Not only formal institutions, but individuals' and firms' capacity to work with those institutions, conditioned outcomes. This book offers a broadly similar argument about Thai social organization, government policies, and the responses of Chinese firms in Thailand, suggesting new ways to understand the Thai economic record. Readers may be able to apply the concepts used here to broader comparative analysis of political economies.

A few disclaimers. While I try to make as convincing a case as possible for the usefulness of particular explanatory concepts, these concepts are of course only several among many intellectual tools that scholars find helpful in discerning patterns in complex social phenomena. I emphasize the importance of social organization as an explanatory variable, but do not try to claim that I have unearthed a Rosetta Stone that can unlock all the mysteries about social life that baffle us.

Readers may take exception to the assumption here, perhaps·in places implicit, that for analytical purposes we can on occasion suggest that society precedes the state. While surely most of us believe that society and state mutually constitute one another, denying the state its accustomed causal primacy may be a useful antidote to much of the work by political scientists in the field of political economy. In fact most studies of Southeast Asia's political economies do not offer state-centered explanations.[14] The disparity between the apparently only moderate capacities of Southeast Asian state institutions and their very strong economic performances perhaps encourages a search for other explanations. Doner, for example, invokes the impact of private sector governance on economic growth in the region.[15] Other scholars emphasize the ersatz[16] or derivative[17] nature of economic growth in the region. The present study, however, treats state weakness not only as cause of particular outcomes but also as result of specific patterns of social organization.

Some readers may be put off by what they discern here as the assertion of a Thai national character. In fact I discuss two national characters – those of the ethnic Thais and the immigrant Chinese. I do not assume that these characters are immutable, that their roots lie in genetic codes, or that ecological, economic, and political conditions cannot help us to identify their origins,[18] but I do argue that broad norms and patterns of acquired behavior condition the responses of groups of people to frameworks of material incentives.

These broad concepts are developed in Part I. In Part II they are used to explain the organization in Thailand of policymaking, private–public interaction, and market responses to state policies in three different economic sectors. To account for variation across these sectors, the book uses an analysis of structural factors, such as the number of actors involved and the ease with which they can detect cheating, that influence the ability of individuals and firms to cooperate with one another. The political economy literature generally refers to such impediments to cooperation as collective action problems. Chapters 4 through 6 examine the financial and textile sectors and the provision of heavy industrial and transport infrastructure. To explain the diverse patterns of interaction among firms and state agencies in the three sectors, I use an analysis of structural obstacles to cooperation, explaining variation in patterns of interaction among firms and state agencies across sectors of the Thai economy. These structural, or utilitarian, variables include the number of firms or state agencies seeking to cooperate, the frequency with which they encounter and seek to overcome shared problems, the duration of such problems and efforts, the extent to which the benefits that derive from cooperation can be divided among the firms and agencies, and the degree to which such benefits regularly arise.

A small number of commercial banks and regulatory authorities facilitated relatively intimate cooperation between private firms and public officials. Together they supported comparatively coherent policies and a domestic industry that served the economy well and generally remained robust until the mid-1990s. In contrast, a larger number of firms in the textile industry and more diffuse authority spread across several government regulatory agencies generally failed to collaborate effectively. The resulting inconsistent public policies, however, did not prevent this industry from growing rapidly and becoming Thailand's most important industry, by most measures, in the 1980s. Coordination between and among public and private agencies and firms was most conspicuously absent in the case of transportation infrastructure and heavy industry policies. The difficulty of parcelling out the "lumpy" benefits in this policy area hindered cooperation and resulted in a policy record whose only strengths came from inaction, which occasionally saved firms and state agencies from commitment to flawed projects.

This book has three central concerns. In trying to account, first, for the emergence of market policies and, second, for the strong response those incentives elicited in Thailand, it draws on an analysis of Thai social organization. The arguments are comparative, often implicitly contrasting the Thai case with other modes of social and economic organization. I emphasize Thai social organization both because such explanations are relatively underdeveloped in the political economy literature and because that literature's explanatory emphasis primarily on either market factors or the managerial capacities of state officials strikes me as not entirely satisfying. The book's third concern, as noted above, is a comparative analysis of patterns of policymaking, public–private interaction, and market responses across sectors of the Thai economy.

To preview the argument briefly, the nature of Thai social organization (the dearth of social capital) induces, all else equal, relatively small firms, some of which are parts of large business groups with interests spread across economic sectors; relatively weak organization among firms, whether to secure the privileges of oligopoly or more economically beneficial forms of cooperation; few and ineffective labor unions, peasant cooperatives, or consumer groups designed to overcome collective action problems among large numbers of geographically dispersed individuals; weak coordination among state agencies; and a diffuse, *ad hoc*, and clientelistic pattern of interest aggregation in which personal relations dominate while broad, participatory institutions such as political parties are weak. These broad patterns, however, manifest themselves in distinctive ways across different sectors of the economy. To sum up the discussion above: that variation results from the number of firms and state agencies involved, the number of times and length of time over which firms and agencies meet in order to cooperate, the degree to which they can share among themselves the gains they achieve, and the number of times such gains recur.

Chapter 1 elaborates the themes introduced here. Chapter 2 offers support for the argument that Thais and Chinese have distinctive endowments in social capital and suggests tentative explanations for those differences. Chapter 3 traces Thailand's political and economic development, sketches the Thai model of political economy, and describes the principal economic policymaking institutions and the key political actors and institutions that produce a distinctive politics of implementation in Thailand. Taken together, the chapters in Part I serve to inform the discussion of the cases covered in Part II.

Chapters 4, 5 and 6 analyze Thai economic policymaking and the forms of cooperation among private and state actors that emerged in different economic sectors. The analysis compares obstacles to collective action – the number of actors, the frequency and duration of interaction, and the divisibility and recurrence of benefits and costs to explain divergent patterns of cooperation within and among private and public institutions. A few commercial banks dominated the financial industry and generally worked closely with the Bank of Thailand (BoT) and the MoF. These state agencies generally eluded "capture" by their "clients," the private financial institutions they regulated.

Together they supported fairly effective state policies and a strong domestic financial sector, achievements which unraveled during the simultaneous transitions to a more liberal regulatory regime and to more open politics in the 1990s. The textile industry twinned poorly organized state agencies (in particular, the Ministry of Industry and the Board of Investment [BoI]) with a disorganized private sector. The resulting public policies were generally ineffectual, but they did not prevent the emergence of an important Thai industry, largely because authoritative state measures were often ineffective, did not hinder firms unduly, and because the scope for market failures in the industry was limited. Competition among government agencies and politicians provided private firms with various ways of getting official support, which they used in some instances to offset the obstacles thrown up by other groups of officials. Finally, in the development of heavy industries and transport infrastructure, the record of achievement was less consistent. Thailand developed a strong petrochemical industry dependent on tariff protection, but failed until the mid-1990s to nurture a fertilizer complex. At considerable cost, officials delayed the construction of ports and related infrastructure. Eventually most of these projects were put in place, but with the initially planned dominance of the public sector giving way to a leading role for the private sector. And at far higher cost, Bangkok's mass transit systems faced an uninterrupted series of delays.

The analysis of different economic sectors in Thailand concludes that the greatest obstacles to cooperative economic activity occurred where no leviathan could impose solutions to collective action problems, where benefits and costs were not easily divided among claimants, and where prospects of gain from future collaboration were limited or the gains were indivisible. Stable and effective policymaking and performance in exchange rate and monetary policymaking until the mid-1990s resulted from the policy dominance of a small set of institutions (the BoT, MoF, and a few dominant private financial institutions). Similarly, though to a lesser degree, a small number of actors shaped financial and fiscal policies. Policy performance generally was less strong in other (nonfinancial) industrial policymaking that targeted particular sectors. Qualified success in the case of the textile industry resulted from efficient market forces and limited private sector governance. The greatest policymaking problems accrued, however, when large actors engaged in zero-sum competition in areas that precluded resort to market solutions, such as the provision of infrastructure.

PART ONE

Chapter 1

The Stock of Social Capital in Thailand

The approach used in this book in trying to understand patterns in Thailand's political economy has similarities to the literature on social capital (discussed below) and that on state embeddedness. Like the latter, the analysis does not draw exclusively on a study of either state or social institutions but situates the institutions or agencies of the state within the surrounding society. While it is at times analytically useful to isolate market behavior and political institutions from their encompassing social contexts, that step carries costs because it distorts our understanding of how markets and institutions actually work.[1]

In thus "embedding" Thai state institutions, I am making three arguments about the reciprocal interaction between state and society.[2] First, the impact of state agencies' autonomy (the extent to which officials can select goals and policies rather than having them dictated by other groups) on their ability to govern well is indeterminate.[3] State officials enjoying autonomy from demands by social groups and able to formulate and implement coherent agendas may enhance broad state capacities to achieve policy goals. The autonomy of some Leninist parties, for example, may have made them better able to transform the societies they governed. But autonomy can mean isolation, and it can undermine state officials' efforts to achieve policy goals.[4] Isolated, officials may have inadequate access to information and be unable to create effective political coalitions that reach out into society and draw on the support of social groups. In *A Suitable Boy*, for example, Vikram Seth depicts a local official facing the prospect of periodic rotation. By rotating officials, central government presumably hoped to make its administrative machinery more effective by checking the development of alliances between its agents and local power-holders. But how, asks the (corrupt) local *patwari*, can an outsider really understand the texture of

9

the life of the village?[5] In short, we cannot, a priori, discern a link between degrees of state officials' autonomy and their ability to select and achieve their policy goals.

Second, state officials draw on traditions of social organization and broad value-orientations similar to those of others in business and society more generally. Officials' worldviews and behaviors are not necessarily distinctive. In such cases patterns of social organization that facilitate or hinder cooperation between private clubs, firms, unions, and a host of other associations should also affect officials working in state agencies. In the Thai case, however, the situation is more complex. Ethnic Chinese with distinctive social capital endowments dominate the private sector, while ethnic Thais dominate state agencies.

Patterns of social organization condition the performance of groups both in society and within the state apparatus. But I do not suggest (my third point) that the state is just one among many social institutions. While analytically we should embed state agencies within broader social networks and value-orientations, and recognize the state's essential social character, the institution of the state remains unique. Its monopoly on the legitimate management of violence, its gatekeeper functions, and its international identity[6] afford its officials potential powers qualitatively different than those of actors situated outside the state. Hence my argument steers a course between ignoring state agency on the one hand[7] and reifying the state and ignoring its social embeddedness on the other. The aim is to draw on the strengths of statist approaches as well as pluralist traditions that often underplay the state's crucial and independent roles.

Embedded analyses of state institutions that use a "state-in-society"[8] or "bring society back in"[9] approach emphasize the ways in which supportive social organization can augment state capacities. Migdal and colleagues argue that particular configurations of state–society relations condition state capacities.[10] This book offers a similar argument, trying to avoid an "undersocialized conception"[11] of the state in accounting for the weaknesses of particular Thai state agencies. States cannot be understood adequately separate from the social context in which they are embedded. The ability of top state officials to shape both society and state depends on their capacity to harness the organizational resources of social groups as well as to create for themselves a degree of autonomy. The embedded state perspective sees state officials drawing on the resources of social groups and authority structures to enhance their power. In short, this is the "judo" view of state capacity in which state officials try to harness the organizational endowments of society to their own ends.

Many academics see the state in functional terms as an artifice designed to overcome collective action obstacles. These obstacles post challenges for which markets may offer no solutions. Who, for example, will pay to provide for national defense, clean water, or the enforcement of contracts? Hence the functions of the state. The state appears, in this view, as a problem-solving institutional innovation that emerges because of a lack of other socially based solutions. For example, Gerschenkron saw the state as substituting for social institutions to address problems specific to late industrializers; private institutions managed on their own to overcome many of the more modest obstacles that confronted the early industrializers.[12] Durkheim, however, argued that where no social groups mediated between the state and atomized individuals, the result would be "a veritable sociological monstrosity."[13]

To some degree, the state's capacity to provide public goods and to satisfy the core interests of capital can depend on the extent and nature of social links with the state. Kohli writes that the simultaneous centralization and powerlessness of state authority in India resulted from the underdevelopment of channels linking central state institutions and society.[14] Making a similar point, Emmerson suggests that as the Indonesian state grew less soft, "less a milieu, more a machine," and "inflicted development" while severing its ties to mobilized social groups, it endangered its capacities.[15] Shue argues that the transformative capacity of the Chinese Communist Party declined over time as links to social groups atrophied.[16] An institutional capacity for mediating conflict, fostering compromise and consensus, and articulating support for a policy direction can be a crucial base for state economic governance.

State officials' links to social groups are important because they afford political support for officials' initiatives and information about general political conditions. They can also provide more specific information necessary in designing, say, effective industrial policies. Japanese state regulators, for example, typically launched policies that gained the support of firms whose interests were affected most directly. Indeed officials typically consulted at length with those firms before enacting policies (and during and after as well). The state's general effectiveness, however, may depend not only on the nature of its links (corporatist, pluralist) to society but also on the nature and extent of organization in society itself. Effective state-led economic growth or a functioning capitalist developmental state may be rooted in a society well enough organized to aggregate and express its interests to state officials and mobilize social support for state initiatives. The active support and participation of business becomes critical where the state is grappling with issues of concern to highly capital-intensive economic sectors. In such cases firms risk large assets that cannot easily be transferred to other productive uses, and as a result rely increasingly on a predictable policy environment. Business firms need to be able to forecast future policy conditions. They need, in short, credible commitments on the part of the state. Obtaining such commitments requires that state officials have information about and understanding of firms' needs.

We can see the dramatic consequences of the absence of such commitments in the tragi-comedy that surrounded plans to provide mass transit in Bangkok (see Chapter 6). Thai state officials' difficulty in formulating clear economic plans or implementing them smoothly resulted, in part, from their inability to rely on the support of a well-organized private sector. No political party or business association was able to act as an authoritative voice articulating the concerns of key business firms. Without organized (business) groups in society able to articulate consensus among firms or various social groups, it becomes extremely difficult for state officials to mobilize support for particular policies. Leadership becomes exceedingly difficult when society does not have in place some organizing building blocks. Sun Yat-sen faced this problem in China early this century. In referring to the daunting task of building institutions based on China's vast but poorly organized population, he drew on the metaphor of sheets of sand. Thai officials confront similar impediments. Because private associations, political parties, or the legislature fail to forge compromises prior to policy formulation, officials must do so at the stage of policy implementation. Only after government agencies announce policies do groups then mobilize, often to throw up obstacles, filibuster, and eventually strike new deals. To a striking degree, the state and its policy outputs remains the only political stage in town.[17]

This context leaves Thai policymakers in a situation analogous to Herbert Simon's watchmaker who found himself, when a single part went awry, having to dismantle all his efforts and begin anew. Simon noted the advantages for the watchmaker of working with modules of assembled parts that could then be put together; in the event of an error, the watchmaker had only to reassemble the bits of the affected module.[18] With a relative dearth of effective interest-aggregating institutions, Thai policymakers make policies with little benefit from such modules, and a single dissenting voice, like the watchmaker's stray part, can send the deliberative process back to square one.

Building Cooperative Links

In addition to the literature on state embeddedness, this book uses concepts developed in the literature on trust and social capital, exploring the institutional consequences of variable affiliational impulses. It suggests ways in which the specific social capital endowments, both of

Thais working within state agencies and of Chinese in private firms and associations, shaped Thai economic and political institutions. The concepts of social capital and trust alone do not lend themselves easily to firm predictions about the nature of state–society relations, the effectiveness of state administration, public policy choice, or the competitiveness of different economic actors. It is nonetheless possible to derive a limited set of analytical tools that offer means of understanding particular characteristics of a country's political economy.

The political scientist Robert Putnam suggests that dense networks of social groups (i.e. social capital) facilitate cooperation in pursuit of common goals in several ways. Networks promote recurrence of co-operative undertakings and the building of linkages among actors in different activities; they inculcate norms of reciprocity, enhance information flows (including reputations for trustworthiness), and establish common understandings of frameworks within which collaboration can occur.[19] The economic historian Carlo Cipolla argues that social capital and state enforcement worked together in the development and spread of credit during the Renaissance in Europe. Identification with communities helped broaden circles of trust and, with the backing of law, facilitated the mobilization of the community's savings.[20] Esman and Uphoff maintain that active social networks are crucial to economic development,[21] and Arrow suggests that poverty may result where there is little trust.[22]

Much of the literature on trust and social capital collapses two analytically separable issues. While the distinction between the two is fairly subtle and not always analytically important, it is worthwhile disentangling them. One concept – let's call it "sociability" – affects the density of cooperative social groups pursuing shared goals that they cannot easily achieve when acting alone. Sociability is rooted in the characteristics of individuals, presumably influenced by individuals' preferences and their social skills. Some (groups of) people may attach more value to affiliation or social identity than others (or, to put it differently, some may cling more tenaciously to autonomy than others). In any event, even if different (groups of) people share preferences, they may differ in their ability to overcome obstacles to effective, sustained cooperation.

Sociability concerns individual attributes, but assumes significance only in the context of social interaction. Differing degrees of sociability affect the propensity to form groups, the longevity of those groups, and their effectiveness in fostering cooperation in pursuit of shared goals. One of this book's central assumptions is that Thais traditionally had a relatively low propensity to form groups and those they formed tended not to endure and were not very effective in fostering cooperation (see Chapter 2). Thais were not very sociable.

The second concept, "social capital," also involves the nature and extent of cooperation-inducing groups. Social capital is a measure of the density of such groups, which constitute a kind of social infrastructure. Enduring cooperative groups constitute social capital. Social capital is the fossil record of successful past efforts to institutionalize ongoing cooperation. The concept concerns not individual attributes but those of a community.

Because the maintenance of already constituted groups may be easier than the formation of new ones, members of a community with limited sociability may be able to draw on accumulated social capital. Since largely conjunctural catalysts may give rise to groups, and their value may induce individuals to make the investments necessary to sustain them, social capital may be greater than we would expect from an analysis of sociability alone. One consequence that flows from this argument is that even if sociability is constant, the distribution of social capital across different sectors of an economy may vary. As noted above, social capital will also vary because of the different obstacles to collective action in various economic sectors.

The concepts of sociability and social capital are tightly interwoven. Social capital may create sociability, because of its use-it-or-lose-it qualities, but sociability also may account for strong social capital. In any case, not only sociability was traditionally limited among Thais, but social capital as well. Subsequent discussion of these concepts generally will not require differentiation between them, and will refer simply to "social capital."

Social Capital

It is convenient to use the term "social capital" in discussing collaboration among groups because of its familiarity among social scientists. But we might just as well use the term "social infrastructure." Like physical infrastructure, social infrastructure can increase economic productivity and has considerable positive externalities. Social capital is also loosely analogous to total factor productivity. Economists recognize that difficult-to-measure conditions (in particular, efficient application of production factors) have important effects on economic growth. Total factor productivity purports to measure these effects. Economists are fortunate. They can assign measures to many of the inputs that combine to produce goods and services, so they can elect to employ as a concept – total factor productivity – a measure of unexplained variance in economic growth. Political scientists who study social capital, as well as economists employing the total factor productivity concept, have some clear hypotheses about the causal links between their variables.

Economists, however, are more confident than most other social scientists that they understand much of what they study and therefore can believe significant a variable defined in terms of unexplained variance.

To offer another simile from economics, social capital may work as a multiplier increasing the stimulus stemming from a given commitment of resources. Yoshihara, for example, noted the superior educational performance among South Korean children compared to Thai children despite comparable commitments of *public* resources.[23] Greater private investments of money and time, the distribution of spending across primary, secondary, and tertiary sectors, and social networks that reinforced norms emphasizing the importance of education explained much of the variance.

Whatever the underlying propensity of a given population of individuals to form and sustain groups for cooperative undertakings (their sociability), the density of such groups is likely to vary in different areas of social, political, and economic life. Although sociability is a deeply ingrained element of culture that does not change instantaneously in response to altered incentive structures, levels of sociability do change. This book makes no assumptions about the pace of such change. In Thailand, however, rapid urbanization and increasing affluence seem to have contributed to an observable increase in business and civil society groups.[24] While it is difficult to quantify either,[25] the argument here conceives of sociability and social capital as continuous variables. Individuals and societies have differing endowments of sociability and social capital, rather than dividing into haves and have-nots. The important point is that particular collective action problems make cooperation to achieve some shared goals easier than cooperation to attain others. Differing sociability and social capital endowments explain why some groups of individuals fail where others succeed in overcoming comparable obstacles.

To recapitulate, by sociability I refer to the relative ease and urgency with which people join and cooperate to achieve goals that would elude them, or could be achieved only at much greater expense, if they were operating on their own. Sociability involves what Fukuyama calls "arational habits"[26] that presumably vary across populations and can grow or wither over time. An accumulated stock of cooperation-facilitating social arrangements constitutes social capital. The existence of a variety of habits of heart and mind (sociability), and of institutional arrangements (social capital), can foster success in cooperative undertakings. Social capital, even with a relative dearth of sociability, can also foster cooperation. All else equal, however, groups are apt to work more effectively where there is sociability.

A couple of additional points are in order here. In discussing sociability and social capital, I make claims about the relative effectiveness of communities in cooperating to achieve their shared goals. As yet, however, I have only tentatively linked sociability and social capital to particular outcomes, whether political democracy or economic growth. As others have observed,[27] ease in forming cooperative groups may be associated as much with communalism, criminality, or fascism as with democracy, as much with conflict as with cooperation,[28] as much with growth-choking distributional coalitions as with small-scale family-based flexible firms or large multinational enterprises.

The ease with which individuals cohere into effective groups (sociability) is intimately linked to levels of trust. The literature on trust distinguishes between trust among communal or family members and trust that extends beyond such groups (generalized morality).[29] As will be evident below, both forms of trust are significant for this analysis, as is the distinction between them. These two types of trust can be inversely related. Trust may be particularly high within social networks characterized by high degrees of closure and high entry barriers.[30] The intensity of group identification that facilitates trust can depend in part on sharp awareness of a boundary that separates us and them. By contrast, low levels of trust may be associated with a relative facility for integrating "others."

Effects of High and Low Levels of Social Capital

The stock of sociability and social capital in a given society influences the institutions that are likely to emerge, the ways in which they operate, and the degrees of success they enjoy in reaching the goals favored by their dominant members. We often argue that where private groups are unable to undertake initiatives on their own, state authorities step in to assume the tasks. This assumption is at the heart of most accounts of the origins of the state. Some political scientists also contend that a pervasive state role is an indicator of social failure. At least implicitly, they give causal precedence to individuals in society: individuals fail, therefore the state moves in. They see the failures of individuals and social groups as triggering a kind of default mode in which the state substitutes for inadequate social institutions.[31] Somewhat confusingly, another broadly held view is that ambitious states can vitiate associations and trust within society.[32] By taking on crucial tasks or suppressing active social groups, the state ensures the atrophy of those groups. In addition to influencing the location of the boundaries between state and society, social capital endowments also may affect the size of businesses,[33] the extent to which they are integrated vertically,[34] and the extent of their commercial success.

What are likely to be the consequences of high levels of sociability and social capital? Putnam has suggested that a community's rich associational life facilitates the tasks of governance and results in more effective democratic government. Fukuyama maintains that trust enables people to work cooperatively in large privately owned firms. We might then expect communities with abundant social capital to exhibit good democratic governance and to have comparatively more large private firms. Using Fukuyama's reasoning, we might argue that large public organizations should also operate more effectively where social capital is abundant. After all, large organizations of any kind need much information exchange to operate effectively. While public agencies can bring to bear the authority of the state, and are therefore different from private associations (trust becomes less crucial where an external referee can monitor compliance), they also depend on the exchange of information and widespread delegation of authority between principals and agents. It seems reasonable to expect, therefore, that as state authorities' dependence on violence diminishes, their ability to coordinate effectively in large groups is likely to vary with the prevailing levels of social capital.

What consequences might we expect to stem from these initial hypotheses? The ability to create large private firms might make it more likely that firms in a given economy are able to establish a presence in economic sectors where scale economies are particularly significant. For reasons discussed below, firm size could also affect the asset portfolios of business groups.[35] Abundant social capital might also be associated with effective state governance if it contributed to coordination among actors within the state and between them and private groups.

Broad networks of enduring social groups are also likely to result in the creation of "distributional coalitions" that organize not to produce wealth but to use political power to influence its allocation. Olson argues that the proliferation of such coalitions would tend to impede economic growth because they would increasingly distort market signals.[36] The extent to which they result in market distortions, and the impact of those distortions, however, may be indeterminate. On the one hand distributional coalitions such as labor unions and industrial associations can use political power to distort market signals and reduce efficiency and flexibility; on the other they may improve state officials' access to information necessary for making and adjusting policies, and provide political support for those policies.

Distributional coalitions that are organized effectively enough to make demands of state officials may stimulate the administrative efficiency of the state. In particular, the articulation and assertion of claims from outside the state can blunt tendencies among state functionaries to pursue their own goals, such as job security or enhanced budgets, which are divorced from their formal administrative functions. Indeed, the notion that public officials unchecked by external demands or monitors would be ineffective was at the heart of Riggs' study of Thai politics in the 1950s and 1960s. Riggs argued that the absence of politically potent groups in society resulted in a "bureaucratic polity" in which the unchecked exercise of state power was of, for, and by bureaucrats.[37] Jacobs also believed that the combination of atomized villages and the "community system" through which officials controlled foreigners in Bangkok[38] resulted, through the same mechanism, in poor administrative performance.[39] Shor speculated that the weakness of local government in Thailand stemmed from the absence of politically active distributional coalitions outside the state.[40] Siffin's study of the Thai bureaucracy noted the impact of weak channels linking businesses to state officials.[41] And Sutton recognized the difficulties in leading an inarticulate society.[42] In essence, these researchers held that Thailand's public administration was weak because the society in which the state was embedded was atomized or, in the case of the Chinese, tightly controlled by the state. The very absence of effective distributional coalitions left the state without interlocutors or external claimants and failed to stimulate the development of administrative capabilities.

A dearth of networks of social groups leaves state officials with few partners when they try to identify and redress social concerns. This may induce poor state performance, although other possible outcomes would include a perfectly insulated state with modest ambitions (a colonial state)[43] or an extremely well-organized state with large ambitions (the early Bolshevik state, perhaps). In Thailand, this dearth of social capital diminished state officials' capacity to foster social change and ultimately facilitated officials' adoption of and reliance on market strategies. The Thai context differs from those that struck political scientist Samuel Huntington, who noted that politically mobilized societies could make so many demands that they choked developing states' administrative machinery.[44]

Where social capital is scarce, what forms of political mediation should we expect to find between individuals and state agencies? If organized social groups beyond kin are not plentiful and cohesive, a social form of corporatism seems unlikely to emerge. State corporatism might develop, but to be effective and to have more than formal significance would require considerable capacities on the part of state officials. The most likely outcome would be a kind of atomized and *ad hoc* pluralism in which many actors could exert influence. In short, a scarcity of social capital might predict something like Samudavanija's characterization of Thai politics as "institutionalized anarchy."[45] In Thailand, where clientage networks are pervasive but more transient

than those in many developing countries, we could expect this pluralism to work through such channels. Where social capital is scarce, we
would expect that the desultory nature of interest aggregation might
also contribute to policymaking patterns in which the main political
struggles occurred in the process of implementing rather than formulating policy. This is in fact an important feature of the Thai policy
process noted above and in later chapters.

In sum, all else equal, high levels of social capital may be associated
with larger firms, a more effective state apparatus, and a large number
of enduring distributional coalitions; elements of corporatist interest
representation are likely. In contrast, low sociability would correlate
with smaller firms, a less effective state, fewer and less successful distributional coalitions, and looser, more pluralistic forms of interest
aggregation. The actual economic impacts of varying levels of social
capital would depend on the economic and technological requirements
of particular economic sectors[46] and the duration of stable economic
conditions.[47]

The impact of distributional coalitions on economic growth, as noted
above, is indeterminate; similarly, the effect of firm size on economic
growth is uncertain. Fukuyama suggested that large firms may be
necessary to gain a competitive presence in particular industries characterized by high research and development costs and other scale
economies.[48] Recent changes in firm organization and the spread of
flexible production around the world, however, cast some doubt on the
importance of firm size for rapid economic growth,[49] and as Fukuyama
himself notes, larger size is not correlated with rates of economic
growth.[50]

But firm size may be important for two other reasons. First, a few
firms of considerable scale in a particular sector should face fewer collective action problems than those confronting a large number of firms
within a sector. Hence large firm size may be associated with more
extensive and effective sectoral organization. Even if this bore no relationship to economic outcomes, it should affect firms' ability to organize for political action and to capture economic rents (profits higher
than those available in perfectly functioning markets). In fact, however,
we cannot assume that firms support the creation of producer cartels.
With high levels of trade dependence, competitiveness, and multinational production strategies, for example, large firms might use their
influence on behalf of low levels of protection and limited state regulation of competition.[51] So we cannot assume that firms in concentrated
sectors will favor limits on competitive pressures.

Nonetheless, we have other reasons for believing that firm size is associated with firms' preferences. If characteristics of social organization

militated against the creation of large firms, in the long run this would imply the creation of more and smaller firms and more diversification, including across economic sectors. As a result, private assets in aggregate would be less dedicated, less asset-specific, more flexible, and their owners would be less apt to invest in political resources in order to protect their assets in any single sector. In short, the intensity of social preferences favoring any particular economic sector or policies would, all else equal, be more moderate than if assets were more concentrated.[52]

We cannot draw firm conclusions about the impact of state effectiveness on economic growth. Certainly state capacity beyond some threshold is necessary to provide a minimum set of public goods, including a modicum of stability, the enforcement of contracts and law in general, the management of macroeconomic policies, and the ability to extract the revenue necessary to pay for those goods. It seems reasonable to suppose that greater state capacity to provide public goods would induce further economic prosperity, even if returns diminished as authorities moved from top-priority to lower-priority goods.

The impact of state capacity on economic performance must ultimately be uncertain, however, because able administration may allow for longer commitments to less effective development strategies than would otherwise be the case. A highly skilled administrative apparatus, for example, might enable an adequate economic performance within a socialist economy and thereby postpone the abandonment of socialism. Or, to offer a more concrete example, the slow pace of economic deregulation in Japan might have resulted in part from the limited degree to which there emerged administrative rigidities that retarded economic growth. Because the system was not entirely broken, it was harder to fix. And, closer to the concerns of this book, the Thai state's extravagant administrative weaknesses helped to explain the relatively brief duration of a quasi-state-led strategy in the middle of this century (although many other countries adhered far longer to demonstrably disastrous policies). We might also suppose that a particularly effective state would be better able to elicit public support, or at least to quell public opposition. Hence its commitment to flawed policies producing weak results might continue longer than would otherwise be the case.

Finally, there are even grounds for hesitating before suggesting any correlation between social capital endowments and state capacities. A propensity to form enduring groups among state officials might hinder effective state performance. For example, officials might form exclusive bonds within smaller state agencies and thereby impede cooperation across such agencies formally subordinate, for example, to ministries. We cannot assume that the impulse leading to the creation of bonds of loyalty within the smaller agencies will also express itself in terms of identification with the larger ministries or state administrative apparatus within which the smaller units are embedded.[53] Officials' capacity for loyalty and identification are unlikely to be infinitely promiscuous. Hence affiliative urges may not induce either cohesion both within agencies and within a complex and hierarchical state administrative apparatus.

To summarize the argument to this point, low levels of social capital may be associated with fewer distributional coalitions, particularly where actors face daunting collective action obstacles and their assets are flexible, as is true of unskilled workers and many labor-intensive firms. Furthermore, if firms subdivide and move into new business activities (the Chinese pattern), rather than grow in size, this may induce asset diversity. With social preferences accordingly less intense, state officials may have a relatively free hand in committing themselves to broad market development strategies. Another plausible outcome would be the emergence of a predatory state exploiting the limited level of effective opposition in order to seize the field for itself. This is a fair representation of the Thai state between the late 1930s and the mid-1950s. Furthermore, as argued above, with limited social capital, an *ad hoc*, weakly institutionalized pattern of interest aggregation is more likely to result than a corporatist one. Such a polity is likely to serve poorly in effecting policy compromises among the interests of different groups. The result is apt to be a politics of implementation, where critical adjustments among interests take place within state agencies as they try to implement policies. This may well diminish policy stability and the credibility of state commitments. State officials, of course, may be relatively more effective in achieving their aims where the obstacles to cooperation among state agencies or between them and private groups are few (as, for example, in coordination games in which it is more nearly possible for all groups to achieve their preferred outcomes); as a result of historically contingent factors; where there are few actors; where task requirements compel frequent intercourse over a long period; and where benefits and costs are recurring and readily divisible. These various probabilistic statements are summarized in Figure 1.

Applying the Argument to the Thai Case

The next chapter argues that Thais traditionally were not joiners; they were not embedded within networks of enduring social groups pursuing shared goals. In this respect Thais differed from the Chinese immigrants. Low levels of sociability help to explain broad patterns of Thai state policymaking, private organization, and interaction between the

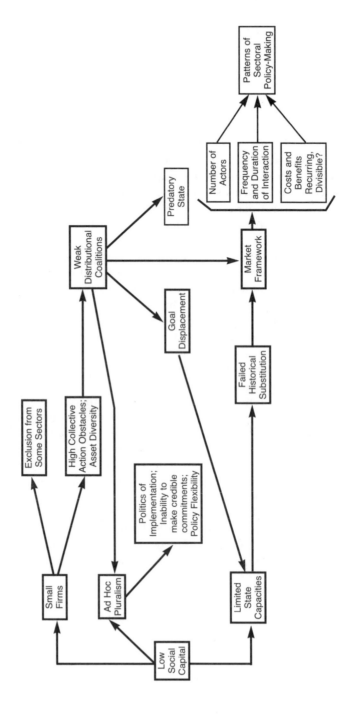

Figure 1 Economic and political consequences of limited social capital

two. We can use the concept of social capital to compare Thailand with other economies characterized by different social endowments. To explain variation in policymaking patterns across sectors in Thailand, however, it is necessary to look at the varying obstacles to collective action, including the number of actors, the frequency of their inter-action, and the extent to which benefits and costs are recurring and divisible. These issues are discussed at greater length in Part II but are briefly foreshadowed here.

Low levels of social capital in Thailand help to account for the ease with which state officials committed themselves to market strategies and the credibility of those commitments.[54] Certainly other factors, including external inducements, the nature of competition within and among elite circles, and the pariah status of the Chinese economic elite, were also important in accounting for Thailand's broadly liberal eco-nomic policies. And clearly levels of social capital alone cannot predict such outcomes. Nonetheless, without pervasive or effective organiza-tion of popular groups, state officials generally did not feel it necessary to steer wealth toward particular social groups (other than themselves). The far richer social capital of Chinese society contributed to the extension of dominant business groups' interests across different eco-nomic sectors (their asset diversity). The Chinese in Thailand were often embedded within social (Overseas Chinese) networks extending beyond Thailand's borders. Their early international orientations, and the fact that their economic interests were spread across different eco-nomic activities, reduced pressures on state officials to provide firms with extensive protection and nurture. Limited social capital in Thailand also helps to account for the weaknesses of state agencies, the small amount of coordination between agencies, and the widespread factionalism, and it appears to be consistent with factionalism within the national elite and its inability to forge an enduring and dominant political coalition. In Thailand, coups and leadership changes were frequent. Unlike most other countries in the region, no stable govern-ing coalition emerged to dominate the country's politics. Intense and unstable intra-elite political competition ensured a plurality of points of access for private interests, resulting in greater competition for eco-nomic rents. The economic inefficiencies were consequently fewer than might otherwise have resulted from cozy (crony) links among offi-cials, politicians, and firms.[55]

The weakness of Thais' urge to affiliate contributed to a general poverty of institutional mechanisms for bargaining among social inter-ests. Political parties, business associations, and labor unions, for example, had only limited roles in governance. As a result, achieving agreement on public policies often followed rather than preceded policy declarations. Political contest concentrated within the state during the policy implementation process. Thai state officials and firms could not rely on political parties, corporatist bargaining arrangements, or policy debate in a parliamentary setting to prearrange compromises before officials articulated public policies. Thai politics not only lacked smoke-filled rooms from which authoritative decisions might emerge but was also without effective forums for bargaining agreements among social groups.

Thai policymakers could not readily fashion credible policy commitments. The frequent reversals of fortune evident in Thailand's distinctive politics of implementation made policy commitments tenuous.[56] In short, without the associated conceptual underpinnings, Thailand was blessed, and cursed, with a politics of checks and balances. These forces, however, acted not so much through formal institutions as envisioned by Montesquieu and Madison, but in *ad hoc* fashion. And these checks and balances operated not so much in the crafting of policies as in their implementation – the actual locus of Thai policymaking.

Markets and Social Capital

States and firms are two examples of institutions that can overcome market failures and increase the scope for cooperative economic behavior. There is a variety of institutions that can play similar roles. Between the level of the individual and that of the state, people come together to achieve common goals. The nature of the institutions that people form to grapple with economic problems varies with the specific economic challenges they face, the preferences of the powerful, and the particular social skills and social capital endowments within a society. Hence even in the face of similar collective action dilemmas, people can make use of different kinds of institutions to achieve shared goals.[57] Markets, states, banks, labor unions, business networks, cartels, business associations, and vertically integrated corporations may all be useful in getting to grips with specific economic tasks. The propensity to form different kinds of institutions results not only from the nature of the tasks confronted, or the distributional consequences of different institutional solutions, but also from the social capital on which members of a given society can draw. A general deficit in sociability may have important economic consequences. From his study of Montegrano in southern Italy, for example, Banfield concluded that the poverty he observed was a consequence of villagers' inability to extend cooperation beyond the nuclear family.[58]

Limited social capital may also influence broad patterns of political economy. Most analyses of Thailand's political economy, for example, perceived a contrast (at least until the baht's collapse in 1997) between relatively effective macroeconomic policymaking and seemingly haphazard, contradictory, and rent-seeking sectoral policymaking. Part of the reason for these divergent outcomes in Thailand was that political leaders delegated authority to technocrats in macroeconomic policymaking agencies, but were less apt to do so elsewhere.

The nature of social solidarity and habits of association, however, may also be important in understanding this issue. Macroeconomic policies tend to cleave social interests across broad economic classes. Tight money policies, for example, may hurt wage and salary earners, as well as those on fixed incomes, while benefiting asset-holders. If people are organized horizontally, in class-based voluntary organizations such as labor unions, occupational groups, political parties, or farmers' groups, they may be more prone to respond to political appeals that differentiate interests along such lines. Some politicians might offer, for example, low interest rates to increase employment by stimulating economic activity. Others might champion tight money policies favoring individuals holding financial assets. If, however, they associate with one another mainly through vertical networks of clientage, politicians seeking political support might find it more useful to be able to distribute discreet favors than to make broad programmatic appeals. They might offer voters, for example, local construction projects, recognizing that more broadly based appeals would fail to mobilize votes. Politicians would employ those policies that seemed best to elicit support, and in doing so would reinforce those patterns of organization. Once established, the relative autonomy of macroeconomic policymaking would in any case compel politicians to look elsewhere for opportunities to reward supporters. Such opportunities were particularly important in Thailand, where political success depended on buying supporters, either through favors or directly buying their votes, and laws limited the extent to which politicians could mobilize funds through legal channels.

Making Sense of the Thai Case

Over the last forty years, political instability, frequent coups d'état and changes in constitutions, and the incapacity of many parts of the Thai government bureaucracy have not prevented the rise of an impressive commercial power. Before massive speculative attacks on the baht in 1997, Thai official foreign exchange reserves exceeded $US35 billion. How should we account for Thailand's economic success since the late 1950s? We can answer that question in highly simplified form, leaving further amplification for subsequent chapters. By the

1950s the traditional Thai nobility, the Thai military, and Chinese business elites (rapidly assimilated as a result of liberal policies, an open culture, and a fluid social structure) had learned to coexist and exchange benefits in the common enterprise of capital accumulation. Economic growth surged, with higher rates of private investment from the late 1950s. Higher levels of investment, in turn, followed the Thai state's adoption of new economic policies that promoted private investment and protected local manufacturing. That new development strategy was linked to Marshal Sarit Thanarat's consolidation of political power and determination to undercut the economic bases of his political opponents in the previously important state enterprise sector. Sarit gave guarantees that the state would not create new enterprises that would compete with private ones. An unmobilized peasantry – the vast majority of the population – was in no position to press demands for redistributive economic policies. And the political weakness of the minority Chinese-controlled business firms prevented them from advancing broad policy demands with any ease. This part of the story begins to sketch the necessary conditions for rapid economic growth in Thailand. The Chinese supplied the entrepreneurial zest and social capital necessary to surmount market failures, the sufficient conditions added to the necessary requisites. Once in place, and without the emergence of significant new political actors, the policy mix of the Sarit years continued: conservative macroeconomic policies, import-substituting industrialization, and minimal additional public articulation of, or intervention on behalf of, specific goals.

While this brief explanation makes good sense of the dynamics that launched Thailand's high-growth era, it fails to account for the economy's sustained rapid growth over a long period. Understanding the long-term commitment to market policies and the strong results that followed requires us to note the effects of path-dependence, the limited degree of political mobilization among social groups, and the ways in which market actors compensated for the limited effectiveness of state promotion initiatives. This book attempts to extend our understanding by exploring these issues as well as the factors that led to sectoral variation in patterns of policymaking and economic outcomes in Thailand.

Chapter 2

Sociability and Social Capital: A Tale of Two Thailands

The previous chapter argued the importance of providing a social per-spective for the study of Thailand's political economy.[1] If economic and political institutions, as well as behavior, are shaped by ongoing social relations,[2] it becomes necessary to look at institutions as dependent as well as independent variables. Adopting such a perspective may shed light on the study of comparative political economy.[3] This chapter undertakes one part of this task by looking at sociability and social capi-tal in Thailand. It also discusses the development of relations between Bangkok and the provinces,[4] and the ways in which these relations affected sociability and social capital as well as the effectiveness of the Thai central administration.

It is important to assess Thailand against other countries along the dimensions addressed so far. While the Thai case is of course unique, it in fact has traits similar to those found elsewhere, including in other Southeast Asian countries. It is possible to contrast the countries of East Asia, as a group, with Western countries, as was popular in debates about "Asian values" associated with rapid economic growth through-out much of the region. Pye argues that there is a tendency in the region to idealize paternalistic leadership and embrace relations of interpersonal dependence.[5] More important for this discussion are the ways in which the politics and societies of Southeast Asia diverge from those of Northeast Asia.[6] State agencies in the former generally have weaker administrative capacities, and their social groups show less effective and enduring organization.

Thai Culture Studies

At the core of this book is an argument about the ways in which habits of behavior influence the formation and survival of cooperative social

27

groups that in turn facilitate particular patterns of political economy. The argument, in its application to the Thai case, rests on the assertion that Thais have low levels of sociability and social capital while the Chinese have higher levels of both. The empirical support for these assertions is indirect and draws heavily on anthropological and socio-logical literature on both groups.

Cultural anthropological studies of Thai culture and society, as well as more casual observations by both Thais and foreigners, long described an easygoing people little encumbered by strict social obliga-tions. Skinner suggests that abundant and fertile land created among many Thais a view that it was senseless to work hard if it was not in fact necessary. He contrasts local ecological conditions with the southern Chinese "Malthusian" context that shaped the ethos of the immigrant Chinese.[7] Not only Thai tourist boards proclaimed a "land of smiles" and a talent for *sanuk* (spontaneous fun).

But it is not these characteristics that stop the Thais forming a system of social institutions. My argument does not rest on differing predis-positions toward work, risk-taking, or other attributes associated with entrepreneurship but concerns the respective Thai and Chinese levels of sociability and social capital. Thais allegedly avoided conflict not only by prescribing appropriate conduct[8] – this was true also, for exam-ple, among the Javanese – but also by limiting participation in volun-tary associations with others, with the result that institutionalized cooperative groups and reciprocal obligations were relatively limited. Narthsupha noted the importance of "anarchism" in Thai social life.[9] Ayal argued that Thai "anarchistic individualism" hurt the economy's development.[10] And in a study both celebrated and scorned (see below), Embree held that Thai society was "loosely structured," allowing individuals considerable leeway in their behavior and only broadly defining roles by delimiting individuals' reciprocal rights and duties. Embree noted the paucity of financial credit associations, of obedience to parents, and of security of property relative to the Confucian societies with which he was familiar.

Embree's work inspired a spirited controversy among students of Thai society. Many of his critics questioned the utility of the "loose struc-ture" concept.[11] More important for our purposes were the critics who held that Thai society was not strikingly free of reciprocal obligations and expectations.[12]

The Historical and Institutional Context

Thai values and social propensities presumably emerged in large part in response to the material environment in which Thais developed their habits of work and association. Perhaps the central ecological conditions shaping traditional Thai societies were low population density and the ease, given monsoon rains and the flooding of the Chao Phraya River, of rice-growing on the central plains. While by no means all Thais lived in this river basin, it served as the center of administrative, political, and economic power. Abundant land, as in all of Southeast Asia until the nineteenth century, and still later in the Thai case, contributed to political and social systems that valued control over labor and water above land ownership. At the same time, however, for some laborers, uncleared jungle made exit from onerous conditions possible. This probably helped to curb the extent of severe exploitation of peasants. While a system requiring differing levels of compulsory labor was widespread in Thailand, even those at the bottom of the social scale also received land allotments under the traditional patrimonial system.[13] Surplus land made it possible to rapidly expand rice production, beginning in the nineteenth century, without major changes in production techniques or in social or administrative organization.[14]

While these broad ecological conditions obtained throughout the region, the relatively small penetration by foreign capital limited the extent of economic and social change evident elsewhere. In what is now Malaysia, for example, conditions of land surplus also obtained, and British colonial policies attempted to "protect" Malay farmers from the impact of disruptive market forces. Nonetheless, peninsular Malaysia experienced large population migrations, some Malay farmers moved into rubber planting, and the roles of officials in local village governments changed as well.[15]

Another important factor differentiating Thailand may have been the relatively limited coastal access for the majority of the population. In parts of Southeast Asia, trading "states" played important parts in the precolonial period, for example in areas of present-day Indonesia and Malaysia. Active merchants emerged in those areas, but had no ethnic Thai counterparts. Political power in these trading regions tended to be less centralized. The relative weakness of the center tended to foster political struggle and, in the nineteenth century, alliances with local Chinese merchants and miners.[16]

Favorable ecological circumstances[17] may have influenced other aspects of Thai culture and personality. Phillips noted Thais' tolerance for nonconformity as well as their lack of drive to affiliate in groups such as voluntary associations. He suggested that Thai individualism drew on fundamental self-acceptance.[18] Benedict pointed to land abundance as a factor encouraging geographic and social mobility in Thailand. She also noted a quality of self-acceptance among Thais: "They have no cultural inventions of self-castigation and many of self-indulgence and merriment."[19]

00.

Traditional Thai social organization, as elsewhere in the region, was patrimonial in nature: the king's domain and the state constituted an identity. Kings granted officials rank and land, but they held no hereditary rights to these. Peasants were not tied to the land but were obliged to render military service to the king (or his local agents). There was no permanent aristocracy. Obligatory labor was widespread. Security and status were dependent on ties with superiors. The patrimonial nature of Thai society may have influenced the subsequent development of Thai central administration, an issue pursued below.

After the Burmese sacking of the former capital in Ayudhya and the founding of the Chakri dynasty in Bangkok in the late eighteenth century, Thai society was remarkably stable until the 1960s. Thailand was never colonized, so in contrast to other areas in the region, no nationalist movement emerged to mobilize Thais in an anti-colonial struggle. The British, and subsequently other colonial powers, compelled Thai officials to adhere to a low-tariff trade regime and to protect the national currency by following conservative fiscal and monetary policies. Full exposure to the international market inevitably put pressure on traditional social institutions and induced the abandonment of the system of slave labor. Thailand became far more of a monoculture (rice) economy than it had been before.

What is remarkable, however, is the extent to which the availability of surplus land moderated externally generated market pressures.[20] Until the middle of this century, economic development was largely extensive in nature, involving the cultivation by more workers of ever more cleared forest land (increasing about fivefold from the middle of the nineteenth to the middle of the twentieth century).[21] State officials did not introduce new ways of organizing production and made relatively few investments in irrigation to stimulate more intensive economic growth;[22] cautious economic policies minimized social disruption. In Malaysia and Indonesia, despite indirect colonial rule and colonial efforts to moderate the impact of administrative and economic changes, these forces had more profound effects on the lives of villagers. In Java they were magnified by enormous population growth, resulting in "agricultural involution."[23] In Malaysia the impact of the world capitalist economy on traditional village life was also greater than in Thailand. Thai elites could accommodate external demands without launching traumatic reforms at home. Wilson described this relative social stasis in the late 1950s and attributed it to conservative economic policies and the abundance of land, which enabled increased population and production without requiring changed social relations.[24]

The scarcity of labor,[25] the availability of surplus land,[26] and the absence of a landlord class[27] also moderated the exploitation of the mass of Thais. While the Thai economy was exposed to the rigors of global markets, the vast majority of Thais were peasants who owned their own land and were able, without significant investments of capital, to grow enough food to sustain themselves.[28] These conditions, however, did not result in rising wealth or rapid socioeconomic change. Far from it. One prominent study suggested that over the hundred years up to the mid-twentieth century, Thais realized no increase in per capita income.[29]

The large immigrations of Chinese during the nineteenth and early twentieth centuries cushioned the impact on traditional rural life of exposure to world markets. The Chinese dominated the new economic roles that emerged with the specialization of productive tasks, including wage labor in the mining and shipping industries. They also moved into wholesale and retail distribution, and financial services, and took on roles in the growing international trade.

The Chinese also reduced the need for state authorities to develop extractive capacities. Officials had little need to survey, monitor, and tax the mass of peasants' consumption, income, or productive activities because the Chinese afforded an easier alternative. Thai officials, like their colonial counterparts in, for example, Singapore, could readily raise revenue by taxing Chinese consumption and leisure (gambling, liquor, opium). Thai authorities also taxed trade (at low levels) and used Chinese tax farmers. One estimate suggested that gambling shops alone at one point accounted for 20 per cent of all state revenues.[30] The combined income realized from Chinese enjoyment of opium, spirits and gambling amounted to about half of all government revenue well into the twentieth century.[31] As Skinner noted, Thais relied on Chinese virtues to boost the economy, and Chinese vices to bolster the treasury.[32]

Finally, it is worth noting the considerable social mobility that many researchers believe was possible in traditional Thai society. For individuals with the predilections and abilities, upward movement in Thai ranks was apparently a real possibility. Major gains in status and role changes generally required entry into one of the two national hierarchies: a (Buddhist) religious order or the (very small) state administration, including the military. More modest ambitions, however, might be accommodated within an individual's village. Anthropological work on Thai village life in the 1950s and 1960s described a diffuse village elite and ad hoc and permeable decisionmaking structures.[33] In short, life in nineteenth-century Siam contrasted with the insecurity and fear of physical violence that, according to Putnam, induced voluntary cooperation and the development of secondary associations in northern Italy seven centuries earlier.[34]

Associational Habits

Traditional patterns of Thai rural life, perhaps bolstered by the tolerant doctrines of Hinayana (Theravada) Buddhism, may have contributed to values and personality patterns inimical to associational life. Steven Piker[35] described Thais as individualistic, given to spontaneity, not adhering to particular roles, wary and suspicious of others, and relying on luck or patronage to secure their material and status needs. These propensities resulted in a relative absence of enduring and binding reciprocal commitments or participation in voluntary associations. Thais were not prone to rely on enduring cooperative groups or dyadic friendships in confronting life's challenges. These outlooks, Piker argued, accounted for the near total absence of ongoing cooperative groups in rural Thailand (other than the Buddhist hierarchy and the, generally nuclear, family).

Mulder observed a similar self-reliance and noted Thais' avoidance of anything but superficial interaction. He differentiated, however, the safety and security of the group close to home from the sphere beyond that narrow circle, which was characterized by the arbitrary and unstable exercise of power.[36] Wijeyewardene emphasized the dominant roles of nuclear family households in rural Thailand, the relatively vague rules defining kinship and obligations, and the absence of either the well-defined local communities exercising corporate control or extended kin groups found in most peasant societies.[37] Wichiencharoen also emphasized Thai individualism, arguing that Thais did not want to be hassled by others or involved in their affairs. The love of freedom reached the point of selfishness, he suggested.[38] Similarly, Somvichian believed that Thais shunned groups because of the great value they set on independence.[39] Klausner also described Thais as wary of submerging themselves in a group and accepting the discipline demanded of group members. As an example, he pointed to the generally weak record of Thai farm cooperatives.[40]

Wit saw rural Thais as largely self-reliant and without strong interest group or class identities.[41] Jacobs contended that in Thailand formal rules were not altogether binding, and that society was free of lasting, significant, goal-oriented, formal organizations not rooted in personal ties. Suspicious of others and eager to avoid interpersonal friction, Thais maintained shallow relations when interaction with others was necessary. With even kinship groups unreliable vehicles for cooperation, Thais were forced to rely on themselves and on fate. By seeking autonomy, they enhanced their flexibility, but they also isolated and weakened themselves.[42]

Blanchard argued that Thais were egoistic, had few obligations to others, and little interest in regularized efforts aimed at charity or social service.[43] Wittfogel reached similar conclusions, seeing these characteristics as results of centuries of state labor exactions that left peasants apolitical, without social consciousness, and that deprived communities of initiative. Intent on disengaging from arbitrary authority, peasants produced atomized political communities.[44] Phongpaichit and Baker also described a distinctive Thai peasant taste for freedom and independence and attributed it to the large numbers among them who were former slaves and recent escapees of onerous labor obligations.[45] A normative injunction warned against avoidable contact with government agents.[46]

In his study of a Thai village, Mizuno found few social groups. Households were independent of one another economically and the village was a community only in the sense that the village dwellings were loosely clustered together.[47] Mizuno found that the village head enjoyed limited authority and could employ no sanctions against free riders who declined to contribute to communal projects. Within families, relative equality prevailed. Mizuno contrasted the patterns he found in Thailand with Western individualism and Japanese collectivism. In Thailand, clientage ties were infused with personal warmth, not authority. Obligations emphasized the superior's need to exercise benevolence more than the inferior's need for loyalty (as was the case in Japan). Mizuno noted various proverbs suggesting low levels of trust: one should not "believe what others say, however nice it may sound"; should not "rely on water from villagers on the other side of the river"; should not look to siblings for help, for "ultimately one will not find anyone but oneself to rely on."[48]

These descriptions concur in noting a relative absence of reciprocal obligations and of regularly constituted groups. It may well be that such conditions would impede the development of cooperation in pursuit of shared goals. Interpersonal trust is a crucial ingredient of cooperation, and its development may depend in part on the extent to which social networks exhibit "closure." In such networks individuals deal with one another across a broad array of social contexts, ranging from the recreational to the educational and productive. By contrast, in an urban, post-industrial society, individuals are apt to encounter others only in specific contexts. Coleman argued that effective norms depend on individuals' actions imposing costs on others and that in "open" networks it becomes difficult to sanction those who impose such costs. So closure tends to promote trustworthiness.[49]

As in Thailand, elsewhere in Southeast Asia societies were marked by pervasive clientage and limited enduring organization of social groups.[50] Generally such groups depended heavily on their leaders. Thailand appeared to have been unusual, however, in the frequency of observations of diffidence toward organized activities and limited reciprocal obligations in villages. In Malaysia and Vietnam, for example, corporate villages were more common than in Thailand. In the Philippines, trust and expectations of reciprocity among villagers appear to have been greater.[51]

The absence of colonialism was probably a crucial factor differentiating Thailand from other Southeast Asian countries. Not only did foreign capital penetrate less deeply in Thailand, but no anti-colonial movement mobilized mass participation. As noted above, political power in Thailand also remained more centralized than elsewhere. Ritual kinship and ritual feasts that served to emphasize bonds of essential equality among participants were less in evidence in Thailand than in the Philippines. Neither did familial models emphasizing fictive kinships play such an important role in the society of small towns.[52]

Still another factor that may help to account for differing patterns of social organization concerns relative homogeneity. If we believe that ethnic boundaries are particularly easily used to mobilize a sense of identity and community, Thais would have been at a disadvantage relative to Indonesians, Malaysians, and Filipinos given their relative ethnic homogeneity.

In any case, whatever the actual causes, popular mobilization appears to have been more of a reality and threat elsewhere in the region than it was in Thailand. The New Order in Indonesia, for example, was vigilant in its efforts to preempt mobilization, suggesting that it saw its potential. In Indonesia and Malaysia, regimes dominated by one party entrenched themselves. Ruling and opposition parties had links stretching down to the village level of a kind that simply did not develop in Thailand. Unlike in Indonesia, most analyses of politics in Thailand do not make frequent reference to the role of groups.[53]

Thais' lack of horizontal networks between equals does not mean that they eschewed all forms of association. The pervasive vertical relations between patron and client were important in all areas of Thai life, and the study of such networks constituted the staple of Thai studies until the 1970s. Patronage remains very important in Thailand today, whether exercised by traditional elites, government officials, wealthy figures in business, or provincial godfathers. Clientage networks and horizontal voluntary associations, however, differ. Jumbala argued that where associations depend on clientage networks they are marked by unequal control over resources among members and heavy dependence on leadership.[54] Furthermore, Thai clientage networks were not particularly stable. The diffuse nature of reciprocity in Thailand left individuals relatively free to shift loyalties.[55] Indeed traditional disinclinations toward binding commitments to groups may have produced weaker clientage networks (or weaker networks may have resulted in less sociability) than in other social settings.[56] In Thailand effective official initiative depended on leadership from the king.[57] This extreme dependence on leaders continued to characterize most of Thailand's voluntary associations that emerged in the 1970s and thereafter.

The importance of clientage in Thailand would lead us to expect the paucity of horizontal association we find there. And if clientage tended to maintain social atomization,[58] the prospects for the emergence of an affiliating urge would appear bleak.[59] Girling argues that the weak impulse toward collective means of tackling social challenges stemmed from fatalism, factionalism, and a long record of unsuccessful experiences with cooperative initiatives, for example in setting up peasant cooperatives.[60]

Many of the descriptions of Thai values and the Thai personality cited above are dated. While they no doubt continue to capture important characteristics of the modal Thai personality, they surely apply less well after the profound changes of recent decades that disrupted traditional socioeconomic patterns and structures. Earlier representations of Thai peasant values were certainly less apt when attached to most of the Thai urban middle class. And prevailing social habits are likely to change further with rapid socioeconomic change and the intermingling of Thais, Chinese, and others. As noted earlier, we have evidence of a strengthening Thai taste for group affiliation, but while we may doubt the applicability of studies of Thai peasants to the contemporary urban middle class, we cannot assume that Thai habits of association have changed fundamentally over the last couple of generations. The vast majority of Thais still live in rural areas and derive a major part of their incomes from agriculture. These Thais, however, are not the subjects of this study. I return to this issue below.

Another facet of Thai society offers admittedly highly indirect evidence of a weak associational impulse. Thais appear to be extremely tolerant of foreigners as well as each other. This characteristic may, in general, distinguish societies in North and Southeast Asia, with the latter having less developed senses of us and them.[61] The Thai willingness to accept outsiders is striking and helps to account for the ready assimilation of the Chinese into Thai society (and the ease that most foreigners feel in Thailand). Indeed, much as in the United States, and with comparable qualifiers, becoming a Thai (in social terms) may require no more than behaving and speaking like a Thai.[62] Typically, such an easygoing delineation of boundaries between us and them is associated with lower levels of trust. In contrast, strong solidarity and bonds of trust are found in communities that have high entry barriers, such as Jehovah's Witnesses, Mormons, or Japanese.[63] This argument is consistent with Coleman's discussion of the effects of social closure noted above.

The weight of opinion cited above supports the notion that Thais traditionally were not preoccupied with formally delineated reciprocal obligations and were not enthusiastic joiners. This by no means suggests, however, that Thais do not have a strong national identity.

Thai Identity

The apparent permeability of the Thai community's borders and the weak urge to associate did not produce the anomic social conditions that Gramsci perceived in southern Italy.[64] Thais did not seem to suffer undue alienation, but rather to enjoy a strong sense of cohesion at the level of the nation (and freedom at the level of the individual).[65] The concept of an integral national community appeared strong. Bunnag noted the strong identification that Thais at all levels of society felt for the Thai state and its symbols.[66] Thais benefited, apparently, from both considerable individual autonomy and a strong sense of national community. Hence while Thais were not particularly prone to associational life, they were tied quite effectively, albeit loosely, by a shared identity. In general, regional identities appear to have been less powerful than in Indonesia, Malaysia, or the Philippines.

Certainly Buddhism played a central role in encouraging the formation of a national identity in Thailand;[67] ceremonies and daily rituals, many linked to Buddhism, contributed to the formation of a national culture.[68] While Thai leaders worked consciously to inculcate an "official nationalism" among Thais in the early twentieth century, it is uncertain that this preempted the role of religion in fostering what Barme calls "nationally-imagined nationalism."[69] Jacobs argued that Buddhism gave Thais a kind of diffuse unity and flexibility while affording means of legitimizing new social undertakings.[70] Wit maintained that the state's centralizing force, unmatched by political mobilization, made the nation's integrity highly dependent on shared cultural traditions.[71] Wijeyewardene contended that Buddhism lent little cohesion at the village level, in part because the national hierarchy operated the temples, but he nonetheless viewed Buddhism as a powerful national integrating force.[72] Indeed Embree argued that loose structure did not imply poor integration but rather facilitated adjustment to change, including that stemming from foreign influences.[73]

The Thai sense of national community was based, certainly since the efforts of King Vajiravudh and Luang Vichit Vadakan in the 1920s, on "Nation, Religion, Monarch." Field Marshal Sarit Thanarat further propagated this trinity in the late 1950s. The Ministry of Education also worked assiduously from the 1930s to promote national unity.[74] The impressive degree to which those values were shared by all Thais provided a solid fount of legitimacy that some leaders (the king, most obviously and dramatically) were able to use even in the 1990s to stabilize the country in times of crisis. But this national identity operated only at a fairly abstract level and did not contribute directly, it appears, to a Thai talent for spontaneous cooperation. A strong national identity did not seem to facilitate meeting the challenge of cooperation to achieve the prosaic goals associated with economic life.

For over half a century, Thais had a weak affiliative urge but a strong national identity. Part of the explanation for both parts of this picture may lie in the weakness of local bases of power relative to the capital. It is worthwhile, therefore, reviewing briefly the traditional patrimonial polity under the Thai monarchy.

Preempting Locally Based Power

Scholars debate the impact on local bases of political power of the extension of centralized power. When the French monarchy built up state power, did it vitiate the power of the traditional nobility with its local roots? Or, on the contrary, did the new central administration succeed in rapidly augmenting its power by working through existing power structures?[75] And what was the impact on voluntary associations of the rapid increase in centralized state power in France and elsewhere?[76]

Just as state-building in France may have decimated voluntary associations in the seventeenth century, the centralization of the Thai monarchy in the nineteenth century could have had a similar effect. We should not, however, overdraw this parallel. After all, we have no evidence that voluntary associations existed in Thailand in any significant numbers before the monarchy centralized power. Furthermore, patrimonialism in Thailand had long worked against the development of strong, locally based power.[77] Nonetheless, regionally based power founded on mining, plantation, and trading economies was more powerful elsewhere in Southeast Asia. So it certainly is possible that the centralization of state power in the nineteenth century undermined the conditions for the emergence of locally based power that otherwise would have emerged at some later time. Narthsupha and Prasertset, for example, contended that the centralizing state retarded the formation of an independent capitalist class.[78] In Thailand such power did not emerge until the 1960s; by the mid-1990s the emergence of that class represented the central story in Thai politics.

In the traditional patrimonial Thai polity, as noted earlier, local lords did not own land but enjoyed its use at the pleasure of the king and were unable to pass on their holdings. With unstable property rights, retaining tenure depended on continuing good relations with patrons.[79]

Under the *sakdina* system dating from the fifteenth century, all Thais were ranked by relatively fine gradations. The mass of people were either slaves or had corvee labor obligations to local lords. The latter, in turn, received labor and produce as agents of the king and passed on a part of those resources to the monarch. In reality the king's capacity to monitor his agents was severely limited. Struggles between monarchs and local lords over the available surplus were a regular feature of the system. Kings tended to need to curry favor with the local lords in efforts to maximize their share of the surplus.[80] Each of the traditional four ministries of the central state operated fairly independently, with their own finances, until the Chakri Reformation under King Chulalongkorn in the latter third of the nineteenth century. Not until early in the twentieth century did the state's administrative controls come close to matching the nominal extent of its authority.[81]

The reforms in the nineteenth century helped to undermine any existing local loyalties. A new centralized bureaucracy replaced the traditional nobility and tax farmers in funneling resources from the provinces to Bangkok. The absolute monarchy's totalitarian face opposed any independent social organization and influenced the dependent development of business, crafts, and ideas.[82] Court laws prohibited private communications among top-level lords.[83] The traditional order specifically barred the formation of private groups.[84] For a time officials experimented with regional boards that served to link the Ministry of Interior with local elites, mostly Chinese. The ministry abolished these boards in 1922, perpetuating the broad trend evident in Thailand in which administrative institutions outran political ones in integrating the nation.[85] Under Rama V and VI the monarchy introduced compulsory education and an official dynastic history and ideology based on nation, religion, and monarchy.[86] The result, then, was a relatively powerful, centralized state facing little local power.

Anderson suggested that the Thai state of this era could be understood most usefully as a type of indirectly ruled principality.[87] No local groups had long experience with political power or extensive landholdings, neither was there a significant commercial class.[88] With the overthrow of the absolute monarchy in 1932, Bangkok's new bureaucratic elites worked to construct an alternative ideology to legitimize their rule. This may help us understand some of the peculiar features of Phibul Songkram's modernization campaigns in the 1940s and 1950s.[89] Like the original secularizing Young Turks, the new lords worked to construct alternative bases of legitimacy.

With the overthrow of the absolute monarchy and the near simultaneous collapse of European influence[90] as a consequence of depression and then war, the new ruling group in Thailand enjoyed considerable freedom, which they used to establish an essentially predatory state. With political competition confined to a very narrow circle of participants, the players did not need to mobilize large resources; the People's Party that overthrew the absolute monarchy comprised a mere score of members.[91] Constant political competition did not spur efforts to mobilize popular support until Phibul's rather episodic efforts in the mid-1950s. Political leaders could deflect resources headed for the state treasury or from the local Chinese. The rise of bureaucratic capitalism (and the Chinese dominance of private markets) surely retarded the emergence of a Thai commercial middle class.[92] Political competition centered on control of the ministries.

From the 1970s the military, prompted by spreading insurgencies, worked at increasing its inroads into rural society. In the early 1980s Prime Ministerial Order 66/2523 promoted the military strategy of mobilizing rural Thais in an effort to preempt competition organizationally. The military, however, like the civil bureaucracy, were primarily engaged in unifying the country administratively. The task of politically integrating rural Thais fell to the rural brokers who dominated political parties by the 1980s.[93] Increasingly, these forces were able to penetrate the state, in Bangkok as well as the regions.

The ideology championed by Thai elites, surviving into the 1970s, employed patronage, controls on organization, and efforts to depoliticize Thais, and thereby may also have served to dampen political mobilization.[94] Given this context, it is possible to see as downright revolutionary Prime Minister Banharn Silpa-archa's truculent insistence in 1996 that "Bangkok is not Thailand."[95] In fact by the 1990s it had become clear that Thailand's democracy was increasingly divided between the rural voters who brought coalitions to power and those in Bangkok who passed judgment on public policies and were able to force the fall of governing coalitions.[96]

The combination of a traditional patrimonial polity followed by the nineteenth-century centralizing regime that tried to preempt autonomous local centers of power may have undermined the state's power in the longer term. Girling suggests that traditional hierarchical attitudes, culture, and acceptance of inferior status by most Thais may have facilitated the state's penetration of society.[97] It may be more accurate, however, to say that these values influenced the terms of state penetration and yielded a less effective state than would have emerged had state authorities been forced to engage mobilized social forces.

Ultimately, state officials need footholds to extend their authority out into society, otherwise they face an undifferentiated, atomized society they must organize themselves with the help of an extensive bureaucratic apparatus. Supporting this point, Chenvidyakarn described the

Thai state's delegation of technical tasks to "functional associations" and suggested that in the absence of such associations, state officials might have had to create them.[98] According to Boone, comparable difficulties faced postcolonial states in Africa. Indeed the parallel may extend further. In many postcolonial African states, as in Thailand in some respects, state officials, and particularly politicians, ultimately had to rely on local power-brokers to serve as their agents.[99] In Thailand the rise of new locally based godfathers reached the point by the 1980s where a police officer in Chonburi, who thought of himself as a part of the centralized state's machinery, complained that in fact he had no authority as all his subordinates and superiors were agents of the local godfather.[100]

The centralization of state power may help us in understanding the relative weakness of voluntary associations in Thailand. Nonetheless, while Thais generally were not active in voluntary associations, such groups did of course exist. Certainly the strongest and most effectively organized groups in Thailand were a variety of business interest associations. In some cases these had roots in Chinese-dialect mutual aid associations.[101] Some of them assumed economic governance functions, such as guaranteeing minimum quality standards.[102] From the late 1970s politicians, and later state officials, mainly in the National Economic and Social Development Board (NESDB), tried to forge corporatist links with business groups. It is worthwhile, therefore, providing a brief overview of links between business, and other social groups, and the state.

Business and Social Organization in Thailand

Riggs drew on data stretching back to the late nineteenth century to trace the development of associations in Thailand. The picture he drew, based on registrations with the police, was far from reliable but gave some idea of relative change over time and differences among ethnic groups in the urge to form associations. The monarchy had specifically prohibited private associations, but had apparently relaxed or removed controls by the late 1800s.[103] From early in this century urban business associations looked to state officials for support.[104] Chinese organizations such as the Association of Industry and Commerce, founded in 1907, organized merchants, manufacturers, and workers.[105] In the 1920s and 1930s the number of associations registered with the police grew; by 1958 there were about 600. The Chinese, Indian, and other foreign groups were disproportionately represented, as were members of the royal household, politicians, and ministry officials serving as sponsors of associations.[106]

By the 1960s several key business associations in Bangkok were increasingly active in consultations with government officials on issues such as export quality control programs. The associations were also active in talks on rationalizing the auto industry.[107] The number of business associations rose from 48 in 1967 to 233 in 1987.[108] The sway of business in general rose steadily after the 1960s as the middle class grew in size and economic growth became an increasingly important goal for Thai leaders. Since the early 1970s business associations took part in the planning process guided by the NESDB.[109] Business influence strengthened during the 1970s as its weight in political parties and parliament grew and officials turned to business leaders for help in finding means of increasing Thai exports and coping with widening current account deficits. Samudavanija suggested that political parties served well as vehicles for the expression of the interests of Chinese business concerns because the parties had no ethnic identities.[110]

The policy influence of business rose dramatically during the 1980s.[111] Business associations themselves, such as the Federation of Thai Industries, provincial chambers of commerce, and the Joint Public-Private Consultative Committee,[112] achieved far greater prominence in the 1980s. They could sometimes exercise voice in policy debates and nudge policy. Generally, both operators of large Bangkok businesses as well as association officials had fairly easy access to state officials. The concerns of these business figures were often consistent with those of technocrats in Government House and bureaucrats in the ministries. With the advent of greater political democracy later in the decade, the roles of business associations themselves declined somewhat, though the unusual 1992 election saw them taking unprecedentedly overt political action.[113] And in subsequent years they became more active again as the Thai economy faced stronger competitive pressures and officials reduced tariffs, encouraging competing sectors to wrangle over those duty cuts.

By the 1970s the middle class was also becoming a significant force in Bangkok's politics. Students took important roles early in the decade in articulating dissent and organizing farmers and workers. The student movement eventually emerged in the tumultuous 1970s as the fulcrum of sharp conflicts within and beyond the military. Building on refugees from the student movement and increased access to foreign financing over the 1980s, the non-government organization (NGO) movement began to grow. Quigley estimated that by the mid-1990s there were in Thailand about 12 000 NGOs with 75 000 to 100 000 members.[114]

Like their business counterparts, labor unions have existed in Thailand since the early twentieth century. As with business groups, the unions were dominated by the Chinese, who controlled most professions other than farming and government service. Labor unions, however, even less than business associations, failed to develop into significant bases of political organization.

Early this century labor was in short supply in Thailand and the infant labor movement was active, frequently using strikes to press demands. State suppression and moves to undermine Chinese control of most occupations in Bangkok eventually weakened the movement. Labor was generally weak and divided thereafter, subject to state clampdowns, including periods when the authorities barred all labor organization.[115] The first labor legislation in Thailand in 1956 allowed workers to organize and bargain collectively, but workers lost these rights immediately after Sarit's coup in 1957 (see page 61). The first significant labor strikes after World War II erupted in the mid-1970s in response to inflation and stagnant wage growth. Nonetheless, labor organizers expressed frustration at the apathy with which many workers greeted unionization efforts.[116]

Only 8 per cent of the Thai workforce in 1990 worked in industry – according to government statistics, in 1990 only one out of four Thai workers was employed outside the family.[117] By 1994 there were about 700 unions representing 300 000 workers, just over 1 per cent of the workforce. The most powerful labor unions were in the state enterprise sector; they were able, for example, to block government privatization initiatives in the 1980s.[118] In 1991 the National Peacekeeping Council (the authors of that year's coup) banned the state enterprise unions. While Prime Minister Chuan Leekpai lifted the ban in 1994, the unions did not regain their former influence.

Private sector unions also grew more active in the late 1980s as unemployment and underemployment diminished. The four largest umbrella organizations increased their joint action, working to back social security legislation and to resist widespread use of short-term contract workers in manufacturing. One labor organizer, however, grumbled about the ongoing difficulty of enlisting workers' support: "the problem boils down to the Thai culture, with workers preferring to do things on their own rather than going for collective bargaining."[119] Nonetheless, layoffs in the 1990s, particularly in the textile industry, helped to spur labor activism.

Bangkok's voluntary associations, other than business and labor groups, were distinctly novel groups that became more prominent beginning in the 1970s. By one count, their number grew from 3300 in 1970 to 12 000 in 1989.[120] Urban population growth, economic expansion, and the temporary end to authoritarian government in 1973 all facilitated the rise in the number and membership of these organizations. The generation of student activists from the early 1970s played disproportionate parts in organizing and leading them. Access to foreign funds and support also helped them grow in number, size, and influence;[121] they were far more active in Bangkok than in other parts of the country. Nonetheless, their rapid development since the 1970s as well as the rise of new Buddhist sects appealing to the urban middle class suggested that Thai society may be becoming more sociable and more richly endowed with social capital (see Chapter 7).

Upcountry Voluntary Associations

Thailand remained a heavily rural country well after its manufacturing sector began expanding rapidly in the 1960s. While the Bangkok region accounted for over half the country's GDP in the 1990s,[122] more than half of all Thais depended on agriculture for their incomes.[123] Agriculture's importance declined rapidly from 22 per cent of GDP in 1982 to 10 per cent in 1994; over that period its share of exports dropped from half to just over a fifth,[124] and disparities in regional income grew more pronounced.

Traditionally, as we have seen, most Thai villagers lived as individuals owing labor to their lords rather than as members of corporate units having joint responsibilities. With integration into international markets in the nineteenth century, the indigenous local elite did not expand much; rather, as elsewhere in Southeast Asia, it was the class of Chinese middlemen that grew.[125] In rural areas of Thailand, however, unlike other countries, there was little elite-based political organization or strong popular movements. When state officials in Thailand worked to sponsor agricultural associations, they reportedly faced greater difficulties than met comparable initiatives elsewhere.[126] The Madras Bank of India sponsored cooperatives in Thailand during World War I in the hope of boosting debt repayment by farmers who were often going into debt and losing their lands; the bank extended loans on condition that farmers establish cooperatives, with the first cooperative running by 1916.[127] For the most part these cooperatives became instruments of individual government officials. New teachers' associations experienced a similar fate.[128] The 1928 Cooperative Societies Act represented an effort to curb Chinese control of rural trade but failed to strengthen the associations.[129] Renewed state efforts in the late 1940s were no more successful.[130] Increased commercialization of agriculture and rising peasant indebtedness also failed to generate spontaneous peasant organization.[131]

Hirsch notes Thai peasants' resistance to officials' efforts to relocate them from outlying areas into "nucleated" settlements. He suggests that peasants not only found their existing dwellings convenient but also did not relish the distractions (*juk jik jai*) of community demands.[132] To this day, peasant cooperatives are generally organized vertically and are closely regulated by state officials.[133] This apparently weak record of rural organization led Chenvidyakarn, while acknowledging the suffocating role of state authority, to wonder whether much rural organization would have arisen in the absence of state interference.[134] In 1997 there were close to 5000 cooperatives covering nearly seven million families. Nearly three-quarters of farm familes were members of at least one cooperative.[135]

Significant rural organization first emerged in the 1970s, when farmers organized to share labor or other production inputs and to make demands of local authorities. The rather authoritarian Thanin government in 1976–77, however, quelled student efforts to organize farmers. In 1975 eighteen leaders of farmers' groups were assassinated.[136] Turton suggests that the activities of the Peasants' Federation of Thailand in 1974 and 1975 showed that farmers were neither diffident toward organization nor unable to cooperate effectively to further political goals (rightists and the military also organized peasants in the 1970s and thereafter). While acknowledging relatively low levels of organization, he rejects Girling's suggestion that any innate peasant aloofness explained this outcome.[137] Nonetheless, in the 1990s, with the exception of sugar-growers[138] and to a lesser extent palm oil and coffee-producers, farmers remained largely unorganized. Large commercial operations dominated the strongest agricultural organizations in Thailand. While rice-growers had no association to coordinate their activities, the (Chinese) millers were organized into the Rice Millers Association. Thai farmers were not only poorly positioned to make political demands but were generally not organized effectively to promote cooperation in facing shared economic challenges. As for rural towns, Chinese groups had long dominated voluntary organizations there.[139]

From the 1980s groups of Thai farmers also organized to oppose the expropriation of land, the building of dams and roads, the establishment of polluting industries, and state efforts to evict squatters from state-owned forests. This mobilization for political action increased in the late 1980s, and conflicts over natural resources became a particularly common cause of popular mobilization in the provinces. For the organizers of this peasant resistance, life could be nasty, brutish, and often short.[140] In the mid-1990s farmers staged large protests in Bangkok, citing a variety of grievances. The Isan Small Farmers' Congress had about 50 000 members and an impressive degree of organization given the intimidation and violence its leaders faced.[141]

Many of these farmers were heavily indebted. The Assembly of the Poor staged marches on Bangkok in 1996 and 1997, protesting against environmental degradation, construction of dams, and endangered access to land in national forest reserves (an issue affecting six million Thais).[142] Like their counterpart business associations, farmers' associations developed more open partisan alignments; the Thai Farmers Federation stood behind the New Action Party in the 1996 elections.[143] By and large, however, and despite a clear trend toward increasing organization even in the countryside, such activities were *ad hoc* in nature and not part of sustained efforts by organized groups.

Thailand's oldest and largest voluntary association was the Buddhist hierarchy. The religion and its temples played a central role in Thailand and helped to define local village communities through most of the country. From the nineteenth century, leaders in Bangkok worked to control the religious orders, in part to centralize power. Prince Mongkut (at the time a monk) led a movement in the mid-nineteenth century to define more clearly the core elements of Buddhism in Thailand. The Thammayut movement worked to rid the *sangha* of sorcerers and potential leaders of peasant millennial movements.[144] Thailand's kings organized the country's priesthood under a supreme patriarch late in the nineteenth century. Governments tried to use monasteries in efforts to boost education and forge a national identity.[145] State officials frequently manipulated the orders to achieve policy goals. Marshal Sarit's government sent monks to proselytize hill-tribe members; monks also went to villages as government agents working for community development.[146] Indeed there were some parallels between the monks' activities and the roles often played in the 1980s and 1990s by NGOs.[147] Nonetheless, the religious orders generally were highly decentralized, and the more overtly political monks worked at both the political extreme left and the extreme right with fairly limited followings.

With rapid economic growth, the monks adapted themselves to their new conditions. There were about 30 000 temples and 200 000 monks in Thailand in the early 1990s.[148] With the economic boom of the late 1980s, many temples in and around Bangkok pulled in large amounts of money. One abbot dispensed millions of dollars a year, via the monarchy and directly, to schools and hospitals. Wat Phra Dhammahaya marketed itself to Bangkok's middle class and, once a month, attracted about 10 000 people.[149] These new and commercially successful temples pointed to possible future forms of association among Thais, even while old religious institutions (young men spending time in monasteries) declined and many temples closed because of a local shortage of monks. The rise of diverse new forms of religious association is of particular interest because it recalls Max Weber's emphasis on Protestant sectarianism in accounting for the prevalence of voluntary groups in the United States.[150]

The most powerful rural force in Thailand was the new political class that grew particularly rapidly from the 1970s (see page 65). Generally ethnically Chinese, these men forged links with state officials and politicians in order to win contracts for themselves and protection from harassment of their various illegal business activities. Politicians and their financiers, at local and national levels, competed for licences and contracts of various kinds. They also worked with, or themselves directed, illegal trades such as smuggling – including drugs and prostitution. By the late 1980s, with the gradual weakening of military dominance over Thai politics, local brokers controlled enough money and votes to dominate Thai cabinets. Banharn Silpa-archa, for example, grew rich in a provincial town in the 1960s and 1970s on construction contracts and other services before rising to leadership of the Chart Thai political party and serving as prime minister in 1995 and 1996.[151] During a 1996 political stalemate, former prime minister Anand captured the consensus Bangkok perception of Banharn when he referred to the "crisis of a shameless leader."[152] The political scientist Chai-anan Samudavanija characterized the disdain that state elites expressed toward the new men of politics as a fear of the latter's potential to act as social forces that could for the first time bind Bangkok and the regions.[153]

The new class of rural political brokers probably established itself readily in part because of the weakness of the Thai central government and its inability to provide local services effectively. Samudavanija emphasized the brokers' role, as with the Chinese secret societies of the past, in integrating the rural masses into a national polity that lacked alternative political channels.[154] In this context elected representatives were probably more than welcomed locally since some of them were spending an estimated $40 000 a month in their constituencies.[155] Butting up against the growing power of the rural brokers was the swelling middle class in the cities, mainly Bangkok. This new class spurred resistance to the rural brokers and their ability to buy political power. Thais grew increasingly uneasy in the 1990s about a widening gulf in attitudes and values between city and country.[156] In the early 1990s, well under a third of all Thais of secondary school age were attending classes, but less than 15 per cent of farm family children were doing so.[157] And traditional unifying forces like Buddhism lost some of their homogenizing force as urban Thais looked for new forms of religious expression that gave them more active roles.[158]

One factor that may have added to the gulf in attitude and outlook between rural and urban Thais was the lingering effect of ethnic differences. In the middle of this century, Skinner estimated that about half of Bangkok's population were ethnic Chinese. That percentage declined considerably as villagers poured into Bangkok (one Thai observed that Bangkok never was a Thai city: first it was Chinese, then Lao – a reference to the migration to Bangkok of large numbers of ethnic Lao from northeastern Thailand).[159] It is time now to look at the roles and social organization of the Chinese.

The Chinese in Thailand

The Chinese were crucial to Thailand's industrialization and, indeed, to economic growth throughout Southeast Asia. As Suehiro notes, the growth of capitalism in Southeast Asia was closely linked to the history of the Overseas Chinese.[160] Phongpaichit and Baker argue that the Chinese in Thailand, relative to those elsewhere in Southeast Asia, represented a particularly powerful economic force, largely independent of political sponsors.[161] In a twist on Williamson's work on the business firm's internalization of markets, I might suggest that in Thailand the Chinese were partially successful in internalizing "state functions," as a result of which they enjoyed lower cost access to production factors, including capital and labor. Given the extraordinary economic roles the Chinese played, it is worthwhile considering separately their habits of association and the specific institutions to promote cooperation that they developed in Thailand. We need to consider both associational links within the Chinese community and institutions that tied the Chinese to the Thai majority.

Successful Thai–Chinese accommodation was fundamentally important for Thai economic growth. Chinese entrepreneurial energy and distribution and trade networks brought the Thai peasantry into the market economy, established and supported manufacturing industries, attracted foreign capital to Thailand, and located overseas markets for Thai exports. Van Roy argued that during the nineteenth-century rice export boom, the Chinese acted as culture brokers, linking Thais to international markets while shielding them from their corrosive impact on traditional forms of social organization.[162] In some ways this same kind of argument held true throughout the twentieth century. The Chinese were clearly outwardly oriented long before the Thais and used their links abroad to develop economic ties between the Thai and international economies. Kinship and informal business networks helped the Chinese raise credit overseas.[163]

The Chinese came to Thailand for centuries in a variety of capacities.[164] From the seventeenth century, Thai monarchs granted royal trade monopolies to the lucky few. The major waves of immigration, however, occurred late in the nineteenth and early in the twentieth century, peaking in the 1920s. Immigration effectively halted in 1949. For the most part the new arrivals were impoverished southern Chinese eager to accumulate capital and return to their families in China. The regular payment of remittances to China probably made Thailand a regular net capital exporter during most of the first half of the twentieth century.[165] Many Chinese succeeded in returning, but large numbers remained in Thailand. Eager to earn money, they were at first free agents operating outside the system of Thai values and obligations and the largely agricultural economy. To some degree, as elsewhere in the region, Chinese with common regional origins tended to go into similar lines of business, a factor that facilitated intrasectoral cooperation.[166] The Chinese diaspora in Thailand was unusual for the prevalence of Teochiu (a group from the south China coast).[167] By the 1990s, although the meaning and significance of ethnicity grew increasingly obscure, the Chinese accounted for something like 10 per cent of the population.[168] This represented far less of the population than in Malaysia, but far more than in Indonesia or the Philippines.

When the Thai kings used Chinese as tax farmers and as their agents for foreign trade (much of it with China), they sometimes granted noble rank to Chinese. As a result of this practice and considerable assimilation into Thai society, Chinese blood is common in Thais at all ranks of society, including the royal family.[169] Zheng Zhao, who paved the way for the founding of the Chakri dynasty,[170] had a Chinese father and Thai mother.

In the nineteenth century the Chinese lost their control over foreign trade to Europeans and began to serve as compradores for the large Western trading houses. They also went into tin-mining, teak-cutting, sawmilling, rice-milling, and building ports and railways. Skinner suggested that tin-mining frequently required group cooperation in working pumps and that the Chinese were careful to keep from outsiders their information on the location of tin resources (though he expressed doubt that others had much interest in that arduous business).[171] The Chinese role in rice-milling increased rapidly and by World War I they were engaged in exporting rice as well.[172]

A typical progression for Chinese entrepreneurs was to begin in trade, then to move into financial activities, and, particularly with the manufacturing boom that began in the late 1980s, into industry. Even in the mid-1990s, some Thai firms remained under the control of Chinese immigrants who had arrived in Thailand as paupers in the 1920s and 1930s. Thaworn Phornprapha represented a typical story. He arrived in Thailand from southern China when about six years old, and before World War II began repairing and selling used Japanese cars. After the war he imported Nissan buses for the city of Bangkok.[173] When his business foundered in the late 1950s, the Bangkok Bank rode to his rescue.[174] By 1962, in cooperation with Nissan, he began to assemble cars locally. In the 1970s Siam Motors moved into the production of various auto parts,[175] and by the 1990s the firm was at the heart of Southeast Asia's leading auto industry.

Despite the difficulties noted above that the Chinese had in extending cooperation beyond extended family groups, they nonetheless managed to create a wide variety of thriving businesses. As with other "middleman minorities,"[176] they showed great solidarity relative to the Thai majority, particularly within linguistic, lineage, or family groups. Their distinct social identity, both assumed and imposed from without, probably contributed to their success in business in Thailand as elsewhere in the region. Bonacich and Modell suggested that high levels of trust in such communities, reinforced by overlapping economic and social memberships that foster community closure and concern to maintain reputations, can result in lower cost funds and in enhanced access to information and economic opportunities, and may even induce workers to accept lower wages if they anticipate later assistance in setting up independent businesses.[177]

There is abundant evidence that the Chinese in Thailand, particularly those from the same speech group, enjoyed such advantages.[178] Doner speculated that shared Chinese ethnicity among owners of firms producing auto parts might have fostered organizational cohesion of those firms.[179] Within the Chinese community there was considerable occupational specialization by speech group. As was the case, for example, in Malaysia, in the face of government harassment or neglect, these groups would form business associations representing the interests of their occupation.[180] In Thailand the local commercial banks emerged out of such groups and were created in response to the need to enlarge the circle of individuals (beyond the family) from which those in business could mobilize funds.[181] While most of the banks rose out of Teochiu groups, the Thai Farmers Bank had Hakka origins (another group from the south China coast). The new banks recruited members from a wide range of occupations in order to broaden their bases of business, in the process, of course, increasing the diversity of their assets. The banks also made extensive use of existing Chinese organizations to further the scope of their businesses.[182] They were able to launch a variety of Chinese businesses that, in part because of the opacity of Chinese bookkeeping systems, could not attract credit from Western banks.[183]

Despite some similarities between the Chinese and Thais in values and social organization, for our purposes it is worthwhile emphasizing the differences. For Thais, surnames were a fairly recent invention. This reflected a fundamental difference in worldview from the more historically rooted and kin-centered outlook of the Chinese. Pye contrasts the ancestor worship of Confucian societies with the dread of the dead in Southeast Asia.[184] For the Chinese in Thailand, prestige required upward socioeconomic mobility, while for Thais, other avenues, such as the monkhood, were widely available. In any event, Thais were long subjected to forced labor obligations and ties to their lords, encumbrances from which the immigrant Chinese were free.[185] While both Chinese and Thais enmeshed themselves in clientage networks, the latter tended to have less of a mutual assistance character and were more hierarchical, as well as transitory.[186] Chenvidyakarn suggested that while Thais were non-joiners, the Chinese were adept in the art of association.[187] Despite the value Chinese typically placed in education, the early Chinese entrepreneurs in Thailand were by and large unconcerned with schooling. Their success seemed to flow from diligence, thrift, and other bourgeois values, including trust, but not education.[188] The capacity to cooperate was also crucial. Yoshihara notes the important role, in the rise of the first extensive Chinese business in Southeast Asia, of an ability to extend trust beyond the family.[189]

The Chinese in Thailand established a rich associational life, generally building on common kin or speech groups, featuring mutual aid societies, guilds, and secret societies that they used to protect their occupations against outsiders. With no public authority to give them adequate protection, they governed themselves.[190] Much the same pattern was evident in Malaya, where the British left the Chinese to manage their own affairs.[191] In much of Southeast Asia, without the backing of formal state authority, the Chinese regulated their businesses, created clinics and community centers, cemeteries and schools, hospitals and temples, and established social security systems. Chinese chambers of commerce offered guarantees of quality control.[192] After Japan's defeat in World War II, the Chinese in Thailand extended assistance to Chinese stranded in Malaya and in Thailand (in some cases finding them local marriage partners) and mobilized funds for famine relief in southern China.[193] This extraordinary record of associational achievement, without parallel in Thai society, was surely facilitated by the high degree of closure within the Chinese communities. Dwellings and places of business generally overlapped and individuals typically entered a business by entering the family.[194]

We also have considerable evidence that the Chinese used this dense fabric of associations to further their business interests. Chinese tax farmers in Thailand in the nineteenth century, for example, managed to increase their takes by manipulating their bids within dialect and kin groups.[195] Yoshihara notes that without particularly valuable resources or colonial control, Thailand was a relative backwater in the world economy and that as a result market institutions developed only gradually. The Chinese in Thailand had to employ their networks to overcome this obstacle, early this century, for example, using networks based on speech groups to mobilize capital. (The Chinese often failed, however, in efforts to extend the circle of trust beyond the family.) Throughout Southeast Asia, the Chinese used networks to provide jobs and labor training, low-cost capital, customers, and supplies on credit. Eschewing enforcement of contracts, the Chinese relied on relations of trust; intimate links between business and social networks facilitated the imposition of social sanctions when necessary. Assessments of trustworthiness were important in gaining business opportunities and, given the closed nature of the networks, a person would forfeit a great deal by tarnishing a reputation for reliability.[196]

Barton's research on Overseas Chinese merchants suggests that trust relations, which afforded access to credit, were more important in differentiating the Chinese from indigenous traders than were traits such as diligence, thrift, long-term horizons, or patience. Barton also offered still another explanation for the asset diversity of Chinese operations: it helped them keep a low profile as a way of avoiding the attention of tax collectors. Extensive networks increased information, thereby reducing risks, and enabled Chinese to get access to cheaper credit than their indigenous counterparts.[197] Dewey, Suyama, Landa, and Lengel also concluded, in separate studies, that Chinese business success was largely a product of their capacities for cooperative undertakings.[198] Landa found in Malaysia that the Chinese could reduce the dangers of free riding, and hence the costs of monitoring, through careful selection of those with whom they undertook cooperative activities.[199] The considerable investment the Chinese made in their reputations led, not surprisingly, to efforts to exploit them by emphasizing their Chinese ethnicity; it may even account, in part, for the 1990s chic among the Chinese in Thailand of embracing their origins.[200]

Building on these extensive networks, the Chinese today control virtually all of the largest firms in Thailand.[201] This has suggested to some that the behavior Le May observed in Thailand in the 1930s continued for quite some time: "Siamese sit by, watching all the requisite services of life being performed by the uniformly impersonal, very vociferous, but intensely industrious celestial."[202] As the discussion above has indicated, however, it was the Chinese ability to build cooperative networks, rather than other behavior differences, that mainly accounted for their disproportionate economic success.

A Modus Vivendi Between Chinese and Thai Elites

Compared to the Chinese elsewhere in Southeast Asia, those in Thailand were easily and fully assimilated.[203] Cooperation between the two communities was crucial to Thailand's subsequent economic development and probably had to do with Thai tolerance as well as the fact that Thailand was never colonized. The absence of colonial control required of Chinese that they curry favor with local elites, rather than colonial ones, in their efforts to advance their interests. It also meant that Thais were not as likely to view Chinese as the agents of a hostile power, a perception particularly common during the independence struggles in Southeast Asia when the local Chinese did not tend to be strong partisans in support of those movements (though many did support either the nationalists or the communists in China). Under Thai law, Chinese born in Thailand become Thai citizens.[204]

Despite a comparatively good record on discrimination, anti-Chinese sentiment in Thailand gained force early in this century and again in the 1930s and late 1940s. It is not entirely clear, however, whether state repression was aimed at the Chinese because of their ethnicity or their high degree of organization.[205]

With a more rapid steamship service from China, Chinese women came to Thailand in large numbers for the first time.[206] This reduced intermarriage between Thais and Chinese and made it easier to maintain a separate Chinese community in Thailand. At the same time both Thai and Chinese nationalisms were on the rise (Sun Yat-sen made a fundraising trip to Thailand in 1908).[207] This had the effect of heightening Thai sensitivity to Chinese economic dominance, a concern propagated by King Rama VI (author of *The Jews of the Orient*). A Chinese strike in protest against a newly instituted head tax in 1910 brought home to the Thai authorities the extent of their economic dependence on the Chinese and eventually led to fairly mild discriminatory measures against the Chinese.[208] Chinese nationalism meanwhile resulted in divisions within the Chinese community between nationalist and communist supporters and also stimulated Chinese boycotts of Japanese goods after the Japanese invasion of China.[209]

In the late 1930s and again in the late 1940s and early 1950s, Thai government policies discriminated against the Chinese. Regulations restricted certain occupations to Thais, limited remittances to China, and required that Thais hold at least half the jobs in any firm with more than ten employees.[210] Postwar anti-Chinese discrimination was wrapped in anti-communist propaganda, the notion being that the Chinese were linked to the largely Chinese communist insurgency in Malaya as well as the Chinese-supported communist movements in Indochina. Indeed efforts by Thai politicians to organize a local labor movement in the 1950s to serve their own ends suffered when Chinese captured the movement and used it to support the Chinese communists on the mainland.[211]

Thai economic nationalism also helped to spur the establishment of state enterprises designed in part to weaken the Chinese stranglehold on the Thai economy. A World Bank report noted in the late 1950s that tension between the two communities could work against state officials adopting a market strategy because of fears that it would tend to increase Chinese economic domination.[212] A perceived overlap of ethnicity and equity issues inclined some Thais to emphasize the trade-off between growth and economic justice.[213] While this ethnic tension exists today in, for example, Indonesia and Malaysia, it is now all but irrelevant in Thailand.

The postwar "Thailand for the Thai" campaign tightened restrictions on Chinese business activities. By and large, however, the better established Chinese suffered less official harassment than those in more modest positions. As Phongpaichit and Baker indicate, the pressure worked to encourage the Chinese to behave politically in Thai fashion (discreet, graceful, oblique).[214] But the overall psychological climate was clearly intimidating and hardly conducive to encouraging investment activities, particularly those of a long-term nature.

A crucial step in realizing a modus vivendi between Thai and Chinese elites was the practice of having leading Thai politicians and bureaucrats serve on the boards of directors of Chinese firms.[215] This gave Thai leaders incomes sufficient to support their political followers and thereby reduced incentives to create state enterprises to serve that function. Doner and Ramsay suggest that this may have been possible in large part because, without secure resources rooted in caste or landed status, the Thai elite was locked in a struggle for resources that created openings for the Chinese.[216] Having Thai elites on their boards offered the Chinese safety from arbitrary state action. Thai leaders also offered inside contracts and privileged information. This arrangement reduced tensions between the two groups at the elite level and established a basis for economic growth in Thailand.

The institutionalization of this system of protection limited competition between Chinese in procuring patronage while establishing cooperation between the two sets of elites.[217] Both elites shared common interests, most importantly the desire to promote the interests of their firms. A less favourable legacy was the tradition of using political connections to assure state protection, monopoly status, or other privileges. The survival of this tradition into the 1990s was evident in former Prime Minister Anand Panyarachun's reference to Thailand's "connection economy."

During Sarit's rule and the launching of a strategy of private investment promotion and import-substituting industrialization (see Chapter
3), relations between the Thai and Chinese improved dramatically.
Sarit himself curried close relations with the Chinese Chamber of
Commerce[218] and by serving on the boards of scores of firms helped
himself accumulate a fantastic fortune. Through these and other channels, Sarit's assets at his death amounted to 2.8 billion baht (about $140
million),[219] a financial base which helped to secure his power and Thai
political stability. Local Chinese responded to investment incentives
by moving resources into manufacturing, often in joint ventures with
foreign firms.

Coexistence between the Chinese and Thai communities, as well as
the communist victory in China in 1949, stemmed capital outflows
from Thailand and made available for local investment the profits
earned in selling goods in Thailand.[220] The easing of communal tensions between Thais and Chinese after the 1950s made possible a
dependence on private enterprise without which Thailand's economy
could not have performed as well as it did. In Indonesia and Malaysia
leaders felt more constrained because ethnically linked equity issues
resonated more powerfully. In Malaysia officials adopted formal policies of discrimination against the Chinese; in Indonesia the smaller
number of Chinese felt highly vulnerable and dependent on secure
sources of patronage. In both countries resentment of the Chinese
remained a latent political force. In the Philippines discrimination
against the Chinese may have significantly hindered economic development.[221] Doner says that smooth assimilation reduced the pressure
for redistributional policies and may help to account for the relatively
strong development by the 1980s of Thailand's automobile industry.[222]
The limits of administrative capacity within the Thai state and the poor
performance of state-owned enterprises in the 1940s and 1950s suggest that the state sector could not have led the way to rapid economic
growth. It is unlikely, for example, that state authorities in Thailand
could have made a commitment to state-led heavy industrialization
that would have lasted as long as that in Malaysia in the 1980s.

Ayal argued that increased trust between the Chinese and Thais
(between business and state officials) was central to the onset of rapid
economic growth in Thailand. The unleashing of Chinese business
energy together with the establishment of limits on the bureaucracy's
patrimonial privileges, Ayal suggested, may have been more important
in ushering in high economic growth rates in the late 1950s than
investment promotion, stable political rule, or crude national planning.[223] Muscat also notes the importance to Chinese entrepreneurs
of credible official policy commitments against nationalization or the

establishment of state enterprises that would compete with Chinese businesses. Such commitments helped to stem the flow of Chinese remittances to China and encouraged the Chinese to move from their highly liquid investments, mainly in services, to longer-term investments that stimulated Thailand's industrial development.[224] In the 1990s, among the top ten firms in terms of sales, only Siam Cement was not a Chinese-owned firm.[225]

Chinese Organization of Thailand's Political Economy

The Chinese role in building links between the Thai economy and foreign capital, markets, and marketing networks was crucial to the country's economic development. The Chinese introduced the sugar industry into Thailand.[226] Bankers often arranged business contacts, foreign buyers, and finance for local firms so that merchants had only to affix their signatures.[227] Further, the external orientation of Chinese business and the asset diversity of their interests may have weakened pressures for protectionist trade policies throughout Southeast Asia.[228] The very nature of Chinese business networks militated against a concentration of interests in any one sector and therefore tended to retard the coalescence of import-substituting industrialization coalitions. This was particularly true in Thailand, where financial interests with strong ties to foreign trade were dominant within the business community. By the 1990s many large Thai firms had major investments overseas, in China and elsewhere. Charoen Pokphand, a conglomerate with roots in the animal feed business in Thailand, was the single largest foreign investor in China. With growing business opportunities, the Chinese returned to their roots, with increasing numbers studying Mandarin. One Thai executive argued that doing business in China through personal connections in China was easier than through legal frameworks in the West.[229]

Chinese firms in Thailand were almost all family-owned enterprises. The quality of management of these firms rose rapidly after the 1950s along with the educational attainments of the Chinese. The practice of polygamy among the Chinese helped to produce large families that could keep pace with the growth in their firms. Equal inheritance, however, meant that expansion was as likely to be horizontal or vertical, into related lines of business, as it was to produce growth in the same firm. With sons often going into unrelated lines of business, enterprise networks linked these diverse interests, building vertical and overseas linkages.

The dominant mode of Chinese business organization in Thailand as elsewhere was the small family-based firm.[230] A survey in the 1980s found that over 90 per cent of manufacturing firms had fewer than fifty workers.[231] In 1990 the Labor Department, reporting on a variety of sectors in addition to manufacturing, found that well over 60 per cent of employees were in firms with ten or fewer workers; only 725 enterprises employed 1000 or more workers. Despite the dominance of Chinese family-owned firms in Thailand, modern corporate organizations were also important. In addition to Thai firms owned by the Crown Property Bureau (Siam Cement, the Siam Commercial Bank) or Chinese-owned firms such as Bangkok Bank or Saha Union,[232] many of these modern corporations in Thailand were foreign-owned.

As already noted, the Chinese in Thailand had stronger affiliating urges (sociability) than the Thais. Riggs noted the disproportionate Chinese presence among registered associations in Thailand in the 1950s.[233] Jacobs suggested that the Chinese had a well-developed network of special-interest groupings to offset the absence of support from Thai officials.[234] Phongpaichit and Baker argue that Chinese entrepreneurs drew on community social capital in developing their economic enterprises.[235] Bonacich and Modell contended that because of higher levels of sociability and social capital, middleman minorities in general have access to production factors at lower cost.[236] This probably has some part in accounting for their economic success. Certainly this was the perception of those Thais who bridled against Chinese clannishness and alleged preferences for doing business with other Chinese. In the future, Chinese sociability and social capital endowments may diffuse among the majority Thai population. The reverse, of course, is also possible. Both groups, however, will be responding to ongoing urbanization, affluence, and a degree of democratization, among a host of profound environmental changes.

The new rural brokers who dominated most Thai political parties were almost all Chinese. With the increasing importance of the ability to buy votes in determining political power, their political roles increased. Indeed between Prem's resignation in 1988 and Chavalit's rise to the premiership in 1996, Thailand had a string of Chinese prime ministers (although General Suchinda, not a Chinese, was prime minister briefly in 1991). The four "Chinese" leaders included a former army general turned businessman, one of the country's most admired businessman-bureaucrats, a southern politician respected for his modest style and integrity, and Banharn, another provincial politician and the first to capture successfully the dominant currents in the country's provincial politics.[237] Prime Minister Prem in the 1980s habitually wore the *chut kharajakan*, the uniform of Thai officialdom. Thereafter, emblematic of the passing of bureaucratic dominance, business suits were increasingly in vogue.

Conclusion

Rather than a strong propensity for associating in continuing groups, Thais had an affinity for retaining their independence and seeking their fortunes through participation in vertical clientage networks. The weakness of the urge for horizontal association may be in part a result of the nature of Thailand's traditional polity and society. Its roots may lie in the traditional land surplus. More important for our purposes are its consequences. Among these, Thais generally were not successful in creating efficient business firms or state agencies. At the same time, the low entry barriers Thais erected against outsiders eased the move toward a market strategy by allowing them to enlist the talents of Chinese immigrants.

The Chinese, by contrast, had the social capital necessary to thrive in business despite the absence of an effective framework of laws and institutions supporting a capitalist economy. The Chinese tendency to leave firms to establish their own operations showed up in Thailand's industrial structure.[238] Mukoyama indicates that small firms in Thailand resisted ties to large firms, fearing a loss of independence.[239] And the Chinese tendency to diversify their assets across economic sectors may have worked against the creation of rigid import-substituting coalitions. The relative absence of popular groups organized to press state officials for political benefits also made the move toward a market strategy easier to effect. Against a background of macroeconomic stability, the Chinese were free to pursue their fortunes. State inefficiency and corruption helped to create something approximating a *de facto* laissez-faire regime for many of these entrepreneurs. Hence by the late 1950s the conditions were there for Thailand's adoption of a market-based import-competing industrialization strategy – and for the Chinese to make the most of it.

In short, the Chinese minority's impulse to affiliate and its creation of networks of social groups, combined with the dearth of sociability and social capital on the part of the Thai majority, produced conditions conducive to economic growth in Thailand. Limited Thai social capital militated against alternatives to a market strategy and helped minimize price distortions. The Chinese penchant for diversifying their business activities worked against concentrations of economic power and the creation of powerful business groups with interests tied to the fortunes of a single sector of the economy. The minority status of the Chinese also contributed to their political weakness, reinforcing the curbs on lobbying by dominant economic interests for specific economic policies that flowed from Chinese business groups' diversification of interests. Their networks of cooperative institutions, bolstered by their minority status, helped them overcome the obstacles to business growth that stemmed from the weaknesses of the Thai state. The missing element in this picture is public goods. Neither the Thai state nor Chinese enterprise produced the collective goods, whether social equity, curbs on a variety of negative externalities, or a stimulus to positive ones. The concluding chapter considers these problems at greater length.

It seems clear that the Chinese and Thai populations in Thailand differed considerably in the ease with which they formed cooperative groups to pursue shared goals. This conclusion holds despite the often noted difficulty among the Chinese of fostering cooperation outside (extended) family groups. Skinner, for example, noted the lack of horizontal solidarity among the Chinese, the hierarchical character of their organizations, and the widespread animosity between different Chinese speech groups in Thailand during the first decades of this century.[240] Siow suggests that while the Chinese (in Malaysia) may have been clannish, they were also very individualistic and that efforts at forging ethnic unity often failed.[241] Within business itself, those cases in which firms successfully integrated members from outside the family circle were often singled out for their ability to do so.[242] Nonetheless, when compared to the Thai majority, we find much greater frequency of association both beyond the family and, perhaps more significantly, within extended family groups.

These points are worth bearing in mind while reading Chapters 4, 5, and 6. Discussion of business in Thailand is generally about Chinese firms. Now that the ethnic divide between Chinese and Thai has largely disappeared, how should we assess the levels of social capital among the business community? Not only are the distinctions between the two communities fading, but both now operate in radically different environments that may tend to diminish further the gap between them.[243] Lim suggests that as firms in Southeast Asia became more export-oriented the significance of Chinese identity either receded or emerged as an obstacle. These firms required more flexible labor markets and access to long-term (impersonal) finance than they could obtain through the traditional institutions of Chinese commercial life. In Thailand, as well, business firms increasingly needed the support of state agencies in creating effective market institutions to support their rapid expansion.

Chapter 3

Thailand's Political Economy

The capacities and orientations of states reflect not only their internal attributes but also the nature of the state's interaction with society. That interaction builds on patterns of organization of social groups and the institutions in state and society. While states can shape social organization and social institutions, they are in turn shaped by them.

For many purposes, analytically separating the state from the surrounding social structure is not fruitful,[1] a point Van Roy made in his analysis of Thailand's economy in the 1960s.[2] Within both private and public spheres, social interaction features collective action problems, although the state's authoritative character can diminish them in public contexts. Without organized groups in society that can articulate consensus among important actors, the state faces greater difficulty in mobilizing support for particular policies. When leaders find themselves without organizational building blocks, leadership becomes exceedingly difficult and is likely to depend heavily on coercion. And when political leaders rely on this, they are apt to see independent social organization as potentially subversive of their goals and therefore to try to undermine it. In short, a self-sustaining cycle can result, and in Thailand this cycle helps to explain the relationship between the state's ineffectiveness and the limited degree to which Thais organize cooperative groups.

As noted in Chapter 2, we might argue that social weakness stems in part from the state's suppresion of social groups, for example labor organizations. The problem with this no doubt valid point is that state suppression of popular movements in most non-democratic regimes seems more a constant than a variable, though of course the vigor of that suppression does vary. It is not immediately clear, however, that the relative success of state elites' efforts to suppress social groups can be explained only in terms of the effectiveness with which they apply their suppressive instruments. That variation may also be a product of the strength of the social forces that the state attempts to subdue. It is worthwhile considering, for example, the relative success of state authorities' efforts to suppress the Solidarity labor union in Poland in the 1980s and the Thai Trade Union Congress.

Even when compared with other Southeast Asian countries, Thai leaders have confronted little effective mobilization of social groups making demands of the leadership. Political parties in Thailand have not had organizations with links to villages comparable to those in Indonesia and Malaysia, for example. Whereas in Indonesia, Malaysia, and the Philippines, state leaders engaged in relatively more suppression of various groups, in Thailand, despite widespread repression, what was more striking was the comparative absence of degrees of organization that would prompt state repression.

A striking feature of Thai public policymaking was the apparent lack of authoritative force granted to most decisions and the ease with which a fairly large number of actors could force the reversal of decisions. The process played out as if participants were not paying careful attention to initiatives percolating within state agencies until affected interests were rudely shocked by officials' announcement of a decision contrary to the participants' interests. Something very like this occurred often. Since groups that could articulate interests, congregate, and bargain were poorly developed, the forging of compromises happened, if at all, at the stage of policy implementation, within the state. Politics was concentrated within state institutions not simply because the state was powerful but also because it did not occur within private associations, political parties, or the legislature.

Another factor contributing to the state's centrality as a political arena was the latitude granted officials in legislation adopted by parliament.[3] As a result, to a striking degree, the state and its policy outputs remained the only political stage in town. In this respect, Thailand continued to resemble what Riggs described in the 1960s as a bureaucratic polity in which officials ruled for, and on behalf of, themselves.[4] What changed after the 1960s was that groups outside the state, business interests in particular, began to develop means of worming their way into the insular state.

Foundations of Economic Growth in Thailand

After the overthrow of the absolute monarchy in 1932, bureaucrats and particularly the army dominated Thai politics. A combination of weak organization and active state suppression blocked the development of powerful actors within society. State officials engaged in factional struggles for power largely unrelated to public policy preferences and free of alliances with actors outside the state. The bureaucracy formed the prime minister's principal constituency, and bureaucrats exercised power by and for themselves. In this Thailand was similar to Indonesia where, Robison suggests, the state faced no social power. The weak organization of socioeconomic classes left officials free of effective pressures from society.[5] The society within which the Thai state embedded itself did not undergo changes politically comparable to the functional differentiation evident within the state.[6] While the narrowly based political system did not undermine social stability, neither did it provide political continuity. Between 1932 and 1997 Thailand had sixteen constitutions and well over 50 cabinets.[7] In the middle of this era of turbulent politics, however, Marshal Sarit briefly concentrated power in his hands and laid the policy framework for Thailand's subsequent decades of economic growth.

Sarit staged a coup in 1957, ousting his two main rivals, and the following year set about reshaping the framework of Thailand's political economy.[8] He established stronger political control than any Thai had been able to wield since King Rama VI, early in the twentieth century. Scholars disagree on whether the Sarit regime represented a Thai style of developmental state or a sort of anachronistic embrace of social stasis comparable to the social order under the absolute monarchy.[9] In any case, under Sarit's autocratic rule Thailand adopted a market-oriented import-substituting industrialization strategy and began its steady and rapid economic expansion. Sarit's development strategy suited his own political purposes by undermining his opponents' political bases in the state enterprise sector. American advisors and the World Bank also advocated greater reliance on the private sector and, together with his anti-communism, Sarit's economic policy changes helped him win considerable financial support from the United States.[10]

The conflation of several factors enabled Sarit to pursue developmental goals: Thailand received substantial economic and military foreign assistance; by the late 1950s a growing number of Thais were well educated and possessed skills necessary for more effective administration; and, probably more important, increasingly they adopted functional values oriented to the performance of tasks.[11]

Sarit granted considerable decisionmaking powers to these new technocrats. Generally they were based in the central bank and the new centralized policymaking institutions Sarit established. The Budget Bureau, established under the Prime Minister's Office in 1959, helped to moderate fierce interministerial battles over the allocation of state resources. The disastrous National Economic Development Corporation Ltd (NEDCOL) affair in the mid-1950s strengthened the hand of Sarit's technocrats. Within three years of creating this holding company, politicians had saddled it with huge government-guaranteed debts. With its collapse, the government was left to pay off the debt through the years of the first five-year development plan.[12] As with Indonesia's technocrats sorting through the economic debris of the Sukarno era, the NEDCOL experience gave Thai technocrats strong incentives to vet politicians' financial policies and also brought in the United States and multilateral financial institutions in support of the technocrats' financially conservative policies. They were able to rein in the politicians because Sarit, until his death in 1963, had centralized power and corruption in his own hands.

Together with Prime Minister Thanom Kittikachorn, a Sarit protégé, Sarit staged a "revolution" in 1958 overthrowing the 1932 political system in favor of a Thai polity dedicated to nation, religion, and monarchy, as well as economic development. The newly established Revolutionary Council threw out the constitution and the national assembly, and banned political parties, trade unions, and strikes.[13]

With power firmly in his hands, Sarit was less dependent on maintaining the state enterprise sector as a source of patronage to reward his followers. In fact he drew heavily on funds from private firms, state monopolies, and the new centralized state institutions he created.[14] He enjoyed such unchallenged political power that the instability associated with incessant jockeying for power among competing factions receded temporarily.

A World Bank survey mission had been in Thailand for a year during 1957–58, and Sarit had read its report before returning to Thailand from the United States (where he had received extended medical care). As in its earlier reports, as well as those of American advisors, the World Bank had called for reducing reliance on state enterprises and monopolies, creating incentives for private investment, and, perhaps in part to boost the influence of the technocrats, more overall planning.[15] Officials implemented many of these recommendations. Most important, they declared that state enterprises would not compete with private firms that received investment promotion privileges. Thai officials strengthened investment promotion laws in 1960 and 1962 (the first law dated from 1954).

The US government approved of Sarit's anti-communism and support for private investment. American assistance increased, particularly economic aid. The US ambassador to Thailand, U. Alexis Johnson, felt that Thailand could serve as a showcase in which US firms would demonstrate the benefits for economic development of openness to foreign capital.[16] American investment flowed mainly into mining and services. Japanese investors also responded to the new investment promotion measures, as well as the higher tariffs hindering their access to the local market, by establishing many of Thailand's modern manufacturing industries.

The new regime increased public investments in infrastructure and created the state's key economic agencies. In 1959 the Sarit government established the National Economic and Development Board (in 1971 it became the National Economic and Social Development Board [NESDB], responsible for development planning) and the Bureau of the Budget within the Prime Minister's Office. That same year the government created the Board of Investment and enacted the Industrial Investment Promotion Act. The new regime launched the first development plan (various infrastructure projects grouped together)[17] in 1961. With a surge in investment, domestic and foreign, the Thai economy began to grow at a consistent pace of over 7 per cent a year.[18]

By the mid-1960s Thailand had in place much of the state institutional and physical infrastructure necessary for economic development. When US spending in the region increased sharply with the commitment of US combat troops in Vietnam, Thailand was poised to exploit the ensuing economic opportunities.[19] Subsequently US spending in Thailand increased sharply, including US aid, spending by troops on rest and recreation, disbursements at US military bases in Thailand, and increased Thai exports to South Vietnam.

For the first time in its history, foreign capital was playing a crucial role in the Thai economy. Compared with many developing countries, Thailand had previously received little foreign investment. Unlike the other resource-rich countries of Southeast Asia, European capital never established significant plantation agriculture in Thailand. Trade, rather than investment, drove Thailand's integration into the world economy. In the nineteenth and first half of the twentieth century, foreign capital inflows to Thailand were lower than those to its neighbors. As late as the early 1970s, one study noted that relative to other Southeast Asian countries, foreign capital's share of total capital formation in Thailand was low.[20]

With its open trade regime, agricultural abundance, and small foreign investment, Thailand was slow to develop a modern manufacturing sector. In 1960 food-processing and tobacco accounted for over half of all manufacturing value. As late as the end of the 1960s, manufactured exports accounted for only 3–4 per cent of the total. Indeed, as late as 1982, primary commodities accounted for 70 per cent of Thai foreign exchange earnings.[21]

If manufacturing developed rather slowly, the Thai economy nonetheless shifted in important ways during the 1960s. One of the most significant changes was the diversification of its agricultural production. Thailand's extreme export dependence on rice declined markedly in the 1960s as maize, sugar, kenaf, cassava and other crops became more important. Agriculture developed mostly without state support, although government programs did extend farmers' access to irrigation. Farmers never launched effective opposition to a rice export tax that lowered rice prices and forced crop diversification by making rice production less attractive. A large government road-building program, financed by US aid largely for counterinsurgency purposes, eased farmers' access to markets in Bangkok and beyond. An increasingly efficient network of Chinese distributors played the key role in moving crops to market.

The labor force grew rapidly in the 1970s at a time when agriculture employment's absorptive capacity was reaching its limit. From about 80 per cent of the workforce in the 1960s, agriculture's share shrank to under 70 per cent in the early 1980s. Meanwhile rapid employment growth in the newly protected manufacturing sector in the 1960s and 1970s began to slow in the early 1980s. For the first time, Thai officials faced serious concerns about widespread unemployment. Nonetheless, migrant workers were still able to return to their villages when they could not find work in Bangkok and other cities. This helped to dampen the political fallout of rising unemployment.

From 1960 to 1985, manufacturing in Thailand grew at over 10 per cent a year. It failed, however, to generate either adequate employment or foreign exchange to offset the cost of rising imports. The exhaustion of easy import-substituting opportunities in the 1970s and the need to continue importing capital goods, parts and components resulted in recurrent trade deficits and rising foreign debt; low public revenue collection and growing public expenditures, particularly for the military and state enterprises, produced larger budget deficits. Mainly concerned about the latter problem, the finance ministry stymied initiatives to restructure tariffs in order to increase the economy's openness because of its desire to maintain or boost existing tax revenue. In this respect Thailand's state differed from its Malaysian counterpart, which, even before independence, had developed considerable revenue-generating capacities. In Thailand, weakness in this constantly restrained the provision of public infrastructure and coherent tax, including trade, policies.[22]

Through the 1970s Thailand's current account deficit mounted. Previously surpluses in services (US military spending, tourism, and Thai workers' remittances from abroad) and capital inflows had offset the trade deficits. Slower export growth in the late 1960s coincided with the beginnings of US military withdrawal from the region and aggravated external deficits. Recognizing the need to move toward a strategy of export promotion, officials tried to push exports by various means from the early 1970s, but the strength of the baht hindered their efforts. Officials also failed to coordinate policies so as to shift incentives decisively away from import substitution. Some growth in the export of manufactures, textiles in particular, came as firms found themselves saddled with excess capacity.[23] But far from strengthening their commitment to an export strategy, in the mid-1970s the authorities bolstered import-substitution incentives in some industries. They did so through tariff increases and failure to coordinate the policy inducements employed by different state agencies.

Until the late 1960s, and even into the early 1970s, Thais enjoyed macroeconomic and political stability. Siamwalla suggested that Thailand's open economy during a period of low global inflation, balance of payments surpluses sustained by US military spending in the region, and a fiscal drag that reduced the possible inflationary consequences of those surpluses, all helped sustain economic stability up to 1973.[24] Then the external stability that underpinned Thailand's macroeconomic performance collapsed. Thailand's economy and its politics followed suit.

During the 1960s the number of university students in Thailand swelled. By the end of the decade they had become a new force in Thai politics. Their activism spelled the end of the bureaucratic polity[25] and, for officials, posed the spectre of political organization by parts of the urban middle class. Students led a campaign resisting bus fare increases in 1969.[26] This experience gave them confidence and organizational skills, which they used to stage demonstrations that ultimately toppled the military government in 1973. During these years military factionalism increased and student activism played into the hands of an intramural power struggle. The years of open politics (1974–76) that followed ruptured Thailand's political stasis, ushering in a period of sharp social and political polarization and instability.

Rapid socioeconomic change, the fall of Sarit's successors, and the expansion of the universities fueled a dramatic upsurge in organized activity in Thailand. With the political opening in the 1970s, business participation in government increased rapidly. Early business inroads came from relatively established Bangkok figures, often with strong links to other power centers, including military personnel. In rural areas, however, a new breed of Thai political figures was emerging. They grew wealthy and built local support bases serving as brokers between Bangkok and the regions. Their importance stemmed in part from both the state's relatively weak administrative reach into local areas and the comparative absence of strong local institutions through which central state officials could operate. These "new men," most of Chinese origin, exploited emerging lines of business, often illegal or requiring political connections. With their wealth and local ties they established the first effective electoral vehicles in rural Thailand. Whether backing candidates or running themselves, buying candidates or buying votes, they emerged by the late 1980s as powerful new political actors.[27]

Other groups played political roles for the first time in the 1970s as well. Students helped to mobilize workers in Bangkok and, initially dispatched by government agencies,[28] farmers in the provinces. Communist insurgencies gained in strength in the countryside, and even the Buddhist clergy became sharply polarized.[29] Newly mobilized rightist forces killed dozens of rural organizers.

In response to instability, radicalization, and fears stemming from communist gains in Indochina in 1975, the military staged a coup the following year. The new prime minister, Thanin Kraivichien, was strongly anti-communist, authoritarian, and an ineffective politician. His government attacked powerful vested interests in the course of anti-corruption and anti-narcotics drives.[30] Polarization grew rapidly and disturbed Thai military leaders, who then arranged another coup in 1977. Army general Kriangsak Chomanand, a more cautious figure, became the new prime minister. Finally, in 1980, a faction within the military forced Kriangsak from office and still another general, Prem Tinsulanonda, assumed the premiership. He held it until 1988.

During the 1970s Thai leaders and officials expanded their economic ambitions. With more Thais mobilized to press their economic and political concerns, politicians attempted to direct fiscal resources toward particular economic sectors, including the rural economy. In this climate officials in the NESDB and the MoF grew less fervent in their support of cautious macroeconomic policies. Even BoT officials gave more attention to distributional issues, ultimately to the detriment of broad macroeconomic health. As public sector deficits widened, bank officials no longer worked as assiduously to stem growing state spending. Meanwhile the central bank in the mid-1970s expanded its control over credit allocation, introducing new rigidities into the financial system.[31] Boonchu Rojanasathien, deputy prime minister in the early 1980s, urged that Thailand adopt the profile of a capitalist development state (Thailand Inc.). Boonchu argued convincingly that Thailand's development suffered from structural weaknesses rooted in the low buying power of the mass of impoverished farmers and tried to use state investment, regulation, and institutional innovation to decentralize Thailand's politics and administration.[32]

By the early 1980s the Thai economy suffered from an accumulation of ills, including high energy prices, low prices for its commodity exports, and global recession and rising protectionism that limited demand for its manufactured exports. Adding to those external difficulties, the 1979 collapse of the Thai stock exchange exacerbated widespread financial institution failures in the early and mid-1980s. Thailand continued to run public sector deficits and its foreign debt grew rapidly, the debt service ratio reaching over 27 per cent in the mid-1980s.[33]

To offset these trends, Thai firms needed to deepen the economy's industrial structure and to expand their own export capacities; export industries by and large had few links to the rest of the Thai economy.[34] During this period more Thais in the business world were enticed by the "Japanese model" of capitalism. They wanted to be able to lobby more actively and effectively to change government policies. Thai government officials, academics, and multilateral development agency officials agreed on the need to restructure tariffs, to improve access to export finance for smaller exporters, and to enhance the efficiency of revenue collection. Many observers were aware of the pressing need for increased efficiency in tax collection, infrastructure development, and spending on education and rural development. A lack of resources, however, prevented the public sector from expanding its investments, although World Bank Structural Adjustment Loans in 1982 and 1983 facilitated modest steps toward these goals.[35] Top-level leaders and officials were also stymied by their inability to coordinate the disparate agencies of the Thai state and the cacophony of conflicting private sector voices that greeted officials' efforts to gain greater input from business. Nonetheless, as noted above, officials were able to implement important policy changes during these years.

The sixth development plan (1987–91) called for an enlarged role for the private sector in Thailand's industrial development. This reflected both a growing consensus in Thailand on the limits of the state's administrative capacities and the straitjacket constraining public finances that resulted from its inability to collect adequate revenue. The World Bank pointed to the political unwillingness to raise enough taxes to finance public investment needs.[36] The private sector, however, was also constrained. The oil crises and the ensuing economic recession in the early 1980s imposed severe pain, and many firms were heavily indebted or failed.[37] There was a great deal of hand-wringing about the economy's future.

These particular worries proved misplaced. With only modest policy changes, in particular the currency devaluations of 1981 and 1984, imposition of a ceiling on the public sector's borrowing abroad, and simplification of duty drawback schemes for exporters, Thailand's economy began to record very rapid growth rates in the latter 1980s. Changes in the East Asian economy during this period brought large inflows of direct foreign investment to Thailand and helped to drive its growth. Lower oil prices also helped to restore external equilibrium to the Thai economy after 1986.[38]

Stable politics helped Thai policymakers take some of the steps necessary to adjust to the economic shocks of the 1970s. Presided over by a single prime minister from 1980 to 1988, the regime under Prem made a compromise between bureaucratic dominance and wider political participation, particularly during the years after 1983, which were marked by coalition governments.[39] Political parties and parliament enjoyed greater influence over policy, although technocrats with cabinet portfolios or serving as economic advisors tended to dominate macroeconomic policymaking. The military maintained a check on political parties through their influence in the unelected upper house of parliament.

The military, of course, had dominated Thai politics since the 1930s. Many observers argued that regular military coups undermined the entrenchment of democratic political process or, indeed, of any political regularities. These frequent military intrusions into politics and the coalitional nature of Thai democratic governments help us to understand the fragility of those governments. But parliamentary government has also suffered because of the very limited development of Thai political parties and their inability to overlay an effective party apparatus onto existing organizations in society.

The extension of politics beyond the boundaries of the state posed new challenges for military leaders. So long as they were confined within the state, the military enjoyed superiority based on their control of coercive instruments and their superior, hierarchically based organization. New actors outside the state, however, could use money and, potentially, organization to challenge military dominance of politics.

Beginning in the 1980s, the military, unlike most previous periods of military-dominated parliamentary government, did not associate their interests with those of a political party. Instead the appointed senate served as the legislative expression of military interests.[40] But the lower house of parliament was able to check military efforts to increase the powers of the upper house in 1983, reflecting the growing strength of parliament and the business interests that financed politicians. After the July 1988 elections and the formation of a government under an elected, civilian prime minister, Chatichai Choonhavan, the roles of parties increased and partially eclipsed the military. The civil service and technocrats also saw their roles diminish.

As political groups outside the state grew more active in Thailand in the 1980s, the military increased their vigilance in maintaining surveillance over these groups. They created rural mass organizations and infiltrated interest groups in order to monitor them. This preemptive organization came as a response to the challenges posed by new political players, however, and did not create new, enduring, effective organizations.

In 1986, when parliament tried to diminish budgetary allocation to the military's "secret fund," the military proved their continuing ability to protect their corporate interests. Not only did they defeat the initiative, but, in the face of strong military pressure, parliament increased allocations. The military also occasionally used "loyalty parades" in which the high brass descended *en masse* for a call on Prime Minister Prem. These exercises served to insulate him from strong political pressures from groups that did not enjoy the confidence of leading military officers. Top soldiers used similar means to intimidate their critics, and they maneuvered behind the scenes to forestall a no-confidence motion against the prime minister in 1987.[41]

Many military leaders had rural roots and saw themselves as having close links to rural Thais. These men often believed they had legitimate roles serving as the people's advocates. Officers insisted they were responsible for protecting the people from unscrupulous "capitalists" and "dark influences" (references to the new class of rural power-brokers).[42] Military leaders often expressed suspicion of businessmen and political parties who were, for the first time, integrating villagers into national political structures, albeit loosely.

The military's claims of paternalistic concern for Thai farmers reflected, in part, the growing economic dominance of Bangkok and the Central Region of Thailand. In 1980 nearly three-quarters of the labor force remained in agriculture, while about the same percentage of manufacturing was concentrated in Bangkok.[43] Given the large productivity differential between the two sectors in Thailand, income disparities widened. Through the 1980s the gap between the center and the regions was growing. At the same time, however, political power moved away from Bangkok. With political parties' powers increasing, parliament became more important. Among these parties the most influential were rural-based ones using extensive vote-buying and dominated by godfathers. By comparison, the Bangkok-based parties were weak. The vast majority of the rural population, however, gained little share either of the economy's growing wealth or of the provinces' rising political influence. And political parties' power was not based on enduring organization among social groups.

When Chatichai Choonhavan assumed the premiership in 1988, it soon appeared that the parliament was entrenching its power and severely curtailing the military's political role. More groups began to press demands on the government, including state enterprise unions and civil servants. With budget coffers flush, the Chatichai government was able to accommodate those demands while still running fiscal surpluses (about 4.5 per cent of GDP in 1990 and 1991). Politicians' growing hubris apparently went too far, however, particularly given the degree of unity within the military in the early 1990s. Chatichai's aides baited military leaders, and when Chatichai intervened in the military's promotion process, the military struck back, staging a coup in 1991.

The Revolutionary Council under General Suchinda Kraprayoon placed Anand Panyarachun, a former civil servant and major business figure, at the helm of the government, and over the next year the Anand government pushed through an impressive list of long-planned economic reforms.

Following early 1992 elections, the military attempted to keep Suchinda in power. The public, which had acquiesced in the military coup in 1991 with scarcely any dissent, grew restive with this evidence of the military's interest in entrenching its political power. Chamlong Srimuang, a popular governor of the Bangkok Metropolitan Administration, led protests against the new government. The large turnout of middle-class residents of Bangkok represented a significant new development in Thai politics. When these led to bloody clashes, the king intervened and ordered a settlement of the crisis. Anand again assumed the leadership, organized new elections, and by the fall of 1992 Chuan Leekpai, a career politician, became the new prime minister. The military had overplayed its hand and suffered at least a temporary decline in influence as a result. Before leaving office, the Anand government cut back on military leaders' perquisites, such as seats on state enterprise boards. Military representation continued in the unelected upper house, but the military were unable in the mid-1990s to prevent interference in their promotion decisions by Minister of Interior (and former Army Chief of Staff) Chavalit in 1995 and 1996. Prime Minister Chuan almost managed to complete his term of office, but was ousted by a 1995 vote of no confidence.

The new prime minister, Banharn Silpa-archa, marked a new high point for the ascendancy of the political parties and the provincially based power-brokers. As an outsider using money earned in lucrative public infrastructure ventures to gain power over Bangkok's key political institutions, Banharn in some respects resembed Tanaka Kakuei, a Japanese prime minister in the 1970s. Like his predecessor Chuan (but unlike Chatichai), Banharn never served in the military. Like Chatichai (but unlike Chuan), he was a businessman-politician. Irreverent commentary referred to him as a "walking ATM," for the alacrity with which he dispensed cash to attract supporters. Banharn typified many of the qualities in politicians that had long led military leaders to resist "parliamentary dictatorship" and the dominant role it gave to money in politics. Money was indeed the crucial force in Thai electoral politics, though the reference to parliamentary power was misleading – power lay in the hands of individual politicians more than in the institution of the parliament, but their power rested on the latter institution.[44] Pollwatch, a Thai election-monitoring organization, estimated that the Chart Thai political party spent $60 a vote in some tight races during the 1995 election.[45] Estimates also suggested that to buy a shoe-in candidate cost parties about $800 000 and that candidates and parties spent $680 million during the 1995 elections.[46] Estimates ran considerably higher ($800 000 to $1 200 000) for the November 1996 election.[47]

Thai elites and the Bangkok middle class never took to the Banharn government. The press pilloried the prime minister and other Cabinet members. Opposition to this government grew in Bangkok in response to widespread corruption, economic mismanagement, and the onset, in 1996, of serious economic problems. Banharn insisted that "Bangkok is not Thailand,"[48] hoping to rely on his power base in the provinces and to ignore growing calls in Bangkok for his resignation. His prospects were weakened, however, by the collapse of export growth in 1996 and a growing sense of impending economic troubles. Banharn was soon forced from office. The even more expensive election in 1996 returned power to an increasingly familiar cast of politicians, in this case led by general-turned-politician Chavalit. After this economic conditions deteriorated swiftly. The new prime minister had only weak influence over most of the key economic portfolios in the new cabinet. Meanwhile political controversies raged over efforts to amend the constitution. Increasingly, political arrangements no longer appeared irrelevant to Thailand's economic success, but capable of threatening that success.

With military power in decline, Bangkok's plutocrats, technocrats, and the middle class increasingly emerged as forces balancing the political power of the rural power-brokers. Various groups called for constitutional amendments enabling impeachment of parliamentarians and establishment of an administrative court that would enable individuals to have legal recourse to bureaucratic measures. Tension among these different groups was evident in the battles over what procedures to employ in rewriting Article 211 of the constitution, which would determine how Thais could amend the charter in the future. The Ministry of Interior and political parties attempted to maintain control over, or at least participate in, amendment procedures. Pitted against these two groups, the middle-class voice in Bangkok rejected working through existing political institutions (parties and parliament) and wanted nationwide elections of unaffiliated delegates to work on amending the article. A compromise of sorts emerged in the fall of 1996 (parliament maintained a role in selecting candidates and a veto, which would then trigger a nationwide referendum, over the final draft of the charter) and, through indirect election, delegates constituted a committee of ninety-nine, who set about drafting a new constitution.[49]

Increasing political organization of social groups also emerged clearly by the late 1980s in response to the increasing sensitivity of various natural resource issues. Rural groups began to mobilize against business and government interests intent on building dams, clearing forests, or removing squatters from forests.[50] Much of this increased activity stemmed from the leadership of NGOs, and these in turn depended to a considerable degree on foreign financing.[51] This development clearly reflected the emergence of greater mobilization of rural Thais.

Meanwhile King Bhumipol presided above the struggles between military, parties, and business interests. By 1996 King Bhumipol's reign had lasted fifty years, far longer than any of the previous Chakri kings (or than any other living monarch). Beginning with the unrest of the mid-1970s, he assumed a crucial role in Thai political crises. The king served as the final arbiter in national political dramas and intervened actively three times in the 1980s in order to restrain military challenges to the prime minister. In 1992 he moved to stop bloodshed in Bangkok between protestors and the military. Calling the leaders of the two groups before him, he admonished them to act on behalf of the Thai people and effectively ordered an end to the crisis. Later he occasionally injected himself into public policy debates. This alarmed some observers, who worried about the potential leaching away of the king's charismatic authority through overuse, but the king also had some ability to delegate that authority to aides, like former Prime Minister Prem, known to enjoy the king's confidence.

The Thai economy expanded rapidly and steadily from the late 1950s in a context of unusual price and social stability. This achievement is particularly striking when we recognize the extent of fundamental structural change evident both in Thailand's economy and polity during these decades. By the late 1960s most observers saw the rebuilding of the monarchy under Rama IX as a key ingredient in this successful formula. The institutions of the state, however, did not contribute directly to the country's economic gains beyond public officials' roles in maintaining broad macroeconomic stability.

Thai Economic Policymaking Institutions

As part of the sharp redirection of the Thai economy in the early Sarit years, Thai officials created central economic policymaking agencies, such as the National Economic Development Board (NEDB – later the NESDB, with the addition of "Social" to its name) and the Bureau of the Budget, and established them under the new Prime Minister's Office. These new agencies did not immediately transform the quality of Thai officials' administration. Limited skills, lack of autonomy from political meddling, and particularly the absence of reliable data precluded effective regulation, much less any more ambitious roles.[52] The new agencies, however, did provide the government with enhanced research and analysis capabilities and a greater measure of centralized control over the various ministries, particularly during Sarit's rule. While the extent of policymaking delegation to technocrats varied over the years, relatively insulated and powerful state agencies generally dominated macroeconomic policymaking (see Chapter 4). Furthermore, a rapidly growing cadre of talented technocrats led gradually to improved administrative efficiency and data collection.

Gradually officials and businessmen came to interact more regularly. Particularly important were the roles of business leaders and associations in the late 1970s in getting officials to adopt the rhetoric appropriate to export-led industrialization strategies. While most of the substance of such a strategy had to wait another decade, officials took some important steps as early as the late 1970s. A key step came in 1984 with a dramatic devaluation of the baht that continued, because of the heavy weighting of the weakening dollar in the currency basket to which the baht was tied, through the decade. Nonetheless, the influence of business continued to be stronger through *ad hoc* and clientelist channels than through formal, inclusive associations. Officials generally reached decisions without consulting those most affected. Typically this produced howls of protest and an inability to implement declared policies.

Development planning in Thailand dates back to 1950 when officials established the Thai Technical and Economic Committee and the National Economic Council, largely to administer foreign aid resources.[53] By 1960 NEDB officials were putting plans together in an *ad hoc* fashion, generally following leads from the various ministries. Glen Parker, a foreign advisor dispatched by the United States Aid to International Development agency to the NEDB in the early 1960s, studied the activities of various Thai state agencies and found a sorry state of affairs.

> Generally, it must be concluded that there is no sense of direction whatsoever in the activities of the Industrial Investigation and Experimentation Division, but rather a considerable amount of aimless threshing around partly for the purpose of fooling budget officers who may pass continuing budgets for deadhead projects either because they do not have the time to investigate or do not have any basis for making a critical judgment. This, however, is only part of the problem.[54]

This unflattering portrait of Thai public administration during those years was perhaps atypical in its acerbity, but not in the sense of the problems it described. Wade observed in his study of Taiwan that governments' capacities to accelerate development vary.[55] In the Thai case, that capacity was surely limited. Hence Muscat's conclusion in the 1960s that the Thai government lacked the endowments necessary to foster industrialization. The limitations of Thai public administration prompted Muscat and many others to suggest for Thailand a development strategy minimizing direct government intervention in markets while concentrating on providing infrastructure and other public goods.[56] It is of course possible, indeed clearly quite easy, for authorities to persistently adhere to bad economic policies. In Thailand, however, the failure of earlier policies by the 1950s facilitated the shift toward the more orthodox economic policies long favored by the country's traditional elite.

Dramatic failures of economic development strategies in poor countries are of course not uncommon. In Indonesia under Sukarno, economic disaster facilitated a sharp policy redirection under Soeharto, his successor. There, however, oil wealth repeatedly offered opportunities to diverge from newly embraced orthodox policies. In the Philippines access to US and multilateral assistance had a similar effect. And in Malaysia both greater state capacities and revenues not only encouraged more active state leadership but also produced stronger outcomes. In Malaysia too, however, the failure of state industrialization initiatives in the 1980s forced public retrenchment and the adoption of more liberal policies.[57]

The principal economic policymaking agencies in Thailand outside the Cabinet were the NESDB and the Bureau of the Budget within the Office of the Prime Minister, the Fiscal Policy Office within the MoF, and the BoT.[58] The NESDB was responsible for policy formulation and planning, including Thailand's five-year plans. The Fiscal Policy Office devised fiscal policy guidelines, including tariff policies, and the Bureau of the Budget was charged with allocating budgetary funds consistent with development plans.[59] In general the latter was more successful in refereeing the allocation of funds than it was in evaluating the means by which or the ends to which they were used.[60]

The BoT enjoyed considerable prestige and policymaking independence.[61] During the late 1980s and the 1990s that prestige came under threat from the MoF. As a result of the firings or resignations of central bank governors and charges of official impropriety, the bank's reputation, and perhaps its influence, suffered. The weakening of institutions traditionally associated with control over macroeconomic policymaking raised the danger of a future loss of control over the economy's health. Observers were also concerned that the adjustment buffer long afforded by the countryside's capacity to absorb slack labor resources was about exhausted. The result promised stronger challenges to the maintenance of disciplined macroeconomic policies.[62] By the time the baht collapsed in 1997 amid widespread financial institution failures, some of the costs of these developments became clear.

Since the mid-1950s the BoI has provided firms with investment incentives. This role was particularly important in the 1970s and 1980s as firms sought to export in the face of negative incentives. The board's policies, however, often worked at cross-purposes. It continued to favor large and capital-intensive projects even as it avowed its commitment to an export strategy. Some of these conflicts reflected different emphases on the part of the BoI staff and the ministers and business association representatives who served as board members. The board made no practical use of performance requirements. From its inception, it announced plans to become more selective in awarding investment incentives and to give more attention to issues of industrial structure.[63] It made little progress in either area. In 1983 it issued its first clear criteria for awarding investment privileges, but it continued to operate without the benefit of clear policies.[64] Perhaps its key contribution was a policy of indiscriminate allocation of investment privileges. It simply allowed the firms to fight it out among themselves[65] and avoided strengthening overly cozy ties between firms and their political champions.

The various ministries tended to resist NESDB interference with their policies. At times the board had only weak vetting powers;[66] ministers could often determine the degree to which they heeded board directives and the latter had few means of enforcing compliance.[67] In general Thai public administration was erratic, shifting with changes in personnel. This was true, for example, of efforts to boost agriculture, and rice production in particular.[68] As noted above and in Chapter 5, it was also true of Thailand's trade policies.

Prime ministers with strong (military) bases of support could exercise considerable sway over policies. Most prime ministers, however, were hobbled by the need to keep their balance amid the political free-for-all in which political competition was generally free from the constraints of formal political institutions and processes such as mass participatory parties or elections.[69] Prime ministers were unable to discipline subordinates or coordinate the work of different ministries. Civil servants, prizing caution and stability, and hoping to survive and advance in a system rewarding seniority, often resisted new policy initiatives. As a result, important issues often remained unresolved until overtaken by events, opposition weakened, or an externally induced crisis forced the hands of officials.[70]

During the 1960s the prime minister and Cabinet made all major economic decisions. The NESDB, the BoT, and the Fiscal Policy Office had considerable influence on macroeconomic policies. Ministries

responsible for implementing state policies generally controlled sectoral policies, and no agency was in a position to coordinate them.[71]
Early in 1981, in the face of mounting economic imbalances, officials
considered making changes in the economic planning and implementation processes as part of the fifth development plan. One proposal
envisioned a National Economic Policy Steering Committee to coordinate the work of the NESDB, the Budget Bureau and the Civil
Service Commission.[72] Prime Minister Prem subsequently established
the Council of Economic Ministers, which screened large public investment proposals before forwarding them to the full Cabinet. Under
Prem the NESDB also enjoyed considerable discretion in vetting economic development initiatives. As noted above, however, technocratic
dominance receded over the 1980s in the face of rising influence on
the part of political parties.

By the mid-1990s it appeared that forces were at work to change
some of the decisionmaking patterns described above. In preparing
the eighth development plan, Sumet Tantiwechakun, the NESDB's
Secretary-General, scheduled a wide range of meetings with different
groups of Thais. Significantly, these meetings came before officials
had drawn up the plan. The November 1996 election featured considerable substantive discussion of economic issues, at least in Bangkok,
perhaps because of deepening anxiety about the health of the Thai
economy. Many opinion leaders expressed unhappiness with the
Banharn government's economic management. In the course of the
campaign the leading contenders for the premiership advertised
teams of former economic policymakers who they promised to employ
as advisors and ministers if elected. The new Chavalit government
declared reform of the bureaucracy as a central goal, and in 1997
launched a masterplan promising major cuts in personnel and rises
in salaries.[73] These developments reflected a trend toward increasing
political influence over economic policymaking and hinted at a
dawning recognition that the ability to hold power would be linked,
however loosely, to an ability to meet the demands of a widening circle
of political claimants.

State Performance

By many standards, the Thai economic bureaucracy performed poorly
even after Sarit's rationalizing reforms of the 1960s. Officials were
rarely able to coordinate policymaking or to ensure consistency and
coherence,[74] though monetary, fiscal, and exchange rate policies
generally stood out as exceptions to this trend. It is likely that, as Riedel
suggested was the case in Indonesia, good macropolicies in Thailand

counterbalanced poor micropolicies.[75] The macroeconomic policy-making agencies attracted the most skilled civil servants.[76] Thailand's economic stability also benefited from its great agricultural strength. Siamwalla emphasized the resilience and flexibility of Thailand's small-scale agricultural producers and suggested that, in the case of rice, Thai farmers' comparative advantage was so great that government policies were unable to undermine it.[77]

Administration in Thailand suffered from a disjuncture between planning and implementation. This lack of coordination largely resulted from the dearth of bargaining and coordinating institutions either within state agencies, among them, or between state agencies and private interests. Jacobs noted the weaknesses of Thai public administration in the 1960s. Despite the state's industrial activism, he argued, its interventions were not guided by any underlying coherent conceptual framework; as a result officials tried to implement short-term and contradictory policies.[78] The advent of planning in the 1960s, he suggested, reflected a longing for development but was not grounded in a willingness to compromise the essential patrimonial character of the Thai economy and society.[79]

Riggs saw Thai administrative inefficiency as stemming from the nature of Thailand's bureaucratic polity. While the monarchy had until 1932 subordinated the bureaucracy, when officials overthrew the absolute monarchy they were no longer subject to control by political leaders.[80] Scott noted that thereafter, with administration and politics conflated, influence, connections and loyalty were more important than skills or competence. The granting of ever more bureaucratic concessions to new political allies resulted in the feudalization of administration. The Thai elite, he suggested, had no need to respond to the concerns of an unmobilized peasantry, docile parliamentarians, or a dependent business class.[81] Indonesia, under Sukarno, produced even more extensive administrative balkanization, in part because political competition extended beyond the state, but without institutions able to pattern that competition. In a Huntingtonesque nightmare, Sukarno created ninety-three ministries within his cabinet.[82]

The weakness of Thai state administration threatened serious economic damage so long as officials were setting up numerous public enterprises. The NEDCOL fiasco was the foremost object lesson on how such schemes could damage the Thai economy. Thai public administration of that time recalled Keynes' observation that

> above all, the ineptitude of public administrators strongly prejudiced the practical man in favour of laissez-faire – a sentiment which has by no means disappeared. Almost everything which the State did in the 18th century in excess of its minimum functions was, or seemed, injurious or unsuccessful.[83]

After Sarit's rule, however, public enterprises receded in importance.

The feudalization of public administration in Thailand described by Scott and others probably had advantages. In this decentralized context, no single group controlled access to crucial areas of decisionmaking. In the textile industry, for example, while Ministry of Industry officials controlled access to factory licenses, the Ministry of Commerce could allocate licenses to import machinery. The result was that it was highly unlikely that a single political party (and parties generally were rent by faction and division) would control both ministries and preclude new entrants into the industry. And even if one party ever gained such control, smuggling of machinery or the illegal establishment of factories offered other options.[84]

In the 1960s Silcock saw Thai economic policy as essentially liberal. Policy outcomes resulted from *ad hoc* bargaining among elites pursuing divergent goals. Thailand's liberalism was not so much a product of ideology, a search for efficiency, or an outcome of struggle among socioeconomic classes as it was a result of *ad hoc* pluralism within the state that induced its weakness.[85] A quarter-century later, but before he twice became prime minister, Anand Panyarachun made the same point in referring to Thailand's "laissez-faire by accident."[86]

Particularly after the collapse of NEDCOL in the 1950s, Thai officials clearly understood the limits of the bureaucracy's capacities. In recognition of the constraints imposed by the slow pace of state decision-making and implementation, an economic advisor to Prime Minister Chatichai Choonhavan in the late 1980s argued that neither Thailand's economy nor its society were geared for fast growth.[87] An economic advisor to former Prime Minister Prem Tinsulanonda reflected a similar view in 1987, expressing doubts that Thailand's administrative or political systems were adequate to sustain a capitalist developmental state-like model of growth. And he asserted in the late 1980s that, despite repeated failures of efforts to restructure the economy through public policies, market forces were effecting those changes.[88]

Thailand did not really have an export "strategy" before it became a formidable exporter in the late 1980s. The Thai government promoted exports in the latter 1970s by relaxing export controls and abolishing export taxes, by allowing duty-free import of inputs needed for export goods, by providing income and business tax rebates for exports, and by expanding export credit facilities.[89] But high tariffs remained in place, so the overall tariff structure retained its anti-export bias.[90] In fact officials did not achieve tariff neutrality until the devaluation of the baht late in 1984, if then.[91] Part of the reason officials were so slow to reduce tariff levels, as well as to eliminate the business (turnover) tax, was MoF concern not to sacrifice revenue.[92]

Tariff levels remained quite high even after the 1992 implementation of the value-added tax and a string of fiscal surpluses removed one of their earlier rationales. Thereafter, however, the trend was one of rapid and sharp tariff reductions (non-tariff barriers were never pervasive). Yet even with the long maintenance of high tariff levels, most economists argued that Thailand's industrialization was relatively "natural," that is, consistent with its factor prices.[93] It is possible that business firms' ability to elude distorting regulations helped to account for the coexistence of market-unfriendly policies and a market-conforming pattern of resource allocation. Many observers concluded that state policies contributed relatively little to Thailand's success, beyond the important steps of maintaining an open economy and stable macroeconomic policies, and giving free rein to Chinese entrepreneurs.

The establishment of stable macroeconomic conditions was enormously important, an achievement owed in large part to the skills of Thailand's leading technocrats. But those skills did not run deep in the Thai ministries, nor were they alone responsible for Thailand's stable macroeconomics: that record depended also on keeping open hunting season for politicians plundering other (line) ministries. As the circle of political competitors broadened in the late 1960s, however, there were greater challenges in sustaining autonomous macroeconomic policymaking. By the late 1980s and 1990s it became clear that macroeconomic policymaking was increasingly shaped by short-term political concerns (see Chapter 5).

Thailand's macroeconomic policy record does not shine when compared with the capitalist developmental states of Northeast Asia, but it looks good when compared to most developing countries. This chapter suggests, however, that Thailand's relative success rested less on an abundance of skills, either technical or political, than on the limited nature of the challenges facing officials. Furthermore, in Thailand, ongoing, sharp, intra-elite competition prevented the entrenchment of favored interests to the degree evident in Indonesia, Malaysia, and the Philippines. Hence, even with little insulation of economic policymaking, the competition for rents among politicians, officials, and their clients helped to minimize the associated costs.

With growing prosperity, income inequality, and a changing economy in the 1970s, pressures for government services grew. The needs for physical infrastructure and more technical and secondary education ensured rapid increases in government investment. In 1970 only a quarter of better educated Thais worked in the private sector; by the 1990s the share had increased to about three-fifths.[94] Facing increasingly competitive foreign markets, by the late 1970s and early 1980s many Thais argued the need for coordinated tariff changes, business–government cooperation, and sectoral industrial policies. In fact, particularly in certain sectors, such cooperation increased. Pressures for rapid tariff reductions in the 1990s flowed from Thai commitments within the GATT as well as the ASEAN Free Trade Area. Exporters grew increasingly concerned to reduce the costs of production inputs such as petrochemicals and steel, which received high levels of protection. Businesses also pushed for larger roles in international trade negotiations and demanded more information from government agencies. The Business Economics Department within the Department of Commerce established in 1995 a joint working group with the Board of Trade, a business association, to analyze ASEAN Free Trade Area, Asia Pacific Economic Cooperation, and World Trade Organization agreements.[95]

Business interests' push for more voice in formulating public policy reflected rising frustration with inept economic management, particularly at the sectoral level. Firms were concerned about frequent policy reversals, particularly on large infrastructure projects for which the outcomes depended on shifts in governing coalitions. Growing political influence over even macroeconomic policymaking threatened to aggravate this problem and to make state commitments increasingly incredible. A government white paper on export policy formulated under the Chuan government faced long delays after a change of government in 1995, before eventual adoption by the Banharn government.[96] In the early 1990s a Japanese business executive complaining about the nature of Thai public policymaking was alarmed by the central bank's loud chastizing of the commercial banks for failing to lower interest rate spreads. At about the same time, foreign participants in an expressway consortium had bailed out of the project when the Thai government was unable to honor the terms of the contract. The Japanese executive noted the difficulty of locating the source of ultimate authority in Thailand, contrasting the Thai case with other countries in the region (even the Philippines!), where small cadres of technocrats allegedly made key economic decisions.[97]

Conclusion

In the 1980s many scholars linked the economic achievements of East Asian economies to the institutional attributes of capitalist developmental states.[98] Clearly, however, Thailand industrialized rapidly without an autonomous state playing a vanguard role in identifying, and allocating resources to, priority industrial sectors. In Bangkok no mandarin vanguard controlled the state in order to drag, kick, and haul[99] Thailand from tradition to modernity.

Phongpaichit and Baker rejected the notion that Thai officials differed fundamentally from their counterparts in the capitalist developmental states of Northeast Asia. The key difference between the two, they argued, arose from the availability of land in Thailand in the 1960s, the predominance in the financial sector of private institutions, and the historical absence of mercantilist ideological influences and models. They acknowledged, however, that even if Thai officials shared goals in common with officials in the NIEs, application differed substantially. Part of the difference, they suggested, lay in the relative absence in Thailand of effective policy instruments.[100] This book contends that chief among these missing instruments was a society organized in ways that could facilitate state penetration of and by society.

The state in Thailand lacked a politically insulated yet powerful bureaucratic elite, a clearly articulated development strategy, a full range of discretionary policy tools, and the information that would be necessary to make effective use of such tools. The institutions of state–business (and business–business) cooperation were relatively undeveloped.[101] Rapid economic growth in Thailand was possible not because state officials manipulated incentives intelligently but because they limited their interventions (or, by cancelling each other, curbed the distortions that resulted from those interventions).

Political elites everywhere are subject to an array of pressures that tempt them to intervene in markets and to regulate the flow of labor, technology, and capital between the local and international economies. Officials may want to intervene to foster economic growth, redirect economic activity (from "parasitic" to "productive" pursuits, from lower to higher value-added production), assure that certain groups share in the benefits of growth, gain political support, or undermine the economic bases of support for potential political rivals. The impulse to intervene is that much stronger given the theoretical support for such intervention, from the mercantilism of Colbert to the demand stimulus of Keynes and on to the new trade theory. The attractiveness of the East Asian NIEs as models added further support for dirigiste models of development. Refraining from market intervention, in short, is rarely easy.

Such restraint becomes that much more difficult if, added to the above factors, we take into account social pressures for redistributional policies. Thai officials faced a relatively easy task in committing themselves to market policies because of the comparative weakness of demands, particularly from popular groups, for such policies. Business demands were also weaker than they might otherwise have been because of the diversity of their interests, spread as they were across economic sectors and between import-competing and export-oriented activities. Even when state authorities were not committed to liberal ideas, their weaknesses were so great that firms might be forgiven for having failed to notice.

Clearly, a relatively liberal development strategy (or outcome) has advantages. While it is possible for "growth coalitions" to use market intervention to encourage capital accumulation and foster economic development, these coalitions tend eventually to use political power to defer necessary adjustments to changing economic conditions. In contrast, restraint in market intervention can help to ensure an economy's flexibility of response and its ability to avoid the emergence of debilitating distributional coalitions.[102] Such restraint ensured the Thai economy's flexibility until the mid-1990s.[103]

Thailand's rapid growth offered hope to would-be followers. Thailand industrialized without the benefit of a cohesive, task-oriented administrative elite of the kind associated with the earlier industrialization drives of the East Asian NIEs. Because Thailand's institutional endowments appeared closer to the developing world norm than were those of the East Asian NIEs, it promised to serve as a more realistic model for emulation by other developing nations. The difficulty with this argument is that Thailand's success rested not only on stable macroeconomic policies but on an absence of effective sectoral policies – those elements of a potential "Thai model" most easily reproduced elsewhere. In Thailand, however, economic success depended, in addition to those factors, on the specific assets of the Chinese, their social networks that enabled them to overcome market failures, and the absence of key effective market institutions. These features of the Thai model may not be replicated easily everywhere.

There were, of course, major costs to the Thai pattern of economic development as elsewhere in Southeast Asia. The Thai state did not perform well in providing public goods. The people suffered from dirty air and water, to say nothing of the prevalence of AIDS. The economy labored with poor infrastructure, from labor training to ports and roads. It also failed to develop an adequate number of firms with skilled workers producing parts and components for firms engaged in final assembly. These weaknesses helped to account for the economy's heavy dependence on foreign capital and the collapse of the baht in 1997, as discussed further in Chapter 7.[104]

Low levels of sociability and social capital help to explain the weak public policy performance detailed here. The impact of institutional weaknesses on policy performance (policy formulation, implementation, and realization of goals), however, varied according to the nature and number of active social groups and the obstacles to cooperation evident in different economic sectors.

PART TWO

Chapter 4

Bargains Between Bankers and Bureaucrats[1]

Poor countries lack capital. Any industrialization strategy requires an effective system of gathering savings for investment in production. Joseph Schumpeter saw banking, along with entrepreneurship, as one of the key factors stimulating economic growth.[2] Given the general recognition of the importance of banking, many governments try to create or shape financial systems to foster economic growth, using financial institutions to shape and direct industrial development.[3]

Political authorities in most late industrializing countries guided capital allocation. Johnson's study of Japan's postwar political economy emphasized state officials' ability to direct scarce capital at below-market costs to favored industrial sectors.[4] Officials pursued broadly similar policies in Taiwan and especially South Korea.[5] In part because banks are so central in creating economic prosperity, authorities in many developing countries either established public banks, imposed tight controls over banking activities, or favored banks through public policies. Even where private banks predominated, as in Thailand, their central developmental roles and the regulatory dilemmas specific to financial institutions induced state officials to favor the banks while regulating them more closely than officials regulated firms in other sectors.

The peculiarities of finance encourage extensive state assistance to overcome market failures and limit their consequences. Financial institutions pose severe problems of moral hazard: the danger that explicit or implicit state guarantees against ruin will invite the extreme risk-taking behavior that boosts the likelihood of just such an outcome. Typically this danger induces intimate ties between banks and state officials; even in Thailand the particular characteristics of this sector led to regulatory and political links among bankers, political leaders, and officials that were unusually close by Thai standards. These ties, however, frayed under the pressures of greater political competition and liberalization of the financial and foreign exchange sectors in the 1990s.

The Thai financial system was unusual among developing countries in the very limited role given to public institutions other than the central bank. The absence of large public industrial or development banks exposed manufacturing firms to regular market discipline, though the financial industry's oligopolistic structure also tended to reduce competitive pressures within the industry.[6] While the state eschewed pervasive direct roles in the finance sector, prudential concerns dictated intimate supervision of financial institutions. The threat of imminent collapse of the financial system in the early 1980s induced particularly close cooperation between private institutions and public regulators. Those ties subsequently frayed in the 1990s as a result of several factors, most importantly the shift in the regulatory regime in a liberal direction and the growing influence of political parties over financial and monetary policymaking. These developments paved the way for yet another financial crisis in the 1990s.

Thai financial institutions expanded impressively during the period of rapid economic growth, the Bangkok Bank growing to be the largest financial institution in Southeast Asia. Thai banks played key roles in financing and coordinating the Thai private sector. While not universal banks, the Chinese family-based financial business groups were in some ways similar to universal banks and were able to provide elements of private sector governance.

Finance sector officials had clear goals and generally achieved them through cooperation among state agencies. Private bankers also cooperated with each other, generally working within the Thai Bankers Association. This record differed strikingly from the picture painted in subsequent chapters of failed state initiatives and limited cooperation among private and public institutions.

The unusual patterns of policymaking in the finance sector resulted from regular interaction among a small number of bankers and regulators, officials' ability to block the entry of new financial institutions into the field, and therefore the relative ease with which banks could apportion among themselves the recurring benefits they achieved through cooperation. Furthermore, the interests of bankers and regulators intertwined. When several banks and finance companies faced ruin in the early 1980s, the interdependence of financial institutions and government financial officials became painfully evident.

The character of this interdependence between bankers and regulators changed in the 1990s with financial liberalization. Among the regulatory changes were moves to allow new entry into formerly protected segments of the industry, which had the effect of increasing the number of firms and, to a degree, reduced the interdependence among them. By undermining the cozy cartel created by a few dominant institutions, deregulation made the financial sector in some ways more similar to other sectors of the Thai economy. Yet deregulation also demanded still more careful regulatory oversight of financial institutions, something financial officials generally failed to achieve.

The financial sector was unusual in one further respect that is not captured by the explanatory variables used in the Introduction to compare the finance, textile, and infrastructure sectors. In both private and public spheres, many of Thailand's best and brightest individuals contributed to a fairly rapid reduction in the social space separating Thai financial officials and Chinese bankers. The banks were among the first private institutions to attract members of the Thai nobility and were the first to bankroll some of their employees as they moved into politics. These individuals were not the *arrivistes* associated with the new rural political brokers discussed in Chapters 1 and 2. Many of these bankers later held leading positions in political parties but retained their reputations as technocrats largely free of the unsavory taint attached to most leading Thai politicians.

Financial policymaking in Thailand brought together a small number of very powerful banks and state agencies. Thai commercial banks dominated the country's economy, with about a third of financial system assets by 1970, rising closer to half in the late 1980s (the central bank share dropped from 36 to 16 per cent over those years). By 1980 three private banks held over half of all commercial bank assets.[7] The MoF and the BoT, for their part, housed some of Thailand's most influential technocrats. With relatively few state officials and private bankers controlling this sector, collective action problems were less pronounced than in other sectors. Nonetheless, relations between the BoT and the MoF were not always smooth and grew worse in the 1990s with growing political influence over policymaking and deregulation in the sector.

The financial sector stood out in Thailand because of the prevailing patterns of policymaking marked by relatively high levels of cooperation. It was also distinctive because the politics of implementation was less evident than in other issue areas. This difference resulted from the better development of prebargaining institutions that encouraged relatively seamless policy formulation and implementation. More unusual still, prior to formulation officials consulted with private institutions and made public pronouncements of the directions in which policy would move. For example, even during the 1990s when officials were pursuing major changes in the regulatory regime that ultimately brought on economic collapse in 1997, they were able to implement the new policies with an usual degree of coherence. Despite the need for adjustment in response to changing conditions and pressures, including the changing fortunes of political leaders, authorities advanced specific measures that were generally consistent with an overall masterplan unveiled in 1995. This "plan" included measures already adopted as well as directions for future policy changes. The broad coherence of policies in this sector, and of particular policy plans, contrasted with national development plans produced by the NESDB, various proposals to create a textile intelligence unit (Chapter 5), or plans for the development of the Eastern Seaboard (Chapter 6). That deregulation ultimately helped to bring on the baht's collapse in 1997 was a result of weaknesses in the substance of policy, as well as a growing politicization of the policy process, which began in the late 1980s. The economic collapse stemmed only in part from failures of coordination among state agencies. More significant was the growing ability of politicians to constrain the central bank's prudent oversight of financial institutions at a time when they enjoyed easy access to foreign funds.

The financial sector in Thailand is of unusual interest because, despite their primary engagement in macroeconomic policymaking, finance officials engaged in some of the most ambitious and coherent efforts at sectoral promotion found in Thailand. By the late 1980s financial authorities pursued development of the sector with an eye to job creation and strategic advantage in ways and for goals comparable with Korean officials fostering plans for the development of the shipbuilding industry.[8] They hoped to create strategic strengths and foster high-wage jobs. The collapse of the baht in 1997 showed, however, that ultimately these initiatives were far from successful. Financial authorities' activism also flowed over into other sectors as a result of their jurisdiction over tariff policymaking during the 1990s when Thailand's trade regime changed rapidly. This left finance officials reconciling the competing demands of firms positioned within different segments of industries facing diminished tariff protection.

Thai Finance Before the High Growth Era

Western imperialists in the nineteenth century sometimes used the defense of the value of their investments as a pretext for colonization. Eager to preclude the application of this principle to their country, Thai officials came to equate monetary stability with national sovereignty. Officials gave greater weight to keeping the baht strong than the seemingly futile tasks of building up economic and military power sufficient to confront imperialist encroachment.

Under pressure from Great Britain, Thailand signed a treaty in 1855 under which it extended extraterritoriality to British citizens in Thailand and forfeited control over trade duties. Similar treaties with other foreign powers followed. Thailand only succeeded in maintaining its formal independence at the expense of about 40 per cent of its nominal territory ceded to Great Britain in the south and to France in the east and northeast during the late nineteenth century. To avoid providing a pretext for additional encroachment, Thai officials put a premium on cautious and conservative fiscal policies aimed at avoiding foreign debt and maintaining the value of the baht.[9] Thai leaders limited public expenditure of any kind, even for the development of basic infrastructure such as irrigation works that would have increased production and foreign exchange earnings,[10] devoting their energies to centralizing control over the kingdom.

Given steadily growing exports, ample foreign reserves, and little political pressure to expand public spending, Thai elites did not need to intervene to maintain the baht's stability. During most of the period before World War II, Thailand ran balance of trade surpluses and accumulated considerable foreign exchange reserves.[11] It exported mostly rice and tin, with four-fifths of total exports going to the British Commonwealth. Officials tied the baht to the pound sterling, keeping the baht one of the world's few free and stable currencies up to the 1940s.

European banks dominated the Thai financial system from the late nineteenth century. Local Chinese banks and the Siam Commercial Bank, which state officials established early in the twentieth century, offered weak competition. Officials used regulations enacted in 1906, 1928, and 1937 to monitor the financial institutions. In 1942, to preempt their Japanese allies from establishing a central bank in Thailand, Thai leaders set up a central bank. A new banking law in 1945 made the Bank of Thailand the main instrument for fairly weak control over the commercial banks (its formal powers rested with the finance ministry).

Wartime experience with inflation reinforced Thai officials' concern for monetary equilibrium. To conserve foreign reserves and sustain the overvalued baht after the war, officials put administrative controls on foreign trade and exchange transactions and adopted a multiple exchange rate system.[12] With the return to regular balance of payments surpluses, the baht regained its stability and officials ended the multiple exchange rate system in 1955.[13] Immediately thereafter, however, NEDCOL's large debts threatened to bankrupt the country (see Chapter 3). This experience served to reinforce Thai officials' conviction of the necessity of sound financial practices.

Financial Development During the High Growth Era

By the 1960s Thai officials were no longer preoccupied solely with economic stability. A strong business sector was emerging, and in some areas a communist insurgency gradually assumed significant scale. Increasingly, economic expansion and equity became key goals. Finance officials came to see banks not only as potential sources of economic instability but as means of financing investment for economic growth. Limits on new entry into banking restricted competition and promised stability. Banks and their political champions reaped the advantages of a rapidly growing demand for capital. For the 1960s as a whole, Thais provided over 90 per cent of the savings to finance private capital formation.[14]

The powerful private banks were central in financing growth. Financially based business groups accounted for close to three-fifths of the total assets of the one hundred leading groups in Thailand, and close to three-fourths if we exclude foreign groups.[15] Most of the banking families had extensive networks of business contacts overseas. For Thai authorities, however, the entrepreneurial exuberance of the commercial banks was a mixed blessing.[16] They were bold and free-wheeling in business but not overly scrupulous about observing formal prudential regulations.

The Commercial Banking Act of 1962 aimed to strengthen regulatory oversight of the banks. This legislation increased the BoT's power to license and inspect local banks and gave it wider powers to vary cash and capital reserve ratios. It also limited to 40 per cent of its capital the amount a bank could lend to any one borrower. In an effort to tame the Chinese business panache, the 1962 law tightened a variety of regulations, forbidding banks, for example, to make loans to their directors or their spouses.[17]

Some of the banks were already heavily involved in international finance. The Bangkok Bank opened a branch in Hong Kong in 1954 and served as creditor to Malaysian tycoon Robert Kuok Hock Nien. During much of its history the bank made two-thirds of its loans abroad, where it earned half its profits.[18] By 1968 it also had branches in Indonesia, Malaysia, and Singapore.[19] It made substantial investments in Hong Kong, Singapore, and Taiwan. By the 1980s the Bangkok Bank was financing almost half of Thai exports and about a quarter of its imports.[20]

Through the 1960s the Thai economy remained remarkably stable even as its foreign trade expanded rapidly. The banks did not play major roles in providing long-term capital to industry, but they enjoyed plentiful business opportunities,[21] often in expanding distribution networks in Thailand and overseas through Chinese business groups. US military spending, meanwhile, stimulated the local construction and service industries and added to the banks' business.[22]

By the mid-1970s Thai financial officials were entertaining more ambitious and diverse development goals. This was largely a response to the social fissures that opened up with the collapse of the bureaucratic polity, and the wider range of interests able to make demands of policymakers. As students, farmers, and workers became more active politically in the mid-1970s, economic growth assumed new urgency. Equity concerns gained greater salience given growing communist and Muslim insurgencies. This unprecedented degree of mobilization of Thais posed unfamiliar challenges to officials.

Faced with such demands, officials were unable to devise policies that would achieve non-traditional goals. Neither did they succeed entirely in sustaining the economy's long record of macroeconomic stability. This was hardly surprising given the host of external problems, including higher energy prices and global stagflation, with which they had to cope. Regulating the banks and managing macroeconomic policies became increasingly complex. Interest rate ceilings that had preserved the banking cartel and guarded against incentives for excessively risky lending also limited the flexibility of commercial banks. Authorities began licensing finance companies in the 1970s as a way of increasing competition and flexibility within the financial sector without deregulating the commercial banking sector itself. New policies seeking to boost rural development by allocating credit, however, introduced greater rigidity into the system.[23] This became more important as both international capital flows and the gap between Thai and overseas interest rates rose.

Along with Thailand's rapid growth, the banking industry grew more concentrated. Deposits rose sevenfold from 1957 to 1967 and again during the next decade.[24] Commercial banks' assets increased at an average annual rate of 22.5 per cent from 1962 to 1978.[25] Each bank, meanwhile, came increasingly under the control of a single dominant family, and the top four banks boosted their market share among all commercial banks and the newly introduced finance companies. For all the concern about increasing oligopoly in the financial sector, officials continued to bar new entries to banking. In 1982 the World Bank urged Thai authorities to allow the establishment of new commercial banks. Foreign banks' presence in Thailand in the 1980s, meanwhile, was smaller than in any other large East Asian market economy.

Bankers' powers rested not only on increasing concentration of control over financial resources. Political connections had also been important – bankers were key players in Thai politics long before the advent of rapid economic growth in the 1960s. The bankers' links to powerful politicians complicated the tasks of regulatory officials. Over time, regulatory authorities' powers of oversight expanded, but at the same time bankers became more powerful and diversified their sources of patronage. As the balance of political power shifted toward politicians and away from regulators in the 1990s, this trend assumed great significance.

Profits from the rice trade, parts of which the government Rice Bureau garnered until 1955, helped to finance political competition in the early 1950s.[26] After 1955, however, leading financial officials turned the rice trade over to the private sector, largely preempting other officials' access to the trade as a source of funds. Together with Sarit's turn to private firms later in the decade, this meant that Thai leaders would need to work more closely with Chinese businesses to raise the funds they needed to finance their political ambitions. Banks and other firms provided politicians with revenue by including top government officials on their boards of directors and helping to finance and manage state enterprises, another source of political finance. In 1972 three-quarters of the banks had military-political leaders on their boards.[27] Silcock saw the alliance between Sino-Thai business interests and Thai politicians in the 1960s as a threat to the state's autonomy and Thailand's economic growth. He feared that Thailand's political system lacked the institutions necessary to prevent money from overwhelming it.[28] By the late 1980s many observers of Thai politics were expressing similar worries. And by 1997, with the collapse of the financial system due in large part to inadequate regulatory oversight, those concerns proved fully justified.

As Thailand's politics shifted in the 1970s, the banks adapted accordingly. They had long experienced challenges in getting protection from politicians. Military leaders provided a degree of security from the 1950s, but the extent of factionalism within the military left bankers exposed to the danger of betting on the wrong horse. In the 1970s, as political parties grew more powerful, the banks increasingly worked through these new political vehicles. This strategy became important when some of the banks' former political sponsors in the military grew weaker in the 1970s. The banks appeared to be potentially vulnerable political targets; legislation in 1979 directly challenged the core interests of the powerful banking families, and in 1981 the promoters of a failed coup apparently had plans to nationalize the banks as well as to kill members of these families.[29]

In 1979 parliament amended commercial banking regulations. One of the objectives of the new law was to weaken the financial power of the few dominant Chinese family groups,[30] which were required among other things to dilute their ownership of the commercial banks; the regulations gave the banks five years to effect these changes.[31] The new law also limited the expansion of credit to non-priority businesses and reduced the maximum credit that could be extended to a single borrower to one-fourth of a bank's capital fund. In an attempt to parry these legislative attacks, the banks began to sponsor former employees' forays into politics. In the end, authorities failed to enforce fully the new divestment requirements.

The collapse of the equity market in 1979 made enforcement of divestiture regulations unattractive. Hard economic times in the 1980s had the effect of partially harmonizing the interests of bankers and their regulators. The ensuing shakeout in the financial sector increased concern over the health of the financial system. Bankers and financial authorities, however, continued to clash over regulatory issues.

By the early 1980s Thai officials were increasingly alarmed about macroeconomic instability. In 1983 the economy registered a record high trade deficit, and commercial bank credit grew by 34 per cent. Finance authorities' anxiety led them to attempt new and unorthodox measures. The BoT placed a limit of 18 per cent on commercial bank credit expansion in 1984. This was the first use in Thailand of quantitative controls on bank lending. The banks fought back. They mobilized powerful opposition to this measure, including firms affected by the diminished access to credit, forcing the BoT to relent and lift the ceiling in August 1984.[32] Commenting on his removal of the credit ceiling, the BoT governor at the time acknowledged the weight of these political pressures in forcing his hand.[33] Having paid those pressures insufficient heed, he subsequently left office at the behest of the finance minister.

Thailand's economic fundamentals steadily worsened through the 1970s. Disaster finally hit the financial sector, triggered by the fall of a major finance company and the ensuing collapse of the local stock exchange in 1979. Other financial institution failures followed: beginning in April 1983 and extending through 1984, the MoF had to rescue thirty-two finance companies; fifteen others collapsed and the BoT revoked their licences.[34] Foreshadowing the financial crisis of 1997, many financial institutions' losses came from heavy exposure to affiliated firms, particularly in property speculation.

Thailand's first financial crisis since the NEDCOL fiasco in the mid-1950s eventually encouraged closer cooperation between the leading banks and financial authorities. Surviving the crisis required cooperation and, in particular, a lead role by public officials. To cope with the insolvent finance companies, they created the Fund for the Rehabilitation and Development of Financial Institutions late in 1985,[35] managed by the state-owned Krung Thai Bank. The MoF and the BoT also created a management pool to assist the collapsed finance companies. In return those companies surrendered one-fourth of their shares and half their voting rights to the BoT.[36] Authorities provided over ten billion baht in soft loans and over two billion in working capital to the ailing banks and finance companies.[37]

The financial sector crisis to some extent encouraged a perception among public and private actors that their fates were intertwined and that cooperation was needed to overcome these difficulties. At the same time, however, the banks fought back against the imposition of quantitative lending controls in 1983 and new regulatory measures proposed by the central bank. Finance officials first began to propose revised banking regulations in 1982. Not only financial sector crises but also opposition from the commercial banks and government coalition partners delayed adoption of the regulations. Kukrit Pramoj, a former leader of the Social Action Party, which was part of the governing coalition, was himself the chairman of a commercial bank. In the face of concerted opposition, finance officials deleted several particularly objectionable clauses from the act. Fearful that legislators in parliament would weaken it further,[38] the authorities finally announced the new regulations in 1985 in the form of an emergency decree. They did so without consulting the banks, and while parliament was in recess. The emergency decree increased the powers of the MoF and the BoT to intervene, through a variety of instruments, in the operations of financial institutions in the early stages of trouble.

By the 1970s finance officials had gone beyond their traditional concern for system stability to embrace developmental and equity goals. The harrowing economic and financial conditions of the late 1970s through the mid-1980s then compelled authorities to return their primary focus to system stability. By 1986, however, Thailand's economy had not only recovered but had moved into a new phase of more rapid growth, spurred on by large inflows of foreign investment. Growth hastened the recovery of the financial system. Macroeconomic stability returned, and for the first time since the 1960s the government regularly ran fiscal surpluses. Despite ongoing external imbalances, officials were free to turn to a more proactive regulatory agenda.

Seizing the opportunties afforded by strong growth, officials in the MoF and BoT began to push a comprehensive set of financial reforms. By and large, the more powerful banks supported the reform agenda. The banks were prospering, with total assets rising sixfold between 1985 and 1994 to over $180 billion. Finance companies' assets expanded almost ten times to nearly $50 billion.[39] External pressure from the GATT and, more directly, the United States encouraged the plans for liberalization, as did the expansion of global capital flows. By the late

1980s both bankers and state officials were also hoping to expand Thailand's economic roles in neighboring socialist countries undergoing market transitions and to develop an offshore banking market.

Thai officials no longer pursued only the goal of system stability, or even efficient or equitable financing of economic activity. Increasingly, financial policy became financial industrial policy as officials promoted the industry for its own sake. In his *Treatise on Money*, Keynes wrote: "It is Enterprise which builds and improves the world's possessions . . . if Enterprise is afoot, wealth accumulates whatever may be happening to Thrift; and if Enterprise is asleep, wealth decays whatever Thrift may be doing."[40] Thai bankers and state regulatory authorities, however, increasingly came to see financial sector development as a means of enhancing efficiency, extending Thai economic activity abroad, and as an independent locus of entrepreneurship. Surakiart Sathienthai, finance minister under Banharn in the mid-1990s, argued that Thai financial institutions would stimulate Thailand's trade abroad with its neighbors.[41] The Chuan and Banharn governments tried, as governments had done from the 1970s, to use financial regulatory policies to address the economic concerns of the largely rural electorate. Regulators favored requests from financial institutions to expand into new lines of business, or to establish new branch operations, if the institutions strengthened their business presence in rural areas. Another policy goal, reducing the oligopoly power of a few banks, was partly overtaken by events in the 1970s and 1980s. While officials adopted regulations in 1979 in an unsuccessful attempt to curb the banking families' dominance, both market forces and liberalizing measures in the 1990s achieved that goal. The banks faced increased competition from finance companies and the Stock Exchange of Thailand (SET), while large local firms' access to foreign bank loans grew rapidly.[42] Then, in the mid-1990s, authorities began to license new Thai and foreign banks.

The Context of Financial Reform

The domestic financial instability of the 1980s and international services negotiations in the 1990s shaped Thai financial sector reforms. Cooperation in weathering the financial crises of the 1980s for a time strengthened mutual confidence between the BoT, the finance ministry, and private financial institutions. The indivisibility of the dangers associated with a potentially spreading financial crisis encouraged increasingly frequent interaction. Regulators needed, and by and large obtained, access to ever more information from financial institutions on their banking activities. The new banking legislation in 1985 had increased the BoT's powers to regulate institutions for prudential aims. As financial officials gained greater powers and capacities, they were able to cooperate more effectively with private financial institutions.

By the 1990s financial officials were also well positioned in two-level bargaining games, using external pressures, mainly from the United States, to chart the direction and speed of the Thai financial sector's liberalization. But by enhancing financial institutions' access to foreign sources of funds, reform of the financial sector ultimately undercut the central bank's ability to control them. Deregulation and the increasing number of players in the sector also complicated cooperation. These new factors led in the 1990s to growing worries about Thailand's financial sector governance. State finance agencies faced a loss of talented personnel as the private sector drew them away with far higher salaries. Prestige differences between officials and bankers were no longer enough to compensate for the growing pay gaps between the two.

Private financial institutions supported much of the reform agenda, in part because of their growing offshore financial services and the expanding international orientation of their domestic clients. The big commercial banks moved increasingly into merchant banking, expanding industry's share in their loan portfolios. They also pressed to be allowed to increase their equity participation in industrial firms as Thailand's industrial sector underwent rapid expansion. Manufacturing had emerged as a major profit center for the banks in the late 1980s. While regulations limited financial institutions' direct holdings in other firms, the main banking families established a wide range of affiliated interests in industry, including those developing on the Eastern Seaboard.

Smooth implementation of financial reform required the active cooperation of the major banks. The increasing importance in Thai politics of elections, political parties, and parliament favored businesses, including the banks, that could finance elections. Widespread consensus on the need for reforms enabled officials to sustain policy changes through considerable political turbulence. In fact state financial officials initiated major financial reforms after Chatichai Choonhavan, a leader of the Chart Thai political party, replaced Prem as prime minister in 1988. Despite reduced policy delegation to technocrats in general, and the particular obstacles thrown up by Chatichai's minister of finance, also a Chart Thai party leader, financial officials continued to be able to work with the major private institutions to manage the reform process. Initially, more democratic politics did not seem to reduce the independence of state officials in macroeconomic policymaking. Party politicians by and large were content to trawl from the growing resources afforded by control over the line agencies, including rapidly expanding infrastructure spending. During the Chatichai years political competition over access to the public trough increased rapidly but did not outstrip growth in the revenue pool.

Through the dramatic political turbulence of the early 1990s, financial officials sustained the reform agenda. While governments differed in the degree to which they were able to force through a policy agenda in the face of opposition, each was committed to the same broad set of financial sector policies. This constancy reflected in part the degree to which Thai elites, public and private, had achieved consensus by the early 1980s concerning the appropriate development strategy for Thailand and the specific needs of the financial sector. Scarcity of public resources, the experience of significant economic disturbances, the rising power of exporters of manufactures, and the diminishing social space between public and private sector elites facilitated a consensus emphasizing the leading role of the private sector in the economy's development. The days of Chinese businessmen apologizing to officials for their poor Thai had passed.[43] The divide separating the public and private sectors had largely disappeared. Power concentrated increasingly in the hands of political parties led by businessmen with roots in state-linked rent-seeking and illegal activities. By the time Banharn came to power in 1995, their power was so great that it threatened the country's economic health. Before considering the economic and financial crises that first emerged in 1996, however, it is necessary to gain a more detailed sense of the financial sector reforms that began in the late 1980s.

The Reform Agenda

A series of financial sector reforms in the late 1980s and 1990s had a number of aims: to boost local savings (and reduce current account deficits);[44] to enhance the financial sector's ability to compete in international markets and exploit new opportunities abroad; to meet demands emerging under negotiations on the GATS for increased foreign access to Thai financial markets; to facilitate the creation of a secondary capital market; to encourage local financial institutions to raise long-term funds; to make it easier for state firms to issue debt; to help the central bank manage domestic liquidity; and to create new financial institutions, such as an Export-Import Bank and a credit-rating agency, that would relieve the BoT of some of its policy responsibilities.[45]

To achieve these goals, significant new legislation was necessary. Officials forced through most of the bills required during the final months of Prime Minister Anand's second tenure in 1992, including the Finance, Securities and Credit Foncier Bill and the Securities Exchange

Commission Bill. The former cleared the way for decreases in the segmentation of the financial industry and redefinition of the activities of different kinds of financial institutions; the latter strengthened regulatory oversight of local equities markets.

Officials deregulated capital flows in the early 1990s. In May 1990 the Chatichai government announced Thailand's adoption of the IMF's Article VIII status; by 1993 foreign exchange liberalization was largely complete. These changes assumed great importance in 1996 and 1997 as capital inflows increased authorities' difficulties in controlling the money supply and speculative attacks on the baht culminated in a sharp depreciation in 1997 and collapse of the financial sector. The huge capital inflows to Thailand raised the need for prudential supervision of financial institutions. But political changes that increased the powers of party politicians hampered the extension of such oversight. In Thailand, as proved to be true throughout East Asia in 1997, a financial system adapted to a context of capital scarcity proved inadequate to the stricter regulatory requirements of a financial system coping with abundance.

One of the first steps to induce competition in the financial sector came when financial officials began to deregulate interest rates in the late 1980s. Between June 1989 and June 1990 the BoT removed or raised ceilings on most commercial bank deposits and loans, as well as on promissory notes and loans by non-bank finance companies. Early in 1992 authorities ended deposit rate ceilings and raised the limit on loans to 19 per cent, and by June 1992 they had completed interest rate deregulation with the removal of all lending rate ceilings.

In order to strengthen domestic institutions' competitiveness vis-à-vis foreign banks, state authorities began to allow commercial banks to underwrite debt instruments. To reduce entry barriers and promote competition among local institutions, officials allowed finance companies to expand into areas, such as foreign exchange dealing, previously reserved for commercial banks.

Moves to allow new entry into the banking sector went less smoothly. In September 1989 the MoF selected nine foreign banks as candidates for new banking licenses, then narrowed the list of candidates to four. At that point, however, the government shifted its policy on issuing new licenses (see below). Nonetheless, from 1994 to 1996 financial authorities hectored local institutions about the need to prepare for greater competition, from foreign institutions and others, while gradually reducing the extent of segmentation within the industry. In January 1994 the Council of Economic Ministers approved reforms that would allow finance companies and foreign banks with international banking facilities licenses (see below) to open lending branches in provincial areas. Foreign securities companies would eventually be able to hold up to 49 per cent equity in Thai financial institutions.[46]

Parliament passed the Securities and Exchange Commission Bill in February 1992 and it went into force in May. Authorities hoped to strengthen the local equities market as a way to boost savings and force banks to compete harder for smaller firms' business, assuming that larger firms would have easier access to the SET. The Securities and Exchange Commission (SEC) issued requirements for firms listing on the SET, began regulating the exchange, and issued guidelines on the issuance of debentures, promissory notes, mutual funds, and warrants.[47] The new legislation empowered the SEC to appoint the SET board, which in turn exercised direct regulatory authority over the market.[48]

Of the many other financial sector reforms, the creation of offshore banking facilities was particularly important. In the early 1990s the BoT and MoF wanted to make Bangkok a financial center, particularly for services business with Burma, Cambodia, Laos, and Vietnam. A central bank working group developed ideas that it later refined in launching the Bangkok International Banking Facilities. Authorities used foreign pressure to liberalize the local financial market as an opportunity to establish these new facilities through which foreign financial institutions could increase their business in Thailand. The Thai proposal to the GATT for the creation of offshore banking facilities stalled foreign demands for opening the Thai market while strengthening Thailand's regional financial role. Rather than granting foreign firms greater access immediately, Thai authorities required them first to participate in the development of new offshore banking facilities, thereby strengthening local skills in these new banking activities. The facilities would also enable the Thai economy to cope with its continuing shortage in local savings, which was certain to continue in light of enormous public investment plans under Thailand's Eighth Five-Year Plan (1997–2001) and ongoing high levels of private investment.

The MoF announced the general outlines of an international banking facilities plan in August 1992 and the Cabinet approved it in September, before the Anand government left office. In March 1993 Thai authorities approved forty-seven Thai and foreign applications to establish international banking facilities. These included all fifteen Thai banks, twelve of fourteen foreign banks with branch offices in Thailand, and twenty foreign banks without previous branch operations in the country. During the first year of operations the new facilities handled over $6 billion in business and continued to expand rapidly.[49] By 1995 officials grew concerned that the bulk of new business was out-in lending, Thais borrowing foreign exchange and increasing the local money supply. Lower interest rates made these loans irresistible, particularly because Thailand's exchange rate peg seemed to remove foreign exchange risks. By 1997 the combination of exchange rate rigidity and interest rate differentials proved disastrous.

Thai commercial banks supported the development of the offshore banking services. Thai banks became increasingly interested in new opportunities offshore, following their customers by opening branches in Ho Chi Minh City, Phnom Penh, and Vientiane to handle trade and remittance businesses (with trade carried out in baht or dollars).[50] Thailand was the leading trade partner for Burma, Cambodia, and Laos. By 1994 Thai banks held eleven of twenty foreign banking licenses in Phnom Penh. They also had six branches in Laos, three in Vietnam, and the first foreign branch in Yunnan.[51] The Bangkok Bank, Krung Thai Bank, and Thai Military Bank were particularly active in the region.[52] In 1992 the Bangkok Bank opened the Yunnan branch office, adding branches in Vientiane and Laos and one in Shanghai in 1993.[53] The Thai Military Bank began lending in the early 1990s to Vietnam's Bank for Foreign Trade through its Ho Chi Minh City branch office.[54] Thai financial authorities promoted the use of the baht in the region, hoping to make Bangkok a regional banking center.[55]

Finance authorities issued an overall plan for the financial sector early in 1995. A series of public announcements leading up to the un-veiling of the plan reflected skillful two-level game-playing as officials emphasized to domestic audiences that liberalization would begin in those areas where local firms needed access to foreign technology and the local market was of modest size. Fuller liberalization would come only when Thai firms had grown stronger.[56] US officials played their part in that game, consistently pushing for further, faster liberalization.[57]

The plan called for new legislation to facilitate authorities' prudential supervision of financial institutions and help the implementation of the BoT's monetary policy. Broadly, it aimed to foster greater compe-tition at home to prepare local institutions for increasing penetration of the Thai market by foreign financial institutions.[58] And, for the first time in thirty years, the MoF would issue new commercial bank licenses. Of fourteen new licenses, officials reserved seven for foreign banks.[59]

Authorities hoped that increased financial competition, particularly from the local securities market, would wean industries from their heavy dependence – four-fifths of their capital – on short-term com-mercial bank lending.[60] At the same time officials began to relax some of the restrictions on bank holdings in other businesses. In May 1994 the BoT ruled that banks could not hold more than one-fifth of their total capital in equities or more than 10 per cent in any one company without receiving approval from the central bank. This represented a loosening of regulations (formerly these higher ceilings applied only to banks' first-tier capital).[61] And the regulatory context in which officials implemented them, with politicians increasingly able to obstruct financial officials' oversight of financial institutions, also undermined their effectiveness.

The wide-ranging financial sector reforms of the late 1980s and 1990s were marked by comprehensiveness, coherence, clarity of articulation, and skillful implementation. They also contained, however, a design flaw that proved fatal, particularly when combined with inadequate prudential oversight.

Fending Off Foreign Capital

Deregulated capital flows, large interest rate differentials between Thailand and abroad, and an exchange rate peg created a deadly cocktail that was a key factor bringing on the collapse of the baht in 1997. Other factors also contributed to the collapse of the baht and the broader financial and economic crises. The Thai export sector began to stall in 1996, financial institutions fueled a bubble in the property sector, and a series of quarrels and scandals undermined confidence in public financial officials. Even as the baht crisis gathered force in 1997, Thai leaders were constrained by their narrow political bases of support. They depended most on precisely those interests which stood to suffer the most damage from necessary policy adjustments. We begin with a discussion of these background developments.

Evidence emerged by the late 1980s and early 1990s of increasingly strained relations between the BoT and the MoF. These strains surfaced during Pramual Sabhavasu's tenure as minister of finance under Prime Minister Chatichai in the late 1980s. Pramual was hostile to local financiers and attracted widespread criticism. Despite Pramual's base in Chatichai's party, the latter eventually had to push him from office.

Through the many changes over the late 1980s and early 1990s, officials made no efforts to enhance the statutory independence of the central bank. The finance minister sacked the BoT governor in 1984, and Pramual followed suit in 1990. Subsequent struggles between the central bank and the MoF developed under later governments as well. Some observers felt that Tarrin Nimmanheiminda, a forceful finance minister, intruded into policy areas once reserved for the BoT. When the central bank failed in 1994 to achieve its inflation targets, Minister of Finance Tarrin called for closer coordination in monetary policies through increasing the finance ministry's control over policymaking.[62]

The central bank and finance ministry differed on how to reduce the sector's segmentation[63] and on standards that finance companies would have to meet in order to be candidates for banking licenses.

More general concern about financial sector governance emerged after Banharn Silpa-archa, having failed to attract other candidates, named Surakhiat Sathienthai as his finance minister in 1995.[64] Other candidates were apparently deterred either by Banharn's reputation for unsavory politics or by a reluctance to take responsibility for issuing new commercial banking licenses (see below). Surakhiat had no former experience in the financial sector and quickly became embroiled in controversies with well-established financial technocrats. At a time when increasing fragility of the country's currency and general financial health put a premium on skilled management, the growing macroeconomic policy influence of party politicians complicated the jobs of officials tasked with making financial and monetary policies. BoT officials botched an effort to bring criminal charges against the top executives of the Bangkok Bank of Commerce, which made loans to politicians while running up huge debts that eventually required a $7 billion central bank bailout.[65] Charges later flew over the awarding of commercial bank licenses and played a part, among a legion of scandals, in the fall of the Banharn government in 1996. Deputy Prime Minister Chavalit held up issuing new banking licenses when the MoF did not award a banking license to the War Veterans Organization.[66] Officials postponed yet again, until after the November 1996 election, decisions on awarding further bank licenses. They faced a zero-sum game of high stakes with a wide circle of bidders, including foreign institutions backed up by their respective governments. The finance minister finally awarded seven new foreign licenses in November 1996 and a further three Thai licenses in January 1997.[67] Also under Banharn, at a time when the central bank was following tight money policies, the government increased allocations to the armed forces and rural clients.[68] The finance minister's inability to curb this spending led to his resignation in September 1996.

Not only were officials fending off political influence in financial and monetary policymaking, they were also feuding with one another. This was evident with the fallout from the Mexican peso crisis in 1995. BoT Governor Vijit Supinit unsuccessfully advocated recourse to exchange controls, and Ekamol Khiriwat, head of the SEC and deputy governor of the central bank, opposed him, gaining finance minister Tarrin's backing. In November 1995, again facing Ekamol's resistance, Vijit set up a $400 million fund to refinance margin loans in an unsuccessful effort to prop up the SET. Vijit eventually forced the resignation of SEC head Ekamol in late December 1995.

These scandals and squabbles grew worse in 1996. Surakhiat resigned in May 1996 (the Banharn government would run through two finance ministers and one vice-minister during its brief tenure), soon after the BoT took over the Bangkok Bank of Commerce with its extensive debts resulting in part from loans to figures associated with the Banharn government.[69] After repeated official denials from central bank and finance ministry personnel, the bank's weakness came to light only when an opposition MP revealed it in the course of a censure debate. Critics maintained that for political reasons the central bank waited too long before moving in on the bank.[70] Indeed the BoT had ordered the bank to make changes in its policies earlier in the year and was apparently aware of fraud and the violation of central bank regulations.[71] The ensuing controversy helped induce the resignation of BoT Governor Vijit in July 1996. Vijit was also the target of criticism for having made rulings on, and approved an SET listing for, a finance company in which he held shares.[72]

Financial and monetary officials clearly no longer worked above Thailand's political trenches. The many scandals that embroiled Thai financial authorities assumed significance beyond their titillating appeal. The scandals diminished confidence in Thai financial officials' competence and integrity, and helped thereby to bolster sceptical assessments of the baht's strength. Battles among officials may also have contributed to their failure to regulate the lending activities that underpinned the burgeoning property boom. At the very time that the boom threatened the health of the financial system, the economy's real sector was undergoing severe pressures as well, as evident in the stagnation of exports in 1996. All these factors would combine and aggravate the consequences of the 1997 baht crisis.

An additional factor, ultimately with the longest-lasting impact on Thailand's economic health, was the property sector bubble that built up in Bangkok in the 1990s. Earnings in this sector peaked in 1991 and vacancy rates climbed, but frenzied building continued unabated. A property index on the SET fell from about 2500 in early 1994 to below 1000 by August 1995.[73] In April 1994 the BoT took measures to curb property loans. A shakeout in the industry appeared imminent. Offshore loans continued to fund the sector's expansion, however, as banks, and particularly finance companies, were still tied to the sector. With the property market in the doldrums and turnover virtually nil (the president of a leading bank declared "there are no transactions"), valuing assets became increasingly difficult (prices were not falling), so that officials tried to force sickly firms to merge with government help.[74] Worse, building of office space continued so that even after the July 1997 devaluation the financial sector crisis remained very serious, with significant additional office space in Bangkok due to become available in 1998 and 1999.[75]

Thailand's largest finance company, Finance One, was one of the casualties of aggressive property development. Its announced plan to merge with Thai Danu Bank at the end of February 1997 confirmed the extent of its fragility and pushed still more investors out of the local equities market. Estimates for the cost of bailing out Finance One in June 1997 came to $6.7 billion.[76] The banks had been saddled the previous year with charges of some $400 million to bail out the Bangkok Bank of Commerce (a fraction of the total cost) and to boost the SET.[77]

In addition to crumbling financial sector governance and a financial meltdown, Thailand's very rapid economic growth suddenly looked vulnerable in the mid-1990s given stagnation of the equities market and exports, and the first fiscal deficit in years in 1997. Officials also had to contend with ballooning foreign debt, further exacerbated by the baht's collapse, and current account deficits. The SET stopped growing, and began to sink, early in 1994. It fell through the next two years and into 1997. As the financial sector in Thailand grew ever more shaky, foreigners grew increasingly concerned. Between 30 and 40 per cent of their holdings in Thai equities were in bank shares.[78] Exports recorded almost no growth in 1996[79] after expanding by 24 per cent in 1995. Major exports such as garments and footwear, frozen seafood, and plastic goods dropped in 1996.[80] Foreign debt jumped from $28 billion in 1990 to about $90 billion by 1997.[81] The sudden collapse in export expansion in 1996 seemed to reflect in large part the long anticipated difficulty that Thai firms would have, given weaknesses in human capital, infrastructure, and public sector performance, in moving from labor-intensive to more skill-intensive exports.

Against this backdrop Thai officials had to cope with an exchange rate peg, a large gap between interest rates at home and abroad, and deregulated capital flows. Fortunately, during the first wave of speculative attacks on the baht, the real sector was still enjoying strong growth.

Rising levels of foreign investment beginning in the late 1980s had made the Thai economy more vulnerable to financial shocks coming from abroad. By early 1994 some Thais expressed concern about rising dependence on short-term inflows of capital and suggested that a devaluation of the baht might be necessary. Foreigners were investing in the Thai equity market and Thais were borrowing abroad to take advantage of lower interest rates. Thai firms used the equity market boom, while it lasted, to leverage still more debt, much of it through the offshore banking facilities, rather than diminish their debt burdens.[82] While the trade and current account deficits had peaked in 1990 at 12.2 and 8.9 per cent of GDP respectively, both figures remained high (in 1995 the current account deficit was back over 8 per cent).[83] Interest rate rises abroad helped to spark an abrupt move out of the Thai stock market early in 1994, sending shares plummeting.[84]

Thai financial authorities faced a rude shock early in 1995 when the baht temporarily came under attack as part of the fallout from the Mexican peso collapse. The baht momentarily devalued, the SET slumped, and interbank loan rates jumped.[85] Fears around the region prompted the first ever meeting of the region's central bankers in Hong Kong, in January.[86] Emerging market mutual equity funds around the world had grown skittish about their holdings in developing countries. Nonetheless, the BoT earned plaudits for its successful defense of the baht against speculative attacks. The central bank responded to the crisis by adding liquidity to the system through the repurchase, loan, and swap markets,[87] pushing local banks to take steps to raise local savings and drawing down its foreign currency reserves to defend the baht. The BoT used a special window to make foreign exchange available to local institutions. Through these measures the bank was rapidly able to stabilize local markets. Eventually the bank also moved to try to monitor bank lending more closely, and to curb certain kinds of lending, mainly for consumption.[88] It temporarily put to rest fears that Thailand would follow Mexico as a victim of a loss of foreign confidence and major currency outflows. The central bank spent only $400 million in reserves in defending the baht from attack during the first quarter and by the next quarter was more concerned about the impact of large capital inflows on gathering inflationary pressures than about the baht's strength. To reduce dependence on short-term borrowing abroad, the Bank of Thailand raised cash reserve requirements on foreigners' short-term deposits. And to dampen price pressures at a time when the Banharn government was increasing government spending, it ordered the banks to reduce their total lending (it expanded 29 per cent over the first half of 1995).[89] The adept management of the ripple effects of the Mexican financial crisis strengthened the BoT's credibility within the Thai financial community. Other trends, however, were working to weaken financial authorities' ability to sustain the country's exchange rate and financial systems.

When the Chavalit government came to power in November 1996, the full extent of Thailand's economic, financial, and governance problems was painfully apparent. Confronting the formidable tasks of containing the damage flowing from these problems, Chavalit's closest economic advisor, Amnuay Viravan, secured only the finance ministry portfolio for himself and the commerce ministry for a close ally. Other economic portfolios went to another party in the new governing coalition. The Chavalit government cut government spending in its budgets for the 1997 and 1998 fiscal years, mainly by reducing military expenditures.[90] Officials created a support fund to prop up ailing financial firms and required them to set aside capital to cover bad debts. The BoT announced in March 1997 that ten finance companies had sixty days in which to boost their capital and the following month provided them with incentives to merge, including the lure of commercial banking licenses. As a stick, they threatened to withdraw access to central bank support and to impose new capital adequacy ratios for those small family-owned firms that resisted merger. The institutions remained open, however, and funds flowed out of them. Meanwhile authorities relaxed the 25 per cent ceiling on foreign ownership of finance companies. In June officials suspended the operations of sixteen finance companies. Despite these steps, observers continued to question officials' resolve in implementing these measures.[91] As Siamwalla noted, the bank "could not continue to support the baht internationally and illiquid finance companies domestically."[92] Ultimately, officials were unable to stem the gathering forces working against the Thai financial system and the baht's rigid peg.

Thai authorities had long tied the baht to a basket of currencies in which the dollar's weighting (80 per cent)[93] was far greater than was justified by Thai trade patterns. Officials resisted IMF advice to shift the weighting of the currencies in the basket.[94] The dollar peg severely limited officials' ability to increase interest rates as part of tight money policies. It also hurt exports by inducing modest currency appreciation as the dollar rose against the yen in 1996.[95] The liberalization of capital controls and the rapid expansion of offshore banking services from 1992 enabled local firms to borrow abroad at low interest rates without incurring foreign exchange risks. Capital inflows stimulated monetary expansion and boosted investment in marginal projects, particularly in property.[96] By 1997 about $70 billion of the total $90 billion foreign debt was in private hands.[97] The fragility of the property sector and its financial backers made the use of higher interest rates as a tool of monetary policy an extremely delicate matter.

In the end, the most important causes of the baht crisis were the liberalization of the financial system coupled with the loosening of capital controls over the early 1990s under a fixed exchange rate system. These factors allowed local investors easy access to investment funds and fueled the property boom even when local interest rates were high. Liberalization of the financial markets increased competition for lending and pushed investment toward increasingly marginal projects while reducing the effectiveness of prudential supervision – what the *Far Eastern Economic Review* termed "half-hearted liberalization and imprudent supervision."[98] Financial sector regulations, however, continued to limit finance companies' abilities to compete in various areas, encouraging their concentration on the property sector, with disastrous results. At the end of 1996 estimates suggested that at least one-fifth of their loans were bad (some estimates ran significantly higher and put the share of bad loans held by the banks at near 10 per cent).

Given the many weaknesses of the Thai economy and financial sector, and the baht's overvaluation, it was only a matter of time before speculative attacks began again. These assumed new force in May 1997 and forced the central bank to intervene on a very large scale to shore up the currency. Thai authorities received some assistance from financial authorities in other countries in the region, who honored agreements reached in 1995 and 1996 in the wake of the Mexican peso crisis and its reverberations.[99] The Thai central bank also intervened in the forward market, committing billions of its reserves. In mid-May officials imposed capital controls, instructing Thai banks to desist from lending baht to foreigners or buying baht-denominated offshore bills.[100] Also in mid-May, authorities and the commercial banks set up a $2 billion fund to support the SET. These measures temporarily stabilized the baht and the SET index actually rose. Administrative and political obstacles, however, continued to delay implementation of rescue measures.[101] Political resistance to allowing the property market to fall to market-clearing prices was intense. In June 1997, soon after the resignation from the Cabinet of Finance Minister Amnuay and his failure to push through tax increases,[102] the SET rapidly dropped a further 4 per cent and attacks on the baht were renewed in force.[103]

Officials were, however, able to fend off the attacks, and some observers remained sanguine about the prospects for future successful defensive efforts. The central bank continued to claim that Thailand had large foreign exchange reserves. The sudden slowing of economic growth in 1996 was, at about 6 per cent, still impressive by most standards. Many analysts expected the investment boom, peaking in 1995, to significantly boost local exports and soon to help reduce the current account gap. The ratio of M2 to total reserves was low.[104] Exports appeared to be recovering slightly in 1997, and most estimates suggested that the baht was not dramatically overvalued (but when authorities allowed the currency to float in July 1997, it immediately depreciated 17 per cent against the dollar before falling about as much again later in the year).

The Cabinet bypassed parliament and, hoping to avert the gathering crisis, issued a series of emergency decrees. In late June 1997 officials ordered the sixteen finance companies to suspend business for a month and to seek buyers. These measures failed, however, to ward off further attacks. The devaluation finally came on July 2nd, as officials acknowledged defeat and floated the baht. The SET then climbed 25 per cent over three days,[105] but observers worried about a possible balance of payments crisis caused by the capital controls that could discourage further foreign direct investment or foreign bank lending. The financial sector's weakness remained a grave concern.

While Thai authorities turned to the IMF for advice, they resisted seeking loans with their attendant conditions. A high-level IMF official scolded Thai officials for this reluctance and noted pointedly that the full complement of measures necessary to resolve the financial sector mess was not yet in place.[106] In late July the Thai government finally gave in and sought an IMF rescue involving a line of credit of as much as $20 billion. With that support secured in August, the central bank ordered forty-two more finance companies to stop business. Japan played a major role in extending the financing to Thai authorities – Japanese banks were the main foreign lenders to Thailand. To qualify for the line of credit, Thai officials promised to cut government spending further and drew up a plan to restructure the financial sector. Immediately after announcement of this turn to the IMF, the BoT governor resigned.[107]

Conclusion

From the late 1980s financial authorities moved toward a more purely regulatory role vis-à-vis financial institutions as they began to liberalize the finance sector. Bankers and regulators drifted away from close cooperation to more arm's-length relations. During this period the number of actors able to shape financial markets and regulations was growing, complicating governance. Yet the capacities of the dominant private financial institutions and officials in the BoT and MoF promised for a time a successful transition to an arm's-length regulatory regime. Liberalization, however, reduced the authorities' capacity to shape the behavior of finance companies because of their easier access to foreign funds. With more firms in the sector, the cozy cartel weakened and cooperation became harder. Bankers and regulators were no longer as familiar with one another, and it became far more difficult to manage the allocation of benefits. Deregulation and politicization simply added to these difficulties.

The authorities' diminished influence, and the new style of financial regulation, became evident in the early 1990s. In anticipation of increased competition, the BoT tried in 1993 and 1994 to persuade the banks to reduce their interest rates, maintaining that their interest spreads were exorbitant. Indeed, banks' profits had been climbing sharply. With liberalization, the banks were able to borrow abroad or through the newly created international banking facilities at low interest rates and to onlend with spreads averaging four points.[108] The BoT expressed concern, in particular, about the plight of smaller borrowers and aimed its criticism mainly at the larger banks.[109] Particularly unusual was the BoT's willingness to go public in its campaign to get the banks to lower their lending rates.[110] This prompted at least one independent economist to complain that the central bank was motivated more by politics than by a concern for efficiency.[111] The banks' average return on assets, however, was much higher than in Singapore's more competitive markets,[112] suggesting that the authorities' complaints had merit. The public row between the central bank and the commercial banks was unsettling to at least some onlookers. One Japanese investor expressed alarm over the "apparent failure by the Bank of Thailand to govern the financial system."[113]

Traditionally, such issues had been handled through discreet talks within the Thai Bankers Association. The confrontation over rate spreads was the more striking given the unusual prominence of former bankers in the Chuan government.[114] In 1993 the BoT had asked commercial banks to announce their "minimum retail rates," which could serve as the basis for calculating their lending rates.[115] In March 1993, unhappy with the banks' high profits and failure to lower rates, the BoT threatened to call on the police to investigate the banks' actual operating costs and to impose hefty fines in the event of non-compliance.[116] Finance Minister Tarrin urged BoT Governor Vijit to pressure the banks to reduce their rates, even after a first round of interest cuts in late June 1993.[117]

Whether in response to these pressures or in anticipation of growing competition from international banking facilities, interest spreads did narrow. In the case of the Bangkok Bank, the average spread fell from 4.6 per cent in the first quarter of 1992 to 3.3 per cent by the end of 1993.[118] This open conflict was emblematic of a newly widening gulf between financial institutions and regulators as the system liberalized. By the time of the Mexican peso crisis, the vulnerability of open economies to sharp swings in investors' perceptions had become increasingly clear. This only reinforced some financial authorities' determination to move toward a regulatory policy profile. Others, however, had their doubts. As noted above, the central bank governor favored temporary reimposition of capital controls during the fallout from the peso collapse. While authorities ultimately resisted this move at the time, in June 1997 they imposed capital controls.

By the mid-1990s the financial sector had opened up with a growing number of players in the private sector and politicians increasingly looking over the shoulders of regulators in the central bank and finance ministry. This spurred a shift away from close cooperation and toward more arm's-length dealings within the financial sector. Regulators' preferences had shifted as well, from a focus on stability and regularity to efforts to enhance flexibility and efficiency. The relatively strong record of cooperation in the financial sector and of its robust development collapsed in the mid-1990s.

Chapter 5

Controls and Contestation: the Thai Textile Industry

First England, and then many other countries, launched their industrial revolutions making cloth. Despite the textile[1] industry's accessibility to poor countries, successfully exporting textiles on a large scale is demanding. The garment sector, in particular, requires skills in complex administration, financing, and management, and in the marketing and quality control necessary to serve foreign markets. Hence the industry serves as a training ground in modern industrial management, marketing, and distribution techniques, fostering the development of finance, insurance, and shipping industries.[2] The industry is often the first to socialize peasants into the practices of factory production. In short, the textile industry is a "basic skill infrastructure builder,"[3] socializing labor, training management, earning foreign exchange, and laying down the key institutions in both private and public sectors that can shape future economic trajectories and the nature of business–state interaction.

Thousands of firms working in production, marketing, finance, and insurance can build, without much conscious coordination between them, a successful textile industry. The characteristics of the industry, particularly its labor intensity and for the most part modest capital requirements, pose relatively limited demands for cooperation among firms. Neither does a strong textile industry require particularly large firms. And the low capital intensity and the standardization of technology in certain sub-sectors result, all else equal, in low entry barriers and a large number of actors. The downstream sector of the industry in particular tends to be atomized.[4] These characteristics impede the use of policymaking instruments such as investment cartels to promote the industry. They also militate against the emergence of a small number of powerful private interests able to collude effectively and, in theory, favor state officials' abilities to shape private behavior.[5] At the same time, however, the large number of firms increases collective action obstacles and can frustrate public officials' efforts to organize cooperative endeavors in the industry.

The tasks associated with the development of an internationally competitive textile industry, in particular the garment industry, put a premium on flexibility and rapid adjustment, while demanding relatively less coordination, whether directed by state officials or private sector firms or associations. Firms in the industry face problems of externalities associated with labor training and foreign marketing, but in general entrepreneurs tend to see these as less crucial to the industry's performance than the need, for example, for investment coordination among firms in emerging steel or semiconductor industries. The industry not only matched Thailand's relative factor costs, but in some respects suited the limited capacities of the Thai state and the relative dearth of cooperation-inducing institutions among private firms.

If low levels of social capital inhibit the development of collaboration between firms and state officials or agencies, the costs in the textile industry should be less severe than they might be elsewhere. After all, the industry's decentralized structure, in most sectors, frustrates resolution of collective action problems even where social capital appears to be greater, as in Japan. The industry is less dependent than most heavy industries on state support, coordination among firms, or intimate ties between firms and the state. In general, the textile industry uses standardized technologies and features large and price-elastic local demand. Export markets are potentially huge, though significant transportation costs afford a degree of natural protection, and the industry does not require exorbitantly large capital investments. Many segments of the industry were relatively labor-intensive.[6] The Thai textile industry itself enjoyed inherent advantages: the Thai domestic market was fairly large; in the 1970s and 1980s local producers had privileged access to neighboring country markets where there was a demand for low-quality goods; Thailand had some potential to grow cotton; and, until the 1990s, labor was fairly cheap.

The industry, in short, demands a set of skills that matches rather well the strengths and weaknesses of Thai state agencies and private firms, as described in Part I of this book. Chinese firms in Thailand, linked to foreign producers and distributors of cloth and clothing, were flexible and efficient. State policymakers, loosely implementing a liberal policy framework, exposed firms to competitive pressures.

A successful textile industry can emerge in an institutional environment like Thailand's with good macroeconomic conditions, a rich array

of trade institutions to finance operations and spread risks, and entrepreneurship. Indeed, building on these, Thai firms created one of the
world's most rapidly expanding textile industries. Collective action
obstacles to cooperation in most sectors of the industry were daunting
because of the relatively large numbers of firms involved. Thai firms
did not enjoy unusual success in overcoming these difficulties, but neither, by and large, did firms elsewhere.[7] The strength of the Thai textile
industry reflected the decentralized capacities of the private sector.

The Thai textile industry's remarkable growth was a testament to
the capabilities of Thai private firms and their ability to collaborate
with foreign capital. State policies of protection for local production
and openness to foreign firms were also important. Other state policies,
however, both those of omission and commission, probably hindered
the development which might have resulted from either an informed
and flexibly implemented set of industrial policies or a true hands-off
policy. And while the lack of cooperation among firms was not always
crucial, its absence may also help to account for the industry's weaknesses that were long in evidence and began to have major effects on its
performance in the mid-1990s. The absence of effective state promotion or of cooperation among firms helps to explain why the Bangkok
Bank took it upon itself to foster the limited cooperation that did
emerge.

The Thai textile industry ranked twenty-first globally in terms
of exports in the early 1990s.[8] It was Asia's third leading exporter of
garments (after China and South Korea), with over $4 billion in 1994.[9]
It was Thailand's most important industry in terms of employment
(over one million in 1993), value, and net foreign exchange earnings
(gross earnings in 1994 were over $5 billion, approximately 14 per cent
of total foreign exchange earnings).[10] Over the 1970s and 1980s, the
industry's contribution to manufacturing value-added nearly doubled,
to 24 per cent.[11] Between 1980 and 1992, Thai clothing exporters
outstripped sixteen countries that had been ahead of Thailand in total
clothing exports.[12]

As noted above, in many industrializing countries state policymakers
first grapple with complexities of industrial promotion in their efforts
to foster or strengthen a local textile industry. As a result, officials'
experiences in the sector may influence the broad framework of state–
business interaction in the economy. To the extent that the industry's
characteristics come to define enduring patterns of this interaction,
linkages among private firms, and the nature of private firms, the
industry has the potential to leave a lasting imprint on an economy's
institutional endowments. Gerschenkron made this point in discussing
the institutional requirements associated with industrialization based on

different economic sectors.[13] Shafer's study of the legacies imparted by the characteristics of dominant economic sectors updates this analysis by showing the different requirements associated with decentralized and labor-intensive industries on the one hand and concentrated and capital-intensive ones on the other.[14] In Thailand the first major industry, textiles, and the country's first major commodity and export, rice, had broadly similar features. In both, production was relatively decentralized and the state played very little part in providing infrastructure, research, or other public goods designed to contribute to the respective sectors' development.

A tension in the argument presented above needs to be addressed at this point. On the one hand, it may be that the characteristics of production in the industry lead firms to employ standardized technologies in the context of atomistic competition and that these production conditions are consistent with Thai institutional endowments. On the other, it appears that the limits on cooperation among private firms or state entities, or between the two, hindered the industry's long-term development. How can an industry be well suited to something approaching perfect market competition and yet be in need of cooperative initiatives among firms? As noted above, textile firms face collective action problems. While these are certainly less costly than in many other industries, they are also more difficult to overcome. In any case, in Thailand, state policies both failed to supply collective goods for the industry and introduced major imperfections in product markets. It is quite possible that better public sector-based labor training and consistent liberal policies on the entry and exit of goods into and out of the economy, and of firms into and out of the industry, would have led to a stronger industry in the long run. The absence of effective labor-training initiatives was itself a result of failures to cooperate among firms and state authorities. Hence, in the textile industry too, Thailand's institutional endowments shaped the capacity for cooperation among firms, between firms and state agencies, and between labor and management. With more cooperation firms might have been able to minimize surplus capacity, to speed up the diffusion of information, skills and technologies, and to pool resources to gather information on market conditions abroad.

One means of overcoming obstacles to cooperation in contexts of market failures is for firms to internalize a variety of transactions. Managers then attempt to induce and command effective cooperation within large firms. While textile firms do not generally require great scale, only large firms can undertake major investments in developing new product lines, committing resources to research and development, and reaching foreign markets on their own. Cooperation among firms can help to overcome the disadvantages of small size if businesses can work together to provide collective goods. For example, firms may work together in devising worker training schemes. Within the textile industry, enterprises also can cooperate effectively simply by increasing the availability of information on markets and technologies. Companies also may need to cooperate in implementing managed trade arrangements as mandated under the Multi-Fiber Agreement that governed most international textile trade after the mid-1970s. And firms may choose to cooperate in creating cartels that limit investment in new capacity. In industrializing countries where enterprises are apt to be smaller and market failures more pervasive, cooperation may offer particularly strong advantages.

Where firms fail to invest in these kinds of external coordination, or where such investments ultimately fail, state agencies may be in a position to substitute for them. Officials can support the textile industry in a number of ways beyond providing macroeconomic stability. For example, they can help businesses cope with excess capacity during cyclical downswings, help producers negotiate advantageous technology agreements with foreign firms, promote the production of higher value-added goods and the creation of backward linkages, ensure adequate access to credit, train labor, and provide administrative and physical infrastructure as well as market information to support exports. State participation is necessary in negotiating international trade agreements and is usually crucial in policing cartel arrangements. More generally, state officials can enforce collective action arrangements among producers; they can also, of course, act to provide tax incentives and subsidize investment costs. If state officials assume such roles, they risk damaging the industry by performing them poorly. In Thailand, with state agencies lacking full information, penetrated by rent-seekers and divided against one another, and with companies unable to cooperate, this was often the result.

Any of three alternative models of industrial governance might have served the Thai textile industry better than the Thai approach did. Thai state officials lacked the information that would have been necessary to formulate and implement relatively successful textile industry policies of the kind evident in some other East Asian economies (by and large Thai officials also lacked the necessary enforcement capacities). These weaknesses, however, did not deter them from pervasive intervention in the industry, where they often acted on behalf of the interests of particular interests or sectors at the expense of the health of the broader industry. More effective state guidance, grounded in an adequate understanding of the industry and aided by information officials could use to hazard calculated gambles, might have strengthened technological capabilities and reduced the growing mismatch in the 1980s and 1990s between the burgeoning garment sector and relatively uncompetitive textile firms exporting mainly gray (unfinished) goods (see page 121). At the very least, stronger education policies would have benefited businesses in the textile as well as other industries. Alternatively, closer cooperation among firms within the industry – private sector governance – might have produced similar results. Finally, less state intervention even without offsetting private sector cooperation might have created a stronger industry in Thailand than exists today. If officials had simply offered guarantees for property rights while maintaining a broadly liberal policy framework with, perhaps, a brief period of protection for the industry's initial development, the industry might have fared better.

Many of the government's more selective textile industrial policies hindered the industry's development. For example, despite the booming textile demand that began in 1985, Thai spinners and weavers operating at close to full capacity were unable to satisfy domestic demand because state officials failed to lift controls on spinning and weaving capacity. This situation persisted for months while the BoI pondered which firms would receive promotional privileges. Textile Policy Committee deliberations dragged on and the industry minister, fed up with the bickering, threatened to exclude the textile associations altogether.[15] It is easy to imagine that companies would have seen oscillating market trends as less capricious than the whims of politicians balancing the claims of competing clients. It is important to remember, however, that the relative weakness of the state's nominally authoritative measures worked to limit the extent of damage inflicted by alleged state promotion. Competition among officials and politicians to control authoritative decisionmaking meant that fewer rigidities resulted than would otherwise have been the case. This competition also limited the extent to which leading firms were able to entrench their oligopolistic power within various sectors. Indeed it was the state's weaknesses that accounted in part for the extent to which the industry remained subject to ongoing competitive pressures that fostered rising export capacities in the 1980s and so reaped the advantages of flexibility in the garment sector. In other sectors, however, particularly where technological upgrading was crucial, smaller firms were unable to adjust. As a result, the textile industry in Thailand was not highly integrated.

Throughout the high-growth era, political parties with close links to established firms dominated textile policymaking in Thailand. Pramarn Adireksarn and other members of the Chart Thai political party, including former Prime Minister Chatichai Choonhavan, often controlled the Ministry of Industry. Pramarn's Teijin group,[16] however, had to compete with other textile groups that were able to get their own political champions, often in other ministries. One of Teijin's foremost competitors was able to use political muscle (as well as naked force) to win favors and cow foreign partners.[17]

In sum, because most sectors of the textile industry present low barriers to entry, the potential for crippling market failures is fairly modest, so the rationale for active state policy roles is weaker than in some other sectors. We can expect the market, therefore, to serve as an efficient instrument, particularly if the state enforces competition policies and does not grant particular firms inordinate special advantages.

By and large, none of the key participants in the industry – state officials, industry associations, individual private institutions outside the industry (though the Bangkok Bank was an exception) – provided crucial assistance to the textile industry in Thailand. State policies, most importantly tariff protection and investment promotion, certainly fostered the development of the industry, but it is less clear that other state instruments helped much, and they may well have hurt. Public policies were generally poorly conceived and implemented. The strength of the industry's development was largely the work of independent firms jostling within the constraints of markets, but with minimal cooperation among them. The result by the mid-1990s was an industry confronting serious challenges in the face of competition from lower-wage textile producers. In short, both the industry's success and its limitations appeared to be consistent with the expectations of institutional performance based on Thailand's social capital endowments.

To provide adequate context for the discussion to follow, the section below briefly traces the industry's development, describing its characteristics and weaknesses. This discussion must include a picture of the pervasive role played by foreign, particularly Japanese, capital. Subsequent sections analyze both private and state efforts over the years to overcome coordination and collaboration problems within the industry.

Japanese Firms and Development of the Thai Textile Industry

Before they began importing textiles on a large scale in the middle of the nineteenth century, Thais relied on cottage industries for cloth and clothing. British and, later, Japanese imports of cloth displaced traditional textile industries over the second half of the nineteenth and first half of the twentieth centuries. During the 1920s and 1930s Japanese textile exports spread across Asia, including China, Thailand, and the Philippines (other markets remained largely captives of colonial exporters).[18]

Thailand's modern textile industry began in the 1930s when the Ministry of Defense, anticipating possible loss of supplies with the approach of war, imported German spinning machines in order to produce yarn for the military's use.[19] By 1939 there were twenty-six textile factories in Thailand.[20] But skills and experience from the Ministry of Defense plant were apparently slow to diffuse to the private sector.[21] A degree of tariff protection and the disruption of trade during World War II stimulated the initial development of the modern industry. Toward the end of the war, as part of a larger plan to move 700 000 spindles and 19 000 looms to offshore sites in East Asia,[22] the Japanese army planned to import 10 000 spinning spindles into Thailand to meet clothing shortages there. The Japanese and Thais hoped to begin operations under joint management in September 1945.[23]

The first modern privately owned firm, a cotton-spinning venture using technicians and second-hand machinery from Shanghai, did not emerge until 1946.[24] A former Shanghai textile industrialist established Bangkok Cotton Mills in 1950.[25] State-owned enterprises played an important role in the industry into the 1940s and 1950s. About twenty spinning and weaving firms started operations after the war up to 1960. They received limited protection and some failed. While serving as a finance ministry official, Pramarn turned a deaf ear to local producers' pleas for increased protection, meanwhile cultivating Japanese textile producers.[26] Thereafter, with the shift toward an import-substituting development strategy under Sarit in the late 1950s, the private sector took the lead, led by Japanese multinationals eager to maintain access to the Thai market and to counter emerging competition from exporters in Hong Kong, Pakistan, and Taiwan.[27] In the face of resistance from local industrialists, Pramarn championed the interests of the Japanese firms.[28] Soon another twenty firms were producing textiles,[29] including those of the entrepreneurs who would eventually dominate locally owned production in Thailand.[30]

Following the pattern seen in the development of Japan's textile industry,[31] many of the early Thai textile industrialists got their start in the business as importers and distributors. They later entered into joint ventures with foreign (mostly Japanese) firms for the local production of textiles when Thai officials protected the market with higher tariffs and quotas. Sukree Phothirattanangkun (Hung Yiah Seng), one of the early local textile manufacturers, began his operations producing military uniforms for the government weaving organization.[32] The founder of Saha-Union, Thailand's leading textile giant, started in the business as an importer of Japanese textiles and then joined with a Japanese firm to establish a joint venture in Thailand in the early 1960s.[33]

The new companies enjoyed tariff protection. Rapid economic growth and population expansion enlarged the domestic market. Production increased rapidly for over a decade – manufacture of cotton fabrics rose more than eightfold during the 1960s and 1970s. The introduction of man-made fabrics by Japan's Teijin in 1968 gave the industry a further boost,[34] and production of synthetic fabric soared through the 1970s.[35]

Successive Japanese investments throughout Asia came in response to shifts in relative factor costs. Rising labor and land costs compelled Japanese firms to move offshore to produce cotton yarn (early 1960s); cotton fabric and garments (late 1960s); synthetic stable yarns and fabrics (early 1970s); and synthetic filament yarns and fabrics (late 1970s). By the 1960s the United States was controlling imports of cotton textiles from Japan using Voluntary Export Restraints under the Long Term Agreement and later the Multi-Fiber Agreement. By moving offshore, Japanese companies could expand their exports further, but in Thailand these firms produced only for the local market; among the pioneers were Toray, Toyobo, Yazaki, and Teijin.[36] Eventually production in Thailand substituted for imports, and in the early 1970s exporting began as production levels outstripped domestic demand.

Japanese investment played a key role in the industry's development. Between 1960 and 1973, textile production accounted for 21 per cent of the registered capital of investments granted privileges by Thailand's Board of Investment. Of textile companies receiving investment privileges between 1960 and 1976, more than four-fifths of the registered capital and employment were provided by joint ventures in which Japanese firms held equity.[37] Thailand was the leading recipient, as measured by the number of investments, of Japanese textile investments, until overtaken by Taiwan in 1968.[38] Between 1960 and 1967, the Thai industry expanded with twenty-three new spinning firms, fourteen of which were Japanese joint ventures.[39]

Nowhere in Asia was Japan's role in the local textile industry more pivotal than in Thailand. This reflected both the attraction of Thailand's relatively large domestic market and its openness to foreign capital. Local producers and their political patrons were ultimately unable to forge alliances that effectively limited competition in the industry, including from new entrants. Yoshihara points out that only in Thailand did Japanese textile investment precede the decline of direct exports from Japan. In the latter 1960s Japanese firms hastened that decline by producing in Thailand.[40] Their share of Thailand's spinning production was much higher than it was elsewhere in Asia; in the case of synthetic fibers, only in Indonesia did Japanese firms account for a greater share of total production.[41] By 1975 only twelve of sixty-three promoted textile firms in Thailand were wholly locally owned. Twenty-four of the remaining fifty-one were Japanese-dominated firms.[42] In 1973 Japanese subsidiaries accounted for over 60 per cent of total production in the textile industry.[43] The Japanese also served as the principal suppliers of textile machinery to Thailand, and while Japanese firms' dominance fell after the mid-1970s (investment from Hong Kong and Taiwan picked up), they remained the major recipients of royalties and technology-licensing fees.[44]

While local control over the textile industry expanded during the 1970s and into the 1980s, the role of Japanese capital, technology, and marketing remained crucial. As late as 1978, Japanese joint ventures' exports accounted for about half of total Thai textile exports. And this was at a time when the industry's dominance of Thai manufacturing was reaching its peak, accounting for nearly half the total value.[45] Firms with Japanese equity participation enjoyed better access to marketing channels, superior quality control, and stable procurement of raw materials.[46] In 1980, among the top hundred companies in Thailand, ranked according to gross sales, foreign firms' share of sales in the textile industry came to over 70 per cent.[47] The dominant position of Japanese firms in the industry as a whole declined with the rapid expansion of the garment sector in the 1980s, but this sector too was foreign-dominated (mostly from Hong Kong).

In the mid-1980s Japanese textile investment returned to Thailand on a large scale after a lull of more than a decade. The government was promoting the midstream parts of the industry (spinning, knitting, and weaving), for local as well as foreign production, for the first time in eight years.[48] In the late 1980s the BoI approved dozens of new Japanese textile investments.[49] Thai exports of textiles (including garments) to Japan rose 47 per cent during the first half of 1987 over the previous year, with garments alone increasing nearly 60 per cent.[50] By 1993 Japan accounted for one-fifth of Thai textile exports (over $400 million, second only to the United States which imported over $1 billion from Thailand).[51]

Rapidly growing Thai textile exports to Japan rested on more than changing cost conditions. From the mid-1980s, buyers from Japanese supermarket chains went directly to Thai manufacturers to place orders, providing technical assistance as necessary. The supermarkets were able to import the goods directly into Japan, bypassing cumbersome Japanese distribution networks. Both changes in the structure of demand in Japan (more bargain hunters), and regulatory loopholes that allowed the growth of supermarket chains appealing to such tastes, enabled the stores to place large orders.[52] In the late 1980s Japanese wholesalers also began to help Thai textile producers with funding, storage, distribution, and market development in Japan and third markets.[53] Large Hong Kong firms meanwhile expanded their garment operations in Thailand in the late 1980s and 1990s, investing in new machinery and technology. As a result these firms were better able to compete abroad in higher-quality markets.[54] Clearly, the Thai industry was a major beneficiary of initiatives launched in consuming markets.

While we might expect that the foreign penetration of the local textile industry would have impeded cooperation because of divergent interests between local and foreign firms, there is no evidence for this; in fact limited anecdotal evidence leads to quite the opposite conclusion. Japanese firms were among the most active in efforts to strengthen the local textile associations.[55] Their ability to do so, however, were ultimately limited by nationalist sentiments among both Thai officials and industrialists that tended to limit the influence of even well-established Japanese firms within textile associations. Japanese firms were most influential perhaps in the upstream production of synthetic fibers, a sector dominated by a small number of mostly foreign firms. And while hardly effective compared to counterparts in many other countries, many Thais believed that the Thai Textile Manufacturer's Association (TTMA) was among the most effective locally.[56]

In the 1990s Thailand's textile industry continued to have a dual structure. Of the thousands of firms and subcontracting households, most were small and confined to a single sector of the industry. But the industry was dominated by textile groups linked in the typical Chinese pattern of "chain ownership"[57] in which members of a single family had crossholdings in shares of a group of companies that together provided a considerable degree of vertical integration. With the expansion of the petrochemical sector in the 1980s and 1990s, this integration increased. Saha Union, for example, moved upstream, producing pure terephthallic acid.[58] Among the textile groups, four dominated in the early 1980s, accounting for about half of spinning capacity and total value-added for the industry. Japanese capital had a hand in each of these four dominant groups but a controlling interest in only two of them. As the industry matured there was no marked propensity to diminish dependence on foreign partners. Thai partners continued to look abroad for capital, technology and, in particular, marketing access.[59] Among the ten largest groups in terms of assets, five were foreign: three Japanese (Toray, Teijin, and Marubeni), one Indian (Birla A.G.), and one Taiwanese (Asia Fibre).[60] Foreign investment continued to be important in the industry into the 1990s; early in 1996 Tuntex of Taiwan announced plans for a series of investments to produce petrochemicals, fibers, and fabric totalling nearly $1 billion.[61]

The key role that Japanese firms played in the Thai textile industry complicates an analysis of Thailand's development that employs the concepts of sociability and social capital. Whatever the industry's strengths and weaknesses, we may find it difficult to isolate the influences of local and foreign factors. It is also worth repeating the point made in the Introduction: that Thailand's very openness to foreign capital may have resulted in part from the paucity of its social capital. The social space between officials and Chinese industrialists may also have made easier the adoption of liberal policies toward foreign capital.[62] In any case, it was local firms and officials who dominated bargaining among firms and between them and state authorities. With the industry's expansion, by the 1970s capacity controls had become a focus of contention among firms.

Booms, Busts, and Basta

By 1971 Thailand had surplus capacity in the production of cotton fabrics. Illegal exports – smuggling to neighboring countries – already played a minor part in "local" demand. The Ministry of Industry responded to this surplus in 1971 with a moratorium on issuance of the factory licences required to establish or expand textile capacity. The surplus disappeared the following year as a result of increased global demand, an agreement with the European Economic Community allowing for duty-free imports of Thai cotton fabrics and garments, and government tax credits for exporters. With this early success in exporting, both bureaucrats and textile firms began to look more carefully at the potential of foreign markets.[63] The moratorium on capacity expansion, however, remained for two years.

Official promotion of textile exports began earlier in the late 1960s, but Thai production costs remained high,[64] and domestic demand was sufficient at the time to absorb expanding supply.[65] Textile producers also enjoyed easy access to markets in Indochina. Exports to neighbors served Thai producers as a dumping ground for unanticipated excess supply. By 1973, however, exports were increasing rapidly, rising to three times the 1972 level and registering the first surplus in Thailand's textile trade. As the industry increasingly integrated into the international market, the gaps between domestic and international prices diminished.[66]

The rapid textile growth rates of the early 1970s came to a halt with the first oil shock, world recession, and, in 1975, the closing of trade across Thailand's border with the states of Indochina. The industry suffered large losses between 1975 and 1977[67] – the textile trade recorded a deficit in 1976 – which resulted in restructuring of firms and increasing localization as some foreign investors pulled out. They were discouraged by heavy losses as well as the political instability associated with communist victories in Indochina and polarized and unstable politics in Thailand after the collapse of military rule in 1973. Tightened restrictions on foreign investment also deterred foreign capital. While foreign investment was still not subject to any comprehensive screening, Thai officials extended promotional privileges only to firms in which Thais held at least half the equity. Japanese textile investment in Thailand came to a halt despite BoI promotion in the mid-1970s.[68]

The industry regained its rapid rates of growth in the late 1970s, fueled by the garment industry's uninterrupted expansion through the earlier slump in textile production.[69] By the early 1980s textile exports constituted over half of all Thai manufactured exports and, within those, garments accounted for more than half.[70] The industry, however, slumped again in the early 1980s with the onset of global recession. By late 1982 the ten largest textile firms had accumulated losses of close to half a billion dollars.[71] Synthetic fiber producers complained that Taiwanese and South Korean producers were dumping in the Thai market.[72] After more than two decades of rapid though uneven expansion, the industry was facing major problems.

Industrialists and officials alike expressed concern at weaknesses in the industry. Many smaller firms specializing in weaving or dyeing were unable to produce high-quality textiles or to make deliveries on time. As a result, the large local and foreign vertically integrated firms that dominated production, and, especially, exports, continued to ship mostly gray textiles.[73] In addition, spinning and knitting operations had far outgrown the weaving sector. These imbalances across different sectors of the industry ensured continuing high dependence on imported textiles. Given the protection afforded local producers and the impediments, at least until the early 1980s, to getting refunds on duties paid for textiles imported and then reexported as garments, the weaknesses in weaving and finishing were sources of worry. But it may also be the case that the limited vertical integration enhanced the garment industry's flexibility.[74] Despite general awareness of such problems, private firms, textile associations, and state officials were unable to ameliorate them.

Yet despite considerable pessimism in the early and mid-1980s, the industry came booming back in the latter part of the decade. Over the 1980s exports expanded elevenfold, with an average well over 20 per cent a year between 1988 and 1991.[75] Several factors help to account for this regeneration. Many of the problems that worried textile executives were not specific to the industry but were associated with the economic slump of those years. Macroeconomic factors, mainly the devaluations of the baht in 1981 and 1984, bolstered the industry's competitiveness. Smoother and more rapid implementation of duty drawback schemes were also important. Large infusions of new investment in the mid-1980s, much of it foreign, strengthened the industry. Finally, the increasingly dominant garment sector, including newly established foreign investments from Taiwan,[76] was especially well positioned to exploit rapidly emerging opportunities.

The industry's strong recovery and export boom in the 1980s owed a great deal to shifting factor prices within Asia, the effects of which were magnified by sharp currency realignments beginning in the mid-1980s. The dollar depreciated sharply against the yen, but also against the Korean won and new Taiwanese dollar. The Thai baht rose only slightly against the dollar while falling significantly relative to the other currencies. This resulted in a decisive cost shift favoring Thai firms, a jump in Thai manufactured exports, and a surge of manufacturing-directed foreign investment in Thailand from Japan and the NIEs.

Despite this strong performance, however, the industry's flaws that had concerned observers in the early 1980s persisted into the 1990s. The garment sector recorded tremendous growth, but upstream firms did not post corresponding gains. The petrochemical industry's rapid expansion became a major burden given the high levels of protection officials afforded it. Furthermore, failures to boost labor productivity became alarming as Thailand's labor surplus disappeared and costs rose accordingly. The labor-intensive garment sector was especially sensitive to changing wage rates: Indonesia's labor costs were one-third and China's one-fourth those in Thailand.[77]

The NESDB selected textiles as one of six priority industries for Thailand's Seventh Five-Year Plan (1992–96). Quality problems in the dyeing and finishing sectors, and the shortage of skilled labor, however, consigned Thai firms to exporting mainly in commodity markets where competition grew increasingly stiff. Firms from China, Indonesia and elsewhere expanded their market shares rapidly at the expense of Thai firms in the mid-1990s (Thai labor costs were between 18 and 28 per cent of those in the East Asian NIEs, but well over twice those in China and Indonesia). Thailand faced hurdles in retaining its number three ranking in 1994 among Asian garment exporters. Thai garment producers themselves began to shift the production of low-end goods to northeastern Thailand or offshore to China, Laos, and other low-wage sites.[78] Export expansion for the industry as a whole slowed from 1992 (in 1995 total exports reached about $6.5 billion). Garments accounted for about three-fourths of exports, with yarns around 15 per cent and unfinished gray fabrics contributing 5–6 per cent. Textiles' share of Thai exports fell from 17 per cent in 1991 to 10 per cent in 1995, and the industry's share of Thailand's total manufacturing value-added also declined.[79]

Thai firms continued to be heavily dependent on imports not just of cotton and cotton yarn and fabric but also in sectors such as man-made fibers and knitted fabrics and, throughout the industry, on machinery and parts.[80] Thais imported many of these products from competitors in China and the East Asian NIEs, as well as Japan. To maintain their long-term competitiveness, Thai firms needed either to improve quality in textile production and finishing or to accept the ongoing concentration in garment production. Achieving either rapidly would require changes in government policies or new initiatives by the textile-producing firms themselves. These would have to include strengthening programs of labor training, lowering tariffs on inputs into the industry (including chemicals and dyes), and fostering stronger firms in bleaching, dyeing, finishing, and printing.[81] The garment industry itself was under considerable cost pressures. Many firms, particularly those with links to Hong Kong, remained competitive by investing heavily, using flexible production techniques, and strengthening marketing networks as they shifted their production to higher value-added goods;[82] smaller firms, however, generally suffered. In the mid-1990s the industry as a whole began to lose employment, and this triggered increased labor conflict. These conditions also boosted opposition to officials' efforts to reduce tariffs in the 1990s.

Officials' determination to liberalize trade spurred a variety of conflicts within the industry. In 1996 the National Federation of Thai Textile Industries presented the government Economic Stability and Security Policy Committee with a list of cuts they wanted on raw material import tariffs, particularly in petrochemical products such as fibers and dyes. Similarly, when the finance ministry cut garment tariffs in May that year, local manufacturers complained and forced an upward revision in tariffs.[83]

The challenges were great, and not only because of growing competition. With economic openings in Vietnam, Laos, and Cambodia, as well as Myanmar, Thai producers lost privileged access to border markets that in the past accounted for as much as one-fifth of "domestic" consumption and still took 10 per cent in the mid-1990s.[84] And Thai firms in the mid-1990s also faced the challenges (and benefits) associated with the slow dismantling of managed world textile trade (the end of the Multi-Fiber Agreement) and the liberalization of textile trade under the ASEAN Free Trade Area. Economists, officials, textile association leaders, and bank research institution staff members repeatedly called for adjustments in the industry in 1996. A Bangkok Bank report called for tariff adjustments, help for smaller firms, more private–public cooperation, establishment of a textile institute, development of a long-term plan for the industry, and vertical integration of the large garment firms.[85]

With the spurt in growth during the late 1980s and early 1990s, garments' share of total textile exports increased from less than half in 1980 to about 74 per cent in 1993 (in net terms, the garment industry accounted for over 100 per cent of exports in the sector; that is, the other sectors were net importers).[86] Garment producers, under pressure to provide higher-quality goods, often as subcontractors, frequently rejected locally produced goods in favor of imports to assure product uniformity, superior quality, and regularity of delivery. The garment sector employed three-fourths of those working in the industry and accounted for over half its 7000-plus factories. (This figure does not include many garment production sites – the Ministry of Industry registers only those firms with twenty or more sewing machines.)[87]

State Promotion of the Textile Industry

To put in broader perspective Thai public promotion of the textile industry, it is worthwhile reviewing briefly state policies elsewhere in the region. Public authorities can promote the textile industry in a variety of ways. The industry was crucially important in all of the industrializing economies of East Asia, and state officials promoted it through various means. In Hong Kong state authorities followed a liberal strategy that contrasted sharply with the state regulatory controls evident, for example, in South Korea. Thai officials adhered, however, to neither of these models.

Hong Kong authorities had a laissez-faire attitude toward textiles, as toward most other sectors of the economy. In Singapore, policy became increasingly liberal toward the textile industry during the 1970s and thereafter.[88] In both cases, however, strong state-supplied physical and administrative infrastructures promoted exporting activities. This was not the case in Thailand.

In Korea and Taiwan officials used capacity controls to harmonize the industry's expansion with an overall national plan. Officials projected demand in local and foreign markets, adjusted those estimates, and applied controls accordingly. Thai officials likewise exercised control over textile industry production by regulating the installation and importation of new machinery and granting promotional privileges. A lack of clear goals, reliable data, or an overall policy framework, however, ensured that in Thailand regulatory decisions were more or less arbitrary and driven at times by rent-seeking objectives. While the Thai state could solicit information and advice from textile associations, conflicts of interest within the latter as well as between them made such consultation problematic.

In Korea and Taiwan textile federations were involved in negotiations with foreign governments over the size and allotment of textile import quotas. Representatives from these federations also advised their governments on international quota talks. Particularly in Korea, the government bestowed on the textile federations a great deal of export assistance, market information, and other forms of support. Hong Kong and Singaporean government ministries and councils also supported their respective export industries. In Thailand the associations in general were less influential, though they were more active in international trade negotiations in the 1990s. Also in the 1990s, they regularly protested against tariff reductions, hoping to force officials to lower tariffs on their raw materials such as petrochemicals or to offer side payments such as lower electricity rates.

In Korea, Singapore, and Taiwan, textile associations provided educational and vocational training. In Hong Kong, universities and other institutions provided support designed to boost productivity. In Thailand, universities and the Ministry of Industry provided only very limited training relevant to the industry. For some reason, in the 1980s even those trained as textile technicians had difficulty finding employment in Thailand; one official estimated that there were fewer than thirty Thai textile engineers in Thailand in the early 1990s.[89] Even at lower levels, technical education in Thailand was weak: in 1990 only 24 000 Thais received vocational training, most of those in non-technical fields.[90]

Given the contrast between promotional policies in Thailand and the NIEs, it is tempting to suggest that Thailand's promotional framework most closely resembled that in the Philippines, despite the industry's far stronger record in Thailand.[91] In Thailand, as in the Philippines, misguided state intervention, resulting in part from the political muscle of dominant textile firms and in part from a lack of coordination, expertise, and information on the part of state officials, caused problems for the industry. A crucial differentiating factor, however, was that in Thailand the many centers of state regulatory control and their links to different political factions ensured that no single firm or group of firms could block competition from new entrants. Here we see the workings of Thailand's "laissez-faire by accident."[92] Furthermore, the BoI's promiscuous issuance of promotional privileges ensured new entry into the industry.[93] And Thailand's trade regime generally was far more open than that in the Philippines. The results in Thailand, of course, were altogether different from those in the Philippines. Not only was the Thai policy regime *de facto* more liberal, firms in general more flexible, and the business environment more stable, but Thailand had more of the Chinese entrepreneurs and the Japanese investors who together played such central roles in building up the industry. Not only did Filipino officials discriminate more against the Chinese, but not until after President Ferdinand Marcos declared martial law in 1972 was Japanese investment welcomed in the Philippines.[94]

Textile Promotion in Thailand

While Thai officials used capacity controls, rarely did they employ them intelligently, and in any case firms often bypassed them. But the fact that private interests were often able to evade controls does not imply that regulations were essentially neutral. Their limited effectiveness was sufficient to stifle the industry's capacity to respond to changes in demand, to enhance the positions of dominant firms, and to retard technological upgrading. Further, a business tax on turnover (abandoned in 1992 in favor of a value-added tax) discouraged subcontracting while encouraging vertical integration; tariffs failed to provide incentives for using local inputs; officials mismanaged foreign market quotas; physical and administrative infrastructures were inadequate and impeded exports; and state policies were ineffective in strengthening weaker sectors of the industry or developing technical skills among the labor force.

Despite occasional initiatives from within the NESDB or the Ministry of Industry, Thai state officials never formulated or implemented a coherent set of policies for the development of the industry. Officials' most crucial policy instruments afforded them control over capacity expansion (see below). Officials did not use these controls effectively to promote the industry, in part because few of them understood it[95] (one former minister of industry referred to a ministry official with a doctorate in textile engineering as "a freak" because of his unusual competence and commitment to the industry).[96]

The Thai economic bureaucracy also had at its disposal many of the more familiar economic policy tools such as control over tariffs, taxes, tax rebates, export subsidies, rediscounting facilities, adjustment of utility rates, and so forth, by which to encourage particular economic activities. Of particular interest to garment producers was the allocation of export quotas. The Thai government exercised few controls over foreign direct investment, subjecting it to no comprehensive screening beyond that required for promotional privileges at the BoI. Regulations imposed no provisions for screening technology contracts associated with direct foreign investment.[97] Officials never established any labor-training facilities. Neither did officials in the Ministry of Commerce manage effectively Thai export quota allotments in markets regulated by the Multi-Fiber Agreement. In 1987, for example, Thailand used only four-fifths of the export quotas allotted to it.

Clearly, however, weaknesses in state textile promotion did not stem from a dearth of appropriate policy instruments but from a lack of planning, inadequate coordination, uneven policy implementation, and the absence of data on which informed policies could be based. At least some TTMA officials regarded bureaucrats and their textile plans as entirely capricious.[98] Vested industry interests could often overturn policy initiatives that threatened their short-term interests. These weaknesses in policy implementation resulted from the limited capacity of state institutions, a failure to coordinate among private firms and agencies, and, given these conditions, departures from a more liberal policy that might have delivered better results in the Thai institutional context.

Controls over capacity, direct and indirect, were the most important policy tool available to Thai authorities regulating the textile industry. They used controls to try to minimize disruption to the industry associated with excessive competition. Officials believed the controls were of particular importance when the industry was primarily oriented toward the domestic market, which was subject to seasonal and longer-term fluctuations associated with harvesting seasons, harvest sizes, and crop prices.[99] While the global textile market was also susceptible to demand fluctuations, the rationale for capacity controls appeared especially weak once a significant part of Thailand's textile production was destined for foreign markets. Furthermore, with total capacity much larger, the impact of incremental production increases on total supply was less dramatic. Bans on the establishment of new factories were in force in 1971 and 1978 before officials finally abandoned this policy instrument in 1987 (formally in 1991). In any case, these controls never were entirely effective. As one textile association official noted, some firms simply ignored the controls, knowing from past experience that officials periodically declared amnesties during which firms would be allowed to register the new machines they had installed illegally.[100]

The BoI exercised less direct means of controlling capacity. Firms generally needed investment privileges granted by the BoI (generally including income tax exemptions for a few years, lower business taxes, and reduced tariffs on machinery imports) to offset various existing policy disincentives. The BoI's grants of investment privileges to textile firms, however, generally were not coordinated closely with the

Ministry of Industry's capacity controls. And firms at times made new investments without inducements from the BoI.

The BoI granted the cotton segment of the textile industry full promotional privileges from 1960. Approved investments received full exemptions from import duties and business taxes on imports of machinery, and income tax holidays for five years. The Board suspended promotion of the industry in 1967 but resumed it in 1968 as the local market grew. Also in 1968, the BoI began to promote the spinning and weaving of synthetic fibers for the first time. It stopped promoting the industry again in 1970. And in 1971, with a slump in the expansion of sales, the Ministry of Industry stopped granting factory licenses for new firms.

Growing textile demand in 1973 and pressure from both existing firms and aspiring entrants led the Ministry of Industry to lift the ban on new capacity and the BoI to grant investment privileges once again.[101] That year the BoI approved investments in new machinery that would double the industry's spinning capacity but stipulated that firms would have to export four times the value of the imported machinery within five years. The BoI, however, apparently never enforced these or other performance requirements. Rather, when many companies failed to meet those targets, it adjusted its requirements and the industry was again, temporarily, saddled with excess capacity.[102] In a rare example of cooperation,[103] the BoI was able to help -in forging a temporarily effective agreement among spinners to reduce production during the sharp downturn in the mid-1970s.[104] Given market conditions at the time, the agreement may have been largely self-reinforcing.

The BoI's promotional policies did not serve any policy goals effectively beyond encouraging aggregate investment in the industry by offsetting existing disincentives. The Ministry of Industry's controls, even if guided by coherent goals and supported by adequate information, would probably have been similarly ineffective. While the ministry could deny licenses for the establishment or expansion of factories, the Ministry of Commerce had long had unilateral control over the actual importing of textile machinery (in 1984, for the first time, machinery imports required approval from the Ministry of Industry as well as the Ministry of Commerce).[105] Coordination between the two ministries was rare, as it was within either of them. Because leaders of different political parties generally headed these two ministries, the former kind of coordination tended to be especially difficult.

A concrete case helps to give a sense of the regulatory environment. One textile firm installed over 40 000 spindles in the 1980s without getting Ministry of Industry approval. The Industrial Works Department of the ministry ordered the machines dismantled, but the Textile

Policy Committee within the same ministry cancelled the order, causing the vice-president of the TTMA to resign from the Textile Policy
Committee in protest.[106] Such experiences inevitably discouraged
Ministry of Industry officials from imposing sanctions. As one official
commented, strict enforcement made for squeaky wheels attracting
high-level political sympathy.[107] If the shoe pinched excessively, firms
would have recourse to politicians powerful enough to overturn official
rulings.

Faced periodically with hundreds of illegal plants constituting as
much as one-fifth of total industry capacity in spinning, the industry
ministry developed a tradition of granting amnesties during which it
registered the previously illegal plants; in 1981–82 the ministry registered 840 illegal plants. This practice at least served to improve the
ministry's database on existing capacity and production in different
sectors of the industry.[108]

Had officials managed to enforce capacity controls, the value of controls would in any case have been limited as they were rarely designed
to serve clearly articulated goals for the industry. Capacity controls
failed to address sectoral weaknesses. For example, high tariffs together
with capacity controls supported the existing poor-quality dye producers.[109] Controls also allegedly encouraged perverse behavior. When
officials lifted controls, some firms invested in additional capacity
beyond their expectations of near term demand growth out of fear that
officials would soon reimpose controls.[110]

Other policies governing the textile industry were not appreciably
more effective. In general, rates of protection were quite high, although
there were almost no quotas.[111] Most yarns and fibers enjoyed rates
of protection between 25 and 40 per cent, while garments had a 60 per
cent tariff (lowered in 1996 to 10 and 30 per cent respectively).[112]
Synthetic fiber imports also faced import surcharges. Similar duties
for some raw materials and semi-finished goods failed to provide tariff
incentives to use locally produced inputs.[113] (To encourage local
processing, tariffs on inputs would have to be lower than those on
processed goods.) And until the 1990s there was little consistent reduction in tariff levels to require local producers to meet international
competition. When promotion of exports began in the early 1970s and
officials began to ease export procedures and offer some incentives for
exports, tariffs on some sectors ran as high as 100 per cent.[114]

In the mid-1980s the NESDB pushed for rationalization of the
industry's tariff structure. The Cabinet's Industrial Policy Committee
approved the NESDB proposal and the Cabinet appointed officials
from the NESDB, MoF, Ministry of Commerce, Ministry of Industry,
Customs Department, and BoI to a tariff committee to address the task.
The newly created committee, however, was largely moribund.[115] One

of its obstacles was that MoF officials were concerned to do nothing to reduce revenue given regular budget deficits at the time. Over the 1980s, officials cut some tariffs and import surcharges while raising or maintaining others. Tariffs remained high overall, between 30 and 60 per cent for most goods. In October 1990, however, the government sharply reduced tariffs to 5 per cent on imports of capital goods, including textile machinery. At the time many firms were still using second-hand 1960s vintage spinning and weaving machines.[116] The lower tariffs led to a jump in machinery purchases and the modernization of some spinning and weaving plants, which could as a result produce finer yarns.[117] Another result was layoffs and severe labor strife.[118] In December 1994 the Cabinet approved a two-year program of tariff reductions that included garment and textile tariffs, as part of Thailand's GATT-agreed tariff reduction package. As noted above, implementation of these plans did not always go smoothly as producers complained and officials attempted to balance the needs of upstream and downstream sectors.

Efforts to Restructure the Industry

Officials devoted considerable attention in the early 1980s to trying to rectify the various problems that beset the industry. In 1983 the NESDB undertook a study of the textile industry giving particular attention to the need for restructuring at a time when officials argued that the industry's midstream sector was relatively bloated.[119] The industry's "old tycoons," intent on barring new entrants into the sector, resisted the restructuring recommendations.[120] The NESDB submitted a report to the government in 1985 leading to the creation of the National Textile Committee (in late 1988 officials changed its name to the Textile Development Committee).[121]

While the BoI enjoyed preeminent influence in many areas of industrial policy, the Ministry of Industry was the dominant player in textiles. The industry minister chaired the Textile Policy Committee, which included representatives of the major textile associations and had ostensible authority over capacity controls. Its influence depended, however, on the whim of the minister. At least one industry minister was so irritated by conflicts between different textile associations that he refused to convene the committee.[122] Press reports criticized this move, but the minister may simply have recognized the obvious – that the private interests were not going to be able to agree on a mutually acceptable outcome. Private interests were too powerful to be controlled by the committee and were not committed to the committee's goals. It was largely ineffective.[123]

The Textile Development Committee hired a United Nations Industrial Development Organization (UNIDO) expert to study the Thai textile industry and make recommendations for the industry based on the experiences of Korea, Hong Kong, Singapore and Taiwan. Later UNIDO dispatched three additional study missions between 1987 and 1988 as well as sending Textile Industry Division personnel for study trips to Hong Kong and South Korea.[124] The ensuing UNIDO report called for the formation of a textile intelligence unit among whose functions would be the collection of reliable data on capacity in different sectors of the industry. The report recommended areas for research and information collection. Lacking such information, it noted, the Ministry of Industry was subject to manipulation by rent-seekers.[125] A subsequent report identified the lack of information as perhaps the industry's greatest liability.[126]

A conflict developed between the Ministry of Industry's Department of Industrial Promotion, which wanted the proposed intelligence unit under its jurisdiction, and the NESDB, which wanted to see the new unit autonomous. In the end the government never established the intelligence unit, although the Textile Division within the Ministry of Industry's Department of Industrial Promotion tried to take on some of its functions.

Private firms were often concerned about the influence of the Ministry of Industry, since it was often under the control of the Chart Thai political party, which had long had ties to favored textile firms. For example, when Chartchai Choonhavan was industry minister, a TTMA official expressed his anguish and dismay at the government's lack of support for the industry, suggesting that the government did the opposite of what the TTMA requested and seemed intent on destroying the industry.[127] In part because firms could elude controls, the Chart Thai party was not able to use the industry ministry's nominal control over capacity expansion to pick winners in the industry. Other firms had connections with competing powerful political groups that they were also able to use to their advantage.

In the early 1990s the textile industry was riding a wave of rapid expansion in production and exports. It was also, however, increasingly clear that serious obstacles could put an end to such rapid growth. Increasingly, both within the private sector and between firms and state officials, new initiatives emerged. For example, in trying to deal with labor unrest in 1993, officials took the lead in establishing the National Tripartite Committee, which included labor, government, and industry representatives.[128] After talking about the idea for some ten years, business groups within the industry called with greater regularity in the 1990s for the creation of a technical training institute. The

Thai Garment Manufacturers Association tried to get Ministry of Industry support for such a scheme.[129] Late in October 1995 the TTMA repeated the call, as did the synthetic fiber producers early in 1996, urging creation of a National Textile Institute that would train technical workers.[130]

In sum, limited institutional capacities or cooperation among state agencies and private firms ensured that state officials lacked the information necessary to formulate or implement effective policies for the industry. Information scarcity resulted in part because some firms, for example illegal ones, did not join industry associations. In any case, no regulations required firms to report production information. As a result of the limitations of state regulatory oversight, the industry depended to a considerable degree on private sector institutions to foster minimum levels of cooperation.

Private Sector Institutions

Despite the establishment of producer organizations in the various sectors of the textile industry, these associations did not succeed in fostering a great deal of cooperative activity. The most important textile association was the Thai Textile Manufacturers' Association founded in 1960 by Pramarn Adireksarn, who had interests in the Teijin group.[131] While the TTMA originally represented all textile sectors, spinning and weaving firms dominated it. The TTMA and other textile associations, along with the Bangkok Bank and the Japanese Chamber of Commerce, reportedly collected the most accurate data on the industry in Thailand. The TTMA set up a fund to provide working capital for retailers and exporters,[132] and tried to establish production and price cartels. In general these initiatives were not very successful. In one case, soon after agreeing to cut production, a textile executive announced plans to invest some $100 million building two additional plants, each to have about 100 000 spindles.[133] The TTMA also worked with foreign business associations, particularly representatives of Japanese textile associations. Textile associations on occasion hired consultants to study policy issues, such as the effects of the business tax (since repealed) on the textile industry.[134] The associations also made recommendations to the government on textile promotion policies.[135]

The associations' role in devising trade policies increased in the 1990s. In particular, they faced new challenges as trade officials implemented significant tariff reductions. They also continued to work for the establishment of a Thai textile institute, and they cooperated with Department of Commerce officials in promoting textile exports and revising procedures for allocating garment export quotas.

The MoF cut tariffs on most Thai goods to meet international commitments and in an effort to enhance local firms' competitiveness. The finance ministry, long a force for higher tariffs to keep up revenue flows, found itself increasingly having to balance the competing claims of producers in different sectors of the textile industry. The ministry's involvement in talks on tariff negotiations promised increased coordination of macroeconomic and sectoral policies in tariff policy planning.[136] Garment producers opposed lowered tariffs on garment imports, and synthetic fiber manufacturers sought lower duties on imports of petrochemical raw materials. Local producers held 90 per cent of the Thai garment market, but were concerned when tariffs on garment imports fell in January 1995 from 60 to 45 per cent, with a drop to 35 per cent scheduled in 1997.[137]

Synthetic fiber producers, with the active involvement of Japanese firms producing locally, pushed consistently for creation of a textile institute that would provide information, foster the industry's technological development, and train personnel. The TTMA also regularly supported this initiative.[138] Within the Ministry of Commerce, the Department of Export Promotion in late 1993 hired an Italian designer to create garments for local production. The agency also organized Ready-to-Wear Trade Fairs in 1994 and 1995.[139] Garment producers pressured the Commerce Ministry to change its system of export quotas allocated under the Multi-Fiber Agreement. With changes in the regime's local content regulations expected to favor Thai garment exporters, the ministry announced late in 1996 a review of its administration of these quotas.[140]

Despite considerable evidence of increased activism on the part of the associations in the 1990s, on the whole, and characterizing the development of the industry overall since the 1960s, textile associations did not contribute significantly to the industry's development or help firms cooperate with one another. Perhaps more important than the textile associations, the Bangkok Bank was at times able to induce cooperation among textile firms. Thai commercial banks had long had close links with the textile industry; Phongpaichit and Baker suggest that they acted in ways similar to investment banks, consulting firms, and business associations.[141] This was particularly conspicuous in the case of the Bangkok Bank, Southeast Asia's largest commercial bank. The bank financed the industry's development, bank officials sat on the boards of various textile firms,[142] and the bank provided government officials with textile industry sectoral studies and policy proposals.[143]

The Bangkok Bank was active in promoting the textile industry from the onset of its rapid expansion in the 1960s. Its strong overseas contacts, particularly in Hong Kong, were useful in the garment sector's development. During the industry recession in the early 1970s, the bank helped firms cope with the withdrawal of Japanese capital. Its financing supported the localization of the industry as Thai industrialists took control of formerly Japanese firms.[144]

The Bangkok Bank financed the expansion of Thai Durable, once one of the textile giants, and when the firm faced financial ruin in 1974–75, the bank oversaw the sale of part of the firm to Saha Union.[145] Indeed during the slump that followed oil price increases, the bank played a key role in financing the industry as a whole,[146] and on occasion it was able to forge production cartels. One source of difficulty in reaching such agreements was the antipathy between Thailand's then largest textile tycoon, Sukree Phothirattanangkun[147] and other textile industrialists.[148] Some observers suggested that only the Bangkok Bank's president, Chatri Sophonpanit, had the influence necessary to compel Sukree to cooperate with the other firms.[149] The bank had to mediate between Sukree and Rhone Poulenc, a French joint-venture partner.[150] Chatri also once served as the chairman of Thai Textile Industry, and later was able to use this experience to mediate conflict between two owners of that firm.[151]

In addition to local private financial institutions and the textile associations, private foreign firms, as discussed above, were important in driving the industry's development. Given the role that markets and private institutions and associations were able to play in supporting the industry, it seems possible that officials would have served the industry's development better by adopting hands-off market policies. Certainly it would have been stronger if officials had, for example, found means to strengthen the finishing (e.g. dyeing and printing of fabrics) sector. Even more important, the industry would have benefited from educational policies that supplied more skilled workers and managers. By 1969 only one-third of students went beyond four years of schooling. By 1994 near 90 per cent were completing six years of school, but the need for students with secondary and technical educations remained acute.[152] The failures of supporting government policies suggests that, on balance, a more limited state role might have been more successful. Indeed state policies would likely have caused more damage if firms had seldom been able to ignore them.

The importance of the failures of public policies in the area of labor training suggests the need to look briefly at this issue in more detail. In particular, labor issues came to the fore of policymakers' attention in the 1990s for a variety of reasons. One of these had to do with the disappearance of a labor surplus, the resulting increases in wages (a tripartite committee established a 135 baht per day – at the time over

$5 – minimum wage, causing consternation among some garment producers) without matching productivity gains,[153] and rising labor strife. Thai Durable's layoff of 376 workers in 1993 set off a prolonged strike. As firms like Thai Durable began to invest in labor-saving machinery, older and unskilled workers were particularly concerned about their future opportunities.[154] Thailand's first social security legislation, adopted in the late 1980s, provided for only a slow phasing in of various safety nets.[155]

Sensitivity to labor issues grew after the burning down of a Sanyo Universal Electric plant late in 1996. The arson followed the failure of workers and managers to reach agreement on the size of annual bonus payments. Workers were unhappy with the ongoing use of casual laborers, some of them continuing on that basis after as many as four years of employment. These workers depended on overtime to earn adequate pay, and the 1996 slump in manufacturing cut into their pay.[156] Similar conditions were pervasive in textile plants.

While some Thai firms worked to upgrade their production and train their workforce, a slash-and-burn style of management was also common. As wages rose, firms simply employed more part-time workers or unskilled immigrants, or moved offshore. Workers at times encouraged this approach by resisting the introduction of labor-saving machinery. With labor and capital unable to cooperate to boost labor productivity, state officials clearly had a part to play. By and large, they failed to do so.

Conclusion

By the 1990s the textile industry as a whole still accounted for nearly one-fourth of Thailand's industrial GDP and over 14 per cent of foreign exchange earnings. Garments were Thailand's second largest export in 1996, at about $4 billion.[157] The different sectors were generally poorly integrated, though some groups, including the large garment firms, increasingly moved toward greater integration. The spinning and knitting segments were reasonably competitive, and the garment industry was a regional leader, but the industry was hampered by weaknesses upstream (petrochemicals) and downstream (finishing and dyeing). Fabric exports were modest and consisted largely of gray goods. A 1992 UNIDO study of the Thai industry concluded that the Thai industry would face increasingly severe competition not only from low-wage countries but also from ever more efficient firms in the NIEs as well as OECD countries.[158] This prediction appeared prophetic when the market for Thai garment exports collapsed in 1996.

Most Thai state officials lacked an understanding of the textile industry or the needs of its firms, so officials were in no position to stipulate performance standards in return for state support. Even with such an understanding, they would have been hobbled by powerful firms' influence either within ministries or with their political bosses. Thai Blanket Industry, for example, got its start and secured its expansion through connections with government officials and political patrons.[159]

Officials' unfamiliarity with the industries they regulated facilitated private influence over authoritative decisionmaking. Lacking a clear industrial policy or fundamental understanding of the issues involved, state officials sought only to facilitate, or balance, private sector interests; they had little ability to weigh private demands using independent standards for judgment. When private interests offered contradictory input, officials adopted strategies aimed at balancing competing claims rather than achieving development goals, but to competing sources of input. And where officials could not find areas of compromise, they generally delayed making policies. Furthermore, competition among state agencies encouraged them to reach out to private clients for support in their struggles, which tended to undermine the potential for consistent state action.

The Introduction drew a contrast between consistent macroeconomic policymaking guided by liberal principles and incoherent sectoral policies driven by rent-seeking concerns in Thailand. How can we square the picture of textile trade policies drawn above with the argument that Thailand's macroeconomic policymakers did not have to contend with demands by lobbying interests because of the latter groups' weak organization? Clearly, textile producers were able to organize to press for protective tariffs. It is important to recognize, however, that the main factor inhibiting tariff reductions from the early 1980s was the concern of finance ministry officials not to forgo revenue and thereby enlarge fiscal deficits.

Nonetheless, if the Thai state's textile promotion was not altogether good, neither was it entirely bad. Either because of a residual commitment to agency goals that survived goal displacement, or because multiple points of access in the system produced competition,[160] powerful industrialists did not always get their own way, with the result that the industry did not become overly concentrated or rigid. For example, in the awarding of BoI privileges, officials generally did not entrench the dominance of existing firms. While the process was slow and the reasoning underlying decisions not always transparent, the political influence of existing producers did not solely determine outcomes; new producers could also exercise influence. We can find isolated examples of Thai textile officials applying performance standards. For example, past performance was the single most important determinant in the awarding of export quotas under managed export arrangements (though this had the effect of favoring established producers).[161]

We can find more indirect, but nonetheless compelling, evidence for the argument that Thai state policies, whether by design or by accident, did not introduce undue rigidities into the Thai economy as a whole. The business sector's very mutability, with the rapid rise of new sectors and considerable change in the relative positions of firms within many sectors, supports this conclusion. One factor that may have helped produce this result was the ethnic divide between Thai officials and Chinese entrepreneurs, which may have hindered the development of overly close, sustained, competition-stifling cooperation. In this sense, ethnic identities may have afforded officials a degree of policymaking autonomy. They may also have contributed, as suggested in the Introduction and Chapter 1, to the asset diversity and external orientation of dominant Chinese business groups.

If officials were able to sustain a degree of insulation from private concerns and to apply technical criteria in some isolated areas of their textile policymaking, they were far from being able to secure cooperation with the private sector in jointly tackling problems that beset the sector. The industry's decentralized structure appeared to overwhelm the influence of divisible and recurring benefits as well as ongoing efforts to cooperate. While cooperation among fiber producers – dominated by a few firms, most of them subsidiaries of foreign multinationals – was apparently more common, even there it was difficult to sustain.[162] Calls for longer-term strategies nonetheless continued. In fact, given the industry's rising dependence on foreign markets and the competition it faced from lower-wage producers, the imperative to cooperate grew stronger. In 1993 Industry Minister Sanan Kachornprasart called for talks with academics and industrialists in devising long-term strategies and adjustments in the way the ministry did its work. That same year the TTMA called for long-term planning on how to cope with rising international competitive challenges. Concerns about such challenges grew acute, in part as a result of the initiative in 1992 to create an ASEAN Free Trade Area. Low-end garment producers faced stiff challenges from overseas, and users of synthetic fibers were concerned with the ongoing protection granted the local petrochemical industry that kept raw materials prices high.[163]

Many Thai garment exporters were subcontractors for foreign producers, notably from the East Asia NIEs, and often received specifications as well as inputs from abroad. Clearly, Thai firms needed to increase the quality of their textile exports as their prices rose, or the East Asia contractors would increasingly send the work elsewhere. As the Thai industry faced the need for fundamental adjustments, the advantages of the Chinese organization of business groups were put to the test. Asset diversity and international orientation suggested flexibility, but would they also enhance commitments to existing production facilities? Textile firms in other countries had proved that if productivity increased, higher wage producers could remain competitive in some sectors. In Thailand, however, with weak labor skills and nimble-footed entrepreneurs, it appeared at least as likely that the latter would choose exit over loyalty. The impact on the local industry could prove severe, raising questions of whether or not Thailand might not prove to be, as suggested by a foreign securities analyst in Bangkok in 1993, "the NIC that failed."[164] Or at any rate, the one that failed to sustain long-term development of the industry that propelled its initial industrialization.

Chapter 6

Incredible Commitments and Policy Chaos

After several years of fits and starts aimed at developing a series of infrastructure and heavy industry projects southeast of Bangkok, and less than a month after the Cabinet decided in 1985 to approve $260 million in foreign loans for the projects, the Council of Economic Ministers put the projects on hold. The NESDB secretary-general, Snoh Unakul, recommended that a "neutral party" be appointed to consider the projects and the advisability of going forward with them.[1] The council ordered a three-member review committee, chaired by a minister in the Prime Minister's Office, to study and assess all the projects and issue recommendations in forty-five days.[2]

This decision produced a storm of protest from the projects' supporters, who saw the decision as aimed at derailing the projects. One critic complained:

> What has gone wrong with this country's decision-making mechanism? Why was it that the proposal to freeze the Eastern Seaboard projects was not screened by the Eastern Seaboard Development Committee before it was passed to the Cabinet? . . . Only two weeks earlier, on October 31, the Cabinet had approved loans for the Eastern Seaboard projects. Then, bang! came the surprise decision to freeze everything.[3]

Consider another case. By the early 1990s the average travel speed in the center of Bangkok or anywhere in the city during rush hour could be counted on one's fingers. With the number of cars choking Bangkok's streets jumping upward, the rate at which they could move fell about as quickly. Children were waking up well before dawn to attend schools, many with dangerously high levels of lead in their blood, and necessity induced the invention of a portable toilet commuters could use in the privacy of their cars. As measures to cope with this crisis, the police suggested they might prohibit traffic-inducing funerals and wedding ceremonies. In the mid-1990s the police took to dancing in the streets while they tried to create traffic flow – if they could not beat the traffic, they at least could divert the frustrated motorists.[4]

It was therefore with understandable dismay that Thais saw, when part of Bangkok's second-stage expressway opened in 1993, that only joggers and skateboarders had access to it. A prolonged series of disputes between the private builders and the state enterprise responsible for overseeing the work remained unsettled. The Thai government failed to increase tolls on expressways already in operation as specified in the contract concluded with the private consortium. In fact the Thai government agency that signed the contract had no authority over the tolls. With their chances of recouping their investment at risk, the private consortium refused to open the expressway to traffic.

Both these stories illustrate aspects of Thailand's infrastructure policy planning and weaknesses in implementing it. Thai state agencies and private business firms were active in providing transport infrastructure.[5] Successful planning and implementation of these massive projects put a premium on coordination between them as well as among interests within the state and private sector. The absence of coordinating mechanisms resulted in a spate of conflicts, delays, and non-decisions.

Despite the failures in providing heavy industries and transport infrastructure described below, Thai officials did manage over the decades a reasonably solid record in providing infrastructure.[6] Implementation of infrastructure in many cases required a top-down style of implementation without the need for performance criteria, project evaluations, or extensive coordination among diverse players. These conditions suited local administrative strengths.[7] Even in the more challenging telecommunications industry, despite considerable confusion, the record on service provision was stronger than in the cases described below.[8] Where officials had to balance the interests of many state and private actors, they fared less well, as becomes evident in this chapter.

Certain public policy tasks are inherently more difficult to achieve than others. In some respects providing transport and heavy industrial infrastructure should be fairly easy. As in national security or most macroeconomic policymaking, but unlike most other policy areas, state leaders can at times act alone to provide infrastructure without needing to coordinate the activities of a diverse set of non-state actors. Furthermore, because infrastructure projects often involve large budget outlays, they are attractive to politicians seeking to dispense favors and build political support. This offers the hope of insulating state officials implementing infrastructure projects from inordinate political pressures from outside the state. By dispensing favors, officials and politicians hope to create a powerful coalition supporting their plans. Competition to influence official decisions, however, will be intense, particularly where benefits are indivisible. In the case of the Lavalin contract for an elevated train, discussed below, rumors suggested the firm had paid a bribe of about $40 million to secure the project.[9] Another factor easing the provision of infrastructure is that many developing countries can draw on foreign aid to finance it. Thailand was certainly fortunate in this regard, using Japanese, United States, and World Bank funds.

In other ways, however, state authorities face particularly difficult problems in providing infrastructure. If they attempt to plan for future needs, they risk miscalculation, waste, and returns lower than borrowing costs. This may be the result, for example, with the massive Pudong development in Shanghai.[10] While infrastructure projects present opportunities for dispensing pork, they carry political costs associated with opposition among losers. Not all groups tendering bids will get contracts. Breaking up large projects into many pieces carries its own risks, as discovered by city authorities in Taipei saddled with huge costs, long delays, and countless controversies in building a subway system.[11] When not all bidders can be satisfied, the disgruntled have incentives to back alternative political leaders. Indeed it was probably not entirely coincidental that the coup that overthrew Thailand's Prime Minister Chatichai Choonhavan early in 1991 came soon after the government had awarded several large infrastructure contracts. Even if the consequences are less dramatic, losers have incentives to try to block project implementation in the hopes of reversing decisions.

The complexity of large infrastructure projects may strain state administrative capacities. Coordination problems tax government abilities when an array of different agencies have jurisdiction over a single project or group of schemes. The large scale typical of these undertakings multiplies the difficulties. Furthermore, in Thailand, as in other developing countries, state officials planning infrastructure projects have increasingly used build-operate-transfer schemes under which the private sector finances, builds, and operates a project for a specified period before turning it over to the state. This privatizing approach has increased the need for coordination.

State officials planning to erect ports, roads, industrial estates, telecommunications facilities and so on need information to formulate effective plans. Private firms can help by providing information on future demand conditions and the particular needs of the private sector. When officials try to proceed with these large projects without the benefit of such information, they can easily make expensive mistakes. One Th ai had such concerns in mind when he referred to a proposed fertilizer complex as a "pink elephant sitting by the seaside."[12] Because of their strong vested interests, business groups can not only offer information but also lend political support that becomes crucial if plans are controversial and face strong opposition.

This chapter tells two sets of stories about state officials in Thailand trying to provide transportation and heavy industrial infrastructure. Both stories feature delays, controversies, reversals, and indecision. The planning and implementation in both sets of projects suffered because of the limited divisibility and non-recurring nature of the benefits, jurisdictional conflicts and differences in preferences among state agencies, and the relative unfamiliarity of the actors in working with one another. Rather than the regular interaction characteristic of the financial or even the textile industries, the actors making decisions about infrastructure and heavy industrial projects for the most part wrangled over benefits on offer only once. Despite these problems, once the parameters of games were set (the players selected), the number of actors was limited, particularly among private participants, reducing collective action obstacles. Poor coordination among state agencies and the indivisibility of the projects' private benefits between participants and non-participants, however, proved to be enormous obstacles.

One group of projects saw officials trying to anticipate future demand through heavy public sector spending for a series of infrastructure and heavy industrial projects along the eastern rim of the Gulf of Thailand. These Eastern Seaboard (ESB) projects included industrial parks with associated utilities, two deep-water ports, transportation links, and the development of heavy industries, particularly ones based on natural gas. In the second set of cases, state officials tried to respond to an existing and acute need for urban expressways and effective mass transit systems in Bangkok. In general, the formulation and implementation processes for both sets of projects diverged sharply from those we associate with state planning in countries like France or Singapore. The differences resulted in large measure from the absence in Thailand of forums within which groups could exchange information and balance interests in the planning process. Even within the state, coordination was weak. Given these limitations, state officials' ability to draw on the information and political resources that private groups might have provided became especially important. Thai officials, however, generally failed to do so, with the resulting politics of implementation described in earlier chapters. Officials' announcements of decisions in this game served as the starter's gun signalling a political scramble that ideally would have preceded officials' selection of policy options. To foreshadow the consequences of this policy process, the consequences of delays were far heavier in the cases of the Bangkok transport projects than in the ESB schemes. Despite considerable delays in the latter, the private sector eventually seized on the opportunities that were emerging and completed, indeed expanded on, the original conception.

Policy Goals

Eastern seaboard projects

In the late 1970s government officials began to see a need for a comprehensive development plan for the eastern seaboard southeast of Bangkok on the Gulf of Thailand. They hoped that development along the coast would ease the overconcentration of population and industry in and around Bangkok as well as port congestion at Klong Toey, the Bangkok river port. A more immediate impetus for developing the ESB area, however, was the desire to exploit newly discovered natural gas deposits in the Gulf of Thailand. Officials hoped that the gas could be used to develop in Thailand a heavy industrial base that would deepen Thailand's industrial structure and, by building linkages among Thai firms, reduce the economy's chronic large trade deficits. Still more immediate factors precipitated actual planning for the projects. ESB residents, alarmed at the potential polluting activities of a proposed new rock salt–soda ash plant,[13] had protested against the proposed plant and passed rumors of threats of sabotage against it.[14] Officials took the threat seriously (in 1986 arsonists had destroyed a nearly completed tantalum plant in southern Thailand).

The ESB projects were key elements of Thailand's Fifth Five-Year Plan (1981–86). The plan reflected conflicting currents among Thai officials on the means of strengthening the economy. These officials were increasingly concerned about external and internal imbalances that resulted in part from the external shocks of the 1970s. Conditions only worsened in the early 1980s as a result of depressed commodity prices, global recession, and a local financial sector collapse. Officials differed, however, on how best to address these problems. One group emphasized the saturation of the domestic market and called for greater emphasis on export promotion. They wanted to limit local price distortions, including the BoI's capital subsidies, and generally endorsed the structural adjustment packages backed by loans from the World Bank and a series of IMF standby agreements. A second group of Thai officials, however, were influenced by Japanese and South Korean examples and believed the time had come to seize the bull by the horns and use public policies to shape Thailand's future comparative advantage.[15] One official of the structuralist persuasion complained that the traditional Thai approach to planning consisted of "putting on gum boots when it floods."[16] The offshore gas deposits afforded such officials an opportunity to advance their agenda. And in the end (or, to be more accurate, in the beginning), they prevailed and launched Thailand's first big public investment program since the 1940s.[17] The Fifth Five-Year Plan suggested that ESB development could help to reduce production bottlenecks caused by excessive industrial concentration in the Bangkok area. The plan called for both export promotion and ongoing import substitution, particularly in natural gas–based industries, and industrialization of the ESB was to serve both policies.

Bangkok transportation projects

At least some officials saw the ESB projects as anticipating future demand. By contrast, the transportation projects in Bangkok were efforts to cope with an unfolding crisis. A study backed by the Japanese government suggested that Bangkok was losing as much as a third of its potential production to the impact of traffic congestion.[18] A Thai Farmers Bank report found that average annual costs in lost production, health outlays, and wasted fuel, as well as forgone tourism receipts and investment, amounted to nearly $2.5 billion a year.[19] Citing serious consequences if the government did not act quickly to address transportation problems, the NESDB in 1990 proposed limits on vehicle ownership and use, further efforts to push industry out of Bangkok, and enforcement of zoning provisions.[20] By way of response, a succession of governments pursued a series of uncoordinated mass transit systems and expressways, many provided under build-operate-transfer[21] schemes, and within the jurisdictions of various different government agencies.

The sections below provide separate and simplified chronologies of the implementation of these projects. These tales are necessarily complex and tangled, but they serve to illustrate the problems such projects encountered in Thailand. The first section begins with the ESB plan as a whole, then, looking in more detail at the fertilizer and petrochemical projects, attempts to account for their divergent histories. Thereafter, the chapter moves on to treat separately each of the major Bangkok transportation projects.

Project Chronologies

Eastern seaboard

The existence of a port at Sattahip and an airfield at U-Tapao built by the United States during the Vietnam War, together with its proximity to Bangkok, had for some years made the ESB an area favored for proposed industrial and infrastructure projects. The area gained real prominence as a focus for development projects when officials decided to pipe natural gas from the Gulf of Thailand to a gas separation plant in Map Ta Phut in Rayong Province. Workers completed construction of the world's longest submarine natural gas pipeline in 1981, and officials decided to site gas-based industries nearby.[22] In March of that year a government committee submitted its report, *A Study in Primary Industrial Development and Deep Sea Port in the East Coast*, to the Committee on the Development of Basic Industry on the Eastern Seaboard. The report called for the establishment of the Eastern Seaboard Development Committee (ESDC) and made recommendations on locating the various industries. Recognizing that the planning required for the projects exceeded the experience of Thai state agencies, the report also urged the NESDB to commission Coopers & Lybrand Associates, an engineering consulting firm, to develop a master plan, to be financed by foreign loans, for the area's development.

The Coopers & Lybrand Associates report envisioned a series of projects costing some $4 billion, less than a third of that for infrastructure and most of the rest going to industrial development.[23] Of the total investment, the government would put up about half, relying on foreign financing for near half that share. The private sector, according to the plan, would also draw on foreign loans for close to 90 per cent of its investments.[24] By 2001, the report suggested, the ESB would compete with Bangkok as a magnet attracting heavy, polluting, and natural gas–based industries. The report also envisioned agro-processing and light industries locating in the area, which would relieve Bangkok's worsening industrial congestion and pollution. The report forecast that the development would create close to half a million jobs in the region over the next two decades.[25]

The plan called for the government to build a container port and industrial estate with an export-processing zone at Laem Chabang; water pipelines to Laem Chabang and Map Ta Phut; a deep-water port at Map Ta Phut for bulk goods; a railway connecting Bangkok to Sattahip; and facilities for urban development at both Laem Chabang and Map Ta Phut. The report recognized that the overall economic rate of return would be rather low, at less than 10 per cent. Job creation would be expensive, about ten times the average for industrial employment in Thailand. The projects would soak up scarce capital while bloating already large public sector and foreign deficits (they would account for about 6.5 per cent of public sector investment over the course of the Fifth Plan, 1981–86). Nonetheless, by creating import substituting industries, the projects offered significant foreign exchange savings and, the report argued, rational use of Thailand's available natural gas.[26]

Thai officials had never before attempted projects on the scale of the ESB plan. To implement such a vast set of projects would require departures from accustomed administrative practices. Ministries would need unprecedented coordination. The challenges appeared daunting.

Even as various Thais in government and business expressed doubts about the wisdom of undertaking plans of such scale, others drew inspiration from the examples of East Asia's developmental states. In the early 1980s Depute Prime Minister Boonchu Rojanasathien called for the creation of "Thai, Inc." Snoh, of the NESDB, invoked Japan's postwar development of ports and associated industries and urban areas as a model for Thai emulation.[27] The Japanese International Cooperation Agency (JICA), in its feasibility study for the development of the Laem Chabang coastal area, noted the experiences of Japan, South Korea, and Singapore in regional development programs.[28]

The JICA study recognized that Thai officials would confront institutional obstacles in attempting to launch and coordinate the plans. With admirable understatement, the study observed that with no Thai agency "designated or capable of adequately supervising" the plan, the government's capacity "to coordinate the Eastern Seaboard Program effectively and to react to new conditions is less adequate than would be desired."[29] Reservations about the Thai policy process also were evident in the Coopers & Lybrand report:

> In considering the options for developing institutions capable of undertaking the tasks necessary to control implementation, we first examined the potential for introducing a new form of development agency with comprehensive powers. Despite the attractions of such a solution, we are aware that it would run counter to existing Thai administrative practices and could not succeed, unless fully supported by existing agencies.[30]

"Existing Thai administrative practices" referred to chronic turf battles among ministries and agencies, and their political leaders, and the difficulty technocrats would face in trying to induce those agencies to surrender control of any projects over which the agencies could assert a plausible jurisdictional claim.

At the outset, responding to these concerns, the Cabinet made significant administrative changes aimed at centralizing control over implementation of the projects. These steps included creating the ESDC in July 1981 and, within the NESDB, the Center for Integrated Plan of Operations. The Cabinet earlier established the Council of Economic Ministers to vet large investment projects.[31] With the prime minister as chair, and Cabinet and other senior officials serving on the board, the ESDC assumed major decisionmaking power over the ESB projects, bypassing the Cabinet in many cases.

The novelty of the plan's grand sweep was reflected in some of the rhetoric attending its launch. Snoh, the top NESDB official, underlined the state's leading role: "This time the government has taken the initiative and is ahead of the private sector in this development effort."[32] After walking through the mud on the ESB with former Japanese Foreign Minister Okita Saburo, Snoh remarked that despite the large expenses involved, "we'd rather shoulder the burden before reaping the benefits. If we move too slowly, we might lose the rare opportunity."[33] Another NESDB official described the plan as a "new departure" that would create a "Silicon Valley of Thailand."[34] In 1985 yet another official held that the plan marked an "historic turning point for the country's development process."[35] His earlier judgment in 1982, however, ultimately proved more acute: "Experience shows that large scale economic projects are always realized through the pressure that the private sector brings to bear upon the government, not the other way around."[36] Similarly, a Budget Bureau official, citing Thailand's lack of a tradition of comprehensive planning, flatly dismissed the Coopers & Lybrand report as a utopian dream.[37]

Despite the decisive roles the private sector eventually played in implementing the projects, business enthusiasm for the plans was at first restrained. Business association leaders were apparently disconcerted by evidence that state officials were divided in their commitment to the projects. The absence of wholehearted state backing and the lack of a clear indication as to which state entities would be implementing the projects aroused private sector scepticism about the projects' futures and discouraged commitments of major assets. Having for the most part had no role in formulating the plans and possessing limited confidence that the state would sustain its commitment to them, most private firms were reluctant to be pioneers in the area's development. Hence the dominant posture among business executives was one of wait and see. They understood, apparently, that for all the fanfare accompanying the ESB's launch, the die had not yet been cast.

Nonetheless, by the end of 1982 several key elements of the ESB plan were moving ahead smoothly. The Petroleum Authority of Thailand (PTT), established in 1978, had completed construction of the pipeline that fed natural gas to power plants onshore; a gas separation plant was within two years of completion. After the failure of negotiations with a Scandinavian consortium to establish a turnkey chemical fertilizer plant, the government organized the National Fertilizer Corporation (NFC) in October 1982. With some $2 million registered capital, the NFC undertook a study of the feasibility of establishing a chemical fertilizer production facility with majority private ownership. Later in 1982 the ESDC gave its "final" approval for the construction of a deep-water container port at Laem Chabang.[38] In June 1983, Japan's Overseas Economic Cooperation Fund (OECF) offered concessional loans for the development of the port.[39] The following month the ESDC ordered the Communications Ministry to proceed with plans for ports at Laem Chabang and Map Ta Phut.[40]

Even when, in December 1983, Samak Sunthornwej, the communications minister, threw a spanner in the works, he stalled progress only briefly on the port at Laem Chabang. Samak claimed to be disgruntled with the stipulation in the proposed OECF loan, designed to favor Japanese firms, that only firms from developing countries could compete with Japanese firms in bidding for the engineering design contracts.[41] The finance minister, responsible for negotiating foreign loans (and described as having close links with Japanese officials), was out of the country and Samak used the opportunity to get Cabinet authorization to seek alternative sources of funding.[42]

Early in 1984, however, the Cabinet overcame Samak's opposition and approved the OECF loan for the Laem Chabang port.[43] Previously, in late 1983, the ESDC had approved applications from four firms to produce downstream petrochemical products. And in June 1984 the Japanese Embassy in Bangkok announced that, including a large loan for the NFC, Thailand topped the list of recipients included in Japan's Eleventh Yen Loan package with almost $300 million dollars in low-interest loans.[44]

Later in 1984, however, rumblings of discontent about the ESB projects grew louder. With slower growth of export earnings because of low commodity prices, officials became more concerned about Thailand's burgeoning debt and the size of foreign loans required to implement the projects. The Thai economy was stalling and the government was bailing out dozens of collapsing financial institutions. Within the NESDB, differences of view concerning the projects grew increasingly evident. One official complained that the government was spending money on non-competitive industries and that, with an oil glut and plummeting oil prices, it was time to reconsider the government's commitment to fertilizer and petrochemical projects. He urged more concern for investments that created jobs, in agro-industries and others.[45] Another senior government official worried about Thailand's ballooning foreign debt pointed to the need to learn from the "Philippines lesson."[46] Debate over the projects became even more contentious as the IMF warned of the need to adhere to goals outlined during discussion of standby agreements[47] and critics noted that the heaviest state financial burdens would fall due in 1985–86 when Thailand's external and budgetary imbalances would be most acute.

By early 1985 the ESDC had made small reductions in the plan and was calling for slower implementation of the projects. The Cabinet formally abandoned the long troubled steel and soda ash projects in April.[48] In July 1985 officials prioritized the projects, putting the NFC and Laem Chabang port at the top of the list. Not long afterwards the Cabinet declared it would avoid any additional curtailments.[49]

To head off growth in the foreign debt, in October 1985 the Cabinet imposed an overall $1 billion annual ceiling on public foreign borrowing. The BoT and the finance ministry, concerned for the integrity of the IMF's standby agreements, called for concentrating resources on profitable, labor-intensive projects that would earn foreign exchange.[50] While reassuring to those concerned with Thailand's financial health, this move threatened the ESB projects.

By this time project proponents were growing increasingly frustrated with the constant uncertainty about the fate of the projects. While critics of the projects argued that Thai officials were displaying an admirable willingness to adapt to changing circumstances, particularly Thailand's growing foreign debt,[51] supporters noted a pattern of policymaking not backed by necessary data and showing poor coordination between ministers and an absence of articulated development priorities. These conditions rendered infinitely more difficult what were admittedly complex technical decisions. A (failed) coup attempt in September 1985 compounded concern about the impact of such indecision on the international investment community.

At the end of October 1985, the Cabinet decided to approve $260 million in foreign loans for the ESB projects for that fiscal year. At this point momentum shifted toward the projects' opponents. In the next month the Council of Economic Ministers put the projects on hold and created a three-member committee to review all of the projects. Opponents of the projects were exultant. As one observed: "There are many more projects with quicker return on investments and smaller schemes that will be of direct benefit to the people. We can't just go for big projects under the circumstances. We don't want to become another Philippines." Supporters, for their part, strengthened their case by pointing to possible adverse Japanese reactions to any changes in the plans since the two governments had already signed loan papers, most recently earlier the same month while the Thai finance minister was in Tokyo.[52] The pendulum indeed seemed to shift back their way. To the dismay of project opponents, following the 45-day review in December 1985, the Cabinet met and decided that all the projects would go forward. A member of the review panel reported optimistically that "there will be no delays, cutbacks, or slowdowns. The projects will go ahead as scheduled."[53]

By the time of the July 1986 parliamentary elections, Thailand's economy was moving toward a very strong recovery. At the time, however, this was not yet evident. Just after the voting, the World Bank released the full text of a critical appraisal of the ESB projects,[54] prompting officials to schedule another Cabinet meeting in October to make more final decisions. On this occasion the Cabinet decided to go forward with the port and industrial estate, including an export-processing zone, at Laem Chabang.[55] Thereafter, with the exception of the NFC (once the centerpiece of the entire ESB program), all the remaining projects bumped along, though with considerable delays. As the signs of growth gathered force and investment continued to expand, it became clear that, even without the NFC, the Industrial Estate Authority of Thailand would have enough customers for the proposed industrial estate at Map Ta Phut.[56] Progress on the petro-chemical projects was so great that plans for a second petrochemical complex began to move forward.[57]

Initial studies for the development of the ESB envisioned government investments in infrastructure of about $1.2 billion. By 1985 planners had scaled that figure down by 30 per cent. Total public investment in the projects over the 1980s probably came to only about half initial projections.[58] In the end the government prodded forward those projects that promised significant economic returns under rapidly changing conditions. While the effort to anticipate future demand with transport and industrial infrastructure failed, flexibility allowed for adjustment, even if not always timely, to changing opportunities. And the failure to move forward with the implementation of some projects may have saved Thailand from being strapped with costly and politically sensitive burdens.

From his reading of this history, Muscat praised the outcomes of public sector decisionmaking in Thailand for avoiding the expensive mistakes that plagued ambitious governments elsewhere. An effective Thai consensus, he suggested, avoided big losers as well as winners, to the economy's long-run benefit.[59] He concluded generously that the policy process could be seen as a "socially optimizing" means of making decisions about large projects.[60] The World Bank also praised the Thai government's ESB policymaking.[61]

As Thailand's economic boom gathered steam, the projects gained momentum, driven by private investment. Infrastructure in Bangkok grew hopelessly overstrained.[62] The projects, particularly in the petro-chemical sector, began to benefit from the economics of agglomeration. Most of Thailand's leading firms eventually made major investments in the region, often in joint ventures with foreign capital. Petrochemical projects featured large among the many heavy industrial projects that proceeded at Map Ta Phut. In 1993 Thai Tantalum Company began production there, using tin slag provided by Thaisarco, located in southern Thailand.[63] By the mid-1990s the region was also associated closely with Southeast Asia's preeminent automobile industry. In 1996

General Motors decided to locate a $750 million assembly plant in the area and Toyota started production at its new plant.[64] Over less than three years in the mid-1990s, total investment in four ESB provinces was considerably higher than that in Bangkok and surrounding provinces. Observers were predicting that by the end of the century Thailand's petrochemical industry would outstrip that in Singapore, its steel industry would challenge Korea's, and its auto industry would be second in Asia only to Japan's. By 1997 officials expected the port at Laem Chabang to outstrip the old Klong Toey port. With over thirty industrial estates in the region by the mid-1990s (most of them privately owned), a single sprawling metropolis spreading from Bangkok to the ESB was in the making.[65]

An integrated steel plant, discussed since before the advent of the ESB plan,[66] was one of the first casualties among the ESB projects. But after the surge in manufacturing activity associated with foreign investment in the late 1980s, demand for steel for auto assembly and electrical appliances industries increased rapidly. By early 1988 interest in a steel project had revived and in late 1989 the BoI promoted development of a $735 million integrated steel project.[67] In February 1994 Sahaviriya Steel Industries began to produce hot rolled steel coils and sheets in Prachuab Kirikhan. By November that year the boom in domestic demand for steel was so great that other steel projects began to go forward.

Despite a hair-raising process of selecting, rejecting, and reselecting projects for development, officials were able to implement many of the ESB projects. Although most suffered considerable delays, even those that authorities cancelled eventually reappeared as projects championed by private sponsors. Enthusiasm for the region's development took root in the early 1990s and helped to fuel interest in comparable projects in other regions of Thailand. What was particularly striking, however, was that despite continuing inadequacies in infrastructure, the ESB developed in a manner conforming to the original Coopers & Lybrand plan. Heavy and petrochemical industries located along the coast; downstream industries located nearby. Steel plants supplied a larger-than-anticipated auto industry. Farther north were more labor industries, stretching up toward the poor and labor-abundant northeastern provinces.[68] Exactly such linkages were promised in the original vision for the area's development.

Review of Specific Projects

The policymaking described above featured confusion and costly delays. In the end, however, the process allowed for extensive vetting, helping to reduce the likelihood of costly errors. But cool economic analysis does not explain adequately why officials dropped or delayed some projects while sustaining others. To gain a fuller understanding of these divergent outcomes, we look in greater detail at the histories of the NFC and the National Petrochemical Corporation (NPC).

Fertilizers

Hopes to set up a large chemical fertilizer plant predated plans for the development of the ESB. Many Thai officials had long argued that as one of the world's great food-exporting nations, Thailand should have some chemical fertilizer production capacity (it had only a mixing facility). Local production of fertilizers, went the argument, would help to reduce price fluctuations, assure stability and quality of supply, and encourage increased application of fertilizers. Thailand had among the lowest rates of fertilizer use and agricultural productivity (per unit of land) in Asia.[69] A fertilizer plant also would make effective use of Thailand's natural gas and ameliorate its trade deficits.

A consortium of German firms built a state-owned chemical fertilizer plant in northern Thailand at a cost of about $15 million in the 1960s following lignite discoveries in the area in the late 1950s. Because of mismanagement, poor-quality lignite and changing demand in the direction of compound fertilizers, the plant never ran at even half capacity. Investors claimed foreigners were dumping fertilizers in Thailand and obtained a ban on nitrogen fertilizer imports for six years.[70] Nonetheless, by 1975 the firms' losses had exceeded its investment cost, and its troubles ended only when the plant blew up.[71] Meanwhile, in the early 1970s, the Metro Group built a private fertilizer-mixing plant, Thai Central Chemical Corporation, with 300 000 tons annual capacity. The project received BoI promotional privileges and a monopoly on fertilizer imports lasting until 1973.[72]

In 1981 a Scandinavian consortium won a bid to construct a $590 million fertilizer plant, but disagreements arose over the gas-pricing formula to be used,[73] the extent of the consortium's equity participation, fertilizer-pricing policies, and other issues.[74] Thai officials then decided to undertake the project, by this time seen as an integral part of the ESB plan, without the participation of foreign equity. Under a complex formula, the government would have a minority shareholding with Thai commercial banks, finance and insurance companies, with fertilizer importers holding the balance. The ownership structure reflected an effort by Chatumongkol Sonakul, the NFC's first chair, to have the financial institutions balancing the presumed opposing interests of state and fertilizer importer shareholders.[75] More than one investor dismissed Chatumongkol's careful weighing of interests as "too clever."[76] Chatumongkol's scheme reflected suspicion that at least some private firms gave in to government pressure to participate in the project only to be in a position to sabotage it. The result, however, by exacerbating free riding and reducing the potential for sunk costs to create strong supporters, may have made matters worse. No private participants were strongly committed to the project.[77] But by creating a large number of equity participants he increased the obstacles to cooperation and the number of effective vetoes over the project. Key bank shareholders grew worried as their businesses slumped and principal clients, particularly the Metro Group, backed by the Bangkok Bank, suffered large losses from the 1984 baht devaluation.[78]

Foster Wheeler, an engineering consultant, completed a feasibility study for the fertilizer complex in 1983 and government officials selected engineering and financial consultants. By mid-1984 several firms tendered construction bids, and the surprisingly low price tag of the winning bid held the promise of significantly higher internal rates of return than at first expected.[79] A dazzling assortment of delays, however, dogged the project. These ranged from technical financing details, including the difficulty of finding a guarantor for the OECF's $85 million loan, to prolonged negotiations, following the yen's appreciation after 1985, aimed at establishing a yen–dollar rate at which the Japanese construction companies would be paid for their work. With the government a minority shareholder in the NFC, the MoF was legally barred from guaranteeing the OECF loan. Chatumongkol hoped at one point to have the PTT provide the necessary backing.[80] When the Industrial Finance Corporation of Thailand (IFCT) finally agreed late in 1985 to provide a guarantee, it insisted that investors increase their registered capital over 1000 per cent to a total of almost $100 million. Subsequently the yen's appreciation increased the value of the Japanese loan in local currency and the IFCT opted out of its role. By 1986 the finance minister talked a group of Thai commercial banks into serving as guarantors for the loan. The bank's opposition increased, however, when the MoF decided later that year to seek higher equity commitments from the commercial bank participants to compensate for reduced public shares in the project. With government support for the projects lukewarm, the banks increased their resistance, and the Bangkok Bank weighed in forcefully in opposition. The bank's stance was crucial. As a former chairman of the project put it, "In Thailand, no project goes forward in the face of opposition from the Bangkok Bank."[81]

After lying moribund for some years, the project revived in the early 1990s with backing from a host of new players. The NFC began importing urea fertilizers and listed on the SET in 1996.

Petrochemicals

In contrast to the tortured history of the NFC, the National Petroleum Corporation (NPC) flourished and helped to launch a new and important Thai industry. The petrochemical industry, however, also became a source of major conflicts between different manufacturing industries because of its dependence on high levels of protection. Among the many components of the ESB projects, the petrochemical scheme stood out for its straightforward and successful planning and implementation. Nonetheless, its achievements followed a long and rich history of vague policies, confused guidelines, and unfulfilled goals.

In the late 1960s various Thai and foreign petrochemical interests and the Thai government held prolonged negotiations in an effort to establish a petrochemical industry. Royal Dutch Shell negotiated with a Thai partner to establish a naptha cracker plant. Japanese importers dominated the import of petrochemical products, and Mitsui and Mitsubishi, together with Teijin, a textile firm and maker of synthetic fibers, emerged as the dominant foreign interests in negotiations aimed at establishing a midstream aromatics industry in Thailand. The project would have been Thailand's largest industrial undertaking.[82] The BoI granted the project generous privileges, including protection against imports. Negotiations on the price at which ethylene would be sold to the aromatics plant dragged on for years and through several BoI deadlines.[83] Other obstacles foreshadowed problems faced by the fertilizer project: concerns about what group would hold majority ownership, local market capacity, optimum plant size, global demand conditions, and Thailand's comparative advantage in petrochemical production.[84] Japan's Ministry of International Trade and Industry insisted that the Japanese shareholders' stake be a minimum of 55 per cent since the Japanese government would be guaranteeing the loans. The BoI wanted to limit the Japanese stake to 49 per cent.[85] By the time the parties finally reached agreement in 1973, the subsequent oil shock led the Japanese participants to lose interest.

The establishment in 1978 of the Petroleum Authority of Thailand was a crucial factor in the NPC's later success in pushing the projects. Together with the Crown Property Bureau's 4.5 per cent share in the NPC, the PTT's 49 per cent gave the state effective control. (The Crown Property Bureau is not legally a state entity, but personnel ties and broad interests tend to align the concerns of its officials with those of state technocrats.) While the NPC experienced significant delays, the threat of outright cancellation was less common than in the case of the NFC. And the relatively simple ownership structure eased decision-making. In fact, relative to the NFC or other ESB projects, a small number of actors could make most decisions. The NPC's president and the chairman of the PTT were in regular contact and handled problems quickly, presenting a united front to the private sector equity participants.[86]

A pipeline brought natural gas from the Gulf of Thailand to Map Ta Phut, where a gas separation plant produced ethane and propane for the olefins plant to convert into ethylene and propylene. Downstream producers, in turn, converted these into a range of products, including vinyl chloride monomer, polypropylene, polyethylene, and polyvinyl chloride. The government guaranteed feedstock prices for downstream firms, monopoly production rights for eight years, and high levels of protection.[87] Unlike investors in the NFC project, players in the petrochemicals projects had assurances of significant and ongoing state support. The Thai government identified petrochemicals as one of six priority industries under the Seventh Five-Year Plan (1992–96). The NPC completed construction of its olefins plant at Map Ta Phut in October 1989.[88] The intermediate and downstream producers completed their parts of the complex by 1990.

In 1987 the Cabinet approved plans for a second gas separation plant and the following year selected downstream participants in a second petrochemical complex.[89] The second, larger group of petrochemical projects included ethylene cracker (olefins) and aromatics plants aimed at increasing capacity and producing new classes of plastics. Twelve downstream projects would locate near the refinery at Sriracha, while the new olefins complex would be near the original plant at Map Ta Phut. Thai Olefins Co. secured late in 1992 a $440 million syndicated loan from the Bangkok Bank and several East Asian banks, the largest loan ever secured by a private Thai entity.[90]

Rapid expansion of production and export of products using petrochemicals, including plastic molds, synthetic fibers, and toys, suggested that the second complex would enjoy high domestic demand. In 1987 imports of petroleum products came to $430 million, 95 per cent of it for local use and the remainder going into the production of toys, textiles, and household decorations for export.[91] Projections suggested that local demand would absorb all NPC I and NPC II (a later complex of petrochemical plants) production by 1996–97. As a result, officials began planning a third complex for the south of Thailand involving aromatics and olefins plants, and production for export. By the mid-1990s private firms, including Siam Cement and Thai Petrochemical Industries, took the lead in pushing the new olefins projects. Siam Cement set its sights on emerging as Southeast Asia's leading petrochemical producer.[92]

While officials moved to establish the NFC before the NPC, and the press and high-level officials accorded the former greater attention, it was the petrochemical project that survived and thrived. Both projects faced a major disadvantage in having to use relatively expensive natural gas. For this and other reasons, including the alleged inadequacy of feasibility studies, World Bank officials expressed concerns about both projects.[93] In both cases, however, large domestic demand would consume all of their production if officials protected them from imports.

The chemical fertilizer plant had the advantages of low construction bids and concessional loans to finance the project. Politicians also saw considerable political appeal in claiming to serve the interests of farmers. The political nature of the project, however, also represented a liability given private sector participants' worries that farmers' complaints would lead ineluctably to state intervention to depress fertilizer prices. To ensure that tariffs did not saddle farmers with the costs of supporting the project, officials refrained from promising any protection from imports. In contrast, a 40 per cent tariff on imported feedstocks protected the petrochemical projects.[94] By 1994 the Thai government made commitments to bring these rates down to 20 per cent. The petrochemical producers, however, managed to delay tariff reductions.[95] The high costs of petrochemical products remained a source of complaints from downstream users, including those in the textile industry.

The Thai petrochemical industry's future remains uncertain. The downstream sector had a lead on competitors in Indonesia and Malaysia but, given the latter's cheaper natural gas, the lead appeared vulnerable. Meanwhile, throughout East Asia firms made heavy investments in petrochemicals, and Thailand, unlike the NIEs, faced shortages of skilled workers in the industry. The conclusion of a free-trade agreement among the ASEAN countries, including Indonesia and Malaysia, caused worry in the industry. Dow Chemical, concerned about Thai commitments to reduce tariff protection, dropped its participation in the $240 million Siam Styrene Monomer Company that would produce polystyrene and other products within the aromatics complex.[96]

Differences between the NFC and NPC's respective owners and consumers were also important in leading to different outcomes. The petrochemical project had a simple ownership structure dominated by a government enterprise with considerable political clout. It was able to bargain directly and effectively with private sector equity participants who were also the downstream users of the plant's output. The chemical fertilizer project, however, had a complex ownership structure, with the government holding a minority share. This tended to offset the advantages of concessional loans from Japan's OECF and of equity participation by the International Finance Corporation.

The boom in the petrochemical industry attracted a broad range of Thai private interests. Saha Union, a conglomerate based on the textile business, planned a joint venture with ICI to produce raw materials for the production of polyester. The Bangkok Bank was active in the second petrochemical complex as financier and investor. In fact in the petrochemical fever of the late 1980s and early 1990s, hardly a single significant Thai economic player failed to get swept up in the enthusiasm. Siam Cement used the projects to diversify into a variety of new fields, including petrochemicals. Thai Petrochemical Industries Group established its own industrial estate, complete with power generation, in Rayong. It moved into the production of cement (a $2.8 billion venture), caprolactum (for textile fiber and auto parts production, in a joint venture with Japanese firms), and both up and downstream in the oil business itself.[97]

The fertilizer project did not lengthen the time horizons of participants' cost-benefit calculations. Essentially it represented a one-shot deal. It challenged an existing business and its powerful financial backer. The many owners with diverse interests were not inclined to cooperate, particularly given the state's equivocal backing. By contrast, the petrochemical complex offered the promise of ongoing profit opportunities. Even if the initial projects failed to yield profits, investors would have a foot in the door and be well positioned to exploit future opportunities. Each investor entered into the scheme with different plans for subsequent expansion, often up or downstream. Furthermore, at the time the project was launched in the early 1980s, it was possible to include most of the small number of major players with interests in the industry.

Bangkok Mass Transit Plans

Between 1979 and 1996 Thailand weathered severe economic difficulties and emerged with strong economic growth, rapidly expanding manufactured exports, public sector revenue surpluses, sharply diminished external debt, considerable economic reform and liberalization, and rapidly rising incomes. Thai electoral democracy overcame its own fragilities and a concerted attack by a newly united army leadership to survive more or less intact. We might expect that these developments would have affected favourably the infrastructure policymaking process in Bangkok. A review of the process surrounding implementation of highway and mass transit schemes in Bangkok, however, offers little support for this view.

In Bangkok the consequences of policy failures were dramatic. Rapid economic growth had long made clear the need for effective mass transit. In 1990 57 per cent of all urban Thais lived in Bangkok.[98] The city accounted for 71 per cent of all passenger cars in Thailand, and the average travel speed in the center of Bangkok was about six miles an hour.[99] Over the late 1980s the average speed supposedly dropped on average more than one mile per hour per year. Meanwhile Bangkok's average per capita income was reaching levels that could sustain a rapidly growing automobile market. In the early 1990s the Thai automobile market boomed, with three-quarters of that growth concentrated in the capital. With some two million vehicles, the number grew by 300 000 a year. Road surface made up less than 10 per cent of the city's area, compared to 20–25 per cent in most large Asian cities.[100] And the city's population continued to grow rapidly (projected to reach over ten million by the end of the century).[101] A city strangling on its exhaust and traffic congestion had some time to wait, however, before it would gain any substantial relief.

Bangkok was "Asia's most gridlocked capital,"[102] and Thais looked desperately for solutions. Traffic was reducing bus revenues and interfering with garbage collection.[103] Nearly half of Bangkok residents identified traffic as the leading issue facing the incoming Banharn Silpa-archa government in 1995.[104] Carbon and dust particulate levels in Bangkok were well above Thai safety standards. *A Family in Traffic*, a novel that tells a tale of cars loaded with telephones, faxes, video and audio equipment, stuffed animals, and portable toilets, with the wife becoming pregnant, won the 1993 Southeast Asia Write award. (One former official suggested that these varied amusements accounted for the great popularity of vans.) Even the Thai paintings on display at the National Gallery, insisted one commentator, reflected concerns about traffic.[105]

Several different mass transit plans, together with accelerated building of highways, were under design or construction in Bangkok in 1990. Thailand's Seventh Five-Year Plan (1992–96) envisioned spending over $20 billion on transportation infrastructure, and initial plans called for a further $44 billion during the eighth plan (1997–2001).[106] The Bangkok projects required coordination among the Highways Department, Land Transport Department, and Harbor Department within the Ministry of Transport and Communications, the State Railways of Thailand (SRT), the Expressways and Rapid Transit Authority (ETA), and the Bangkok Metropolitan Administration (BMA), among others.[107] Thai transportation projects were marked by a rich history of conflicts, delays, and particularly in the case of the mass transit schemes, almost no initial progress. A brief review of these projects follows.

Skytrain

Thai officials initiated the earliest of the Bangkok mass transit plans in the early 1980s under the management of the ETA. Not until 1990, however, did the ETA begin to negotiate a contract with Lavalin, a Canadian firm. Initial plans for a $1.6 billion elevated electric train to be completed by 1992 quickly ran into problems. In fact Lavalin was not able to sign a contract until early 1992.[108] It soon faced conflicts with two other subsequent mass transit projects and, because of contract irregularities, opposition from the Anand government, which overturned the agreement in June of that year.[109]

The Anand government nonetheless wanted to push the project forward. In July 1992 officials created a state enterprise, the Metropolitan Rapid Transit Authority (MRTA), to supervise the Skytrain project (renamed the Metropolitan Rapid Transit System) as well as the other two schemes after their thirty-year concessions expired. The authorities scaled back the project, in part with the aim of achieving better coordination with the other two mass transit projects discussed below.

When the Chuan government assumed office in 1992, it ordered the MRTA to turn the Skytrain over to private investors. Committed to addressing rural poverty, officials wanted to avoid unnecessary public spending on the Bangkok area. In seeking new private sector bids, however, the government required a new feasibility study and tendering of bids, causing further delays. This opened the way for reconsideration of an underground project rather than the planned elevated train. Environmental groups pressed to move all three mass transit projects below ground. Bangkok Land, a private firm, and its official sponsors were determined to stick with the existing plans for an aboveground MRTA system. Thanachat Holding, a private competitor, and its friends favoring a subway system, fought for changes. A German consortium, Metro 2000, expressed interest in implementing an underground system in Bangkok. Indecision on whether or not to put the system underground coincided with vacillating on the extent to which the government would privatize the scheme. By 1994 the National Environment Board, backed by a prominent environmental campaign opposed to the elevated plan, was insisting on changes in the MRTA project.[110] Metro 2000 threated to abandon its efforts on behalf of a subway system unless the government provided a clear policy.[111] Finally the Cabinet awarded the project to Bangkok Land in February 1994. The debate over whether to keep the projects visible or tunnel beneath the streets continued, with officials awarding contracts and then withdrawing them because of prohibitive costs.[112]

In the late summer of 1995 the MRTA sent out pre-bid documents for its elevated train. Then, in September, the Cabinet decided to put 21 kilometers of the system underground, with the government assuming the 50 per cent cost increase and facing two additional years for construction.[113] A $250 million Japanese government loan covering 40 per cent of the cost for civil engineering work helped to lessen the pain in arriving at the decision. Officials expected project completion in 2002 (a decade behind the original schedule) at a cost of $2.8 billion.[114] A German-Japanese-Thai consortium won the bid in September 1996 for work on one part of the plan.[115]

The MRTA project, like the others, suffered from corruption and from poor planning and coordination. Frequent changes in government resulted in regular reversals in decisions, making the state's authoritative commitments non-credible. When officials announced contract awards, howls of protest typically ensued. For example, the losing bidders representing Italy, France, and South Korea complained about the September 1996 contract award.[116] A similar pattern was evident in the awarding of other infrastructure contracts.[117] What makes the losers' protests unusual is their vehemence and their usefulness, because in some cases they were able to modify or overturn decisions.

Bangkok Transit System Corporation's elevated train

The initiative for an elevated train under the BMA's jurisdiction came long after the Skytrain, but its progress was comparatively rapid. Early in 1992 the Anand Cabinet approved the project, granting Tanayong Corporation (Bangkok Transit System Corporation, BTSC) a thirty-year concession.[118] At $800 million, the elevated project would include two lines, cover 24 kilometers, and would be completed by 1996. The BTSC was able to hold a ground-breaking ceremony in June 1992 and secured BoI promotional privileges that same year (including an eight-year tax holiday and, like the Hopewell project discussed below, reduced tariffs on its imported equipment).[119] By the following year the BTSC gained financial support for the project.[120] Thereafter the obstacles began to mount.

One of the main problems was the siting of the Tanayong rail yard. Tanayong originally planned to drop it in the middle of Lumpini Park, one of western Bangkok's few public green spaces. This set off a storm of criticism, required the cooperation of other state agencies, and resulted in an eight-month delay as officials scrambled to get an alternative location. Nonetheless, the BTSC was able to break ground in March 1994,[121] just two months before the government decided temporarily to abandon the existing configurations for the various plans and to put all three of the projects underground.

The project also suffered as a result of becoming entangled in party conflicts, including those within the ruling coalition. Using a variety of public agencies, politicians wrangled with one another for control over the project and its contract. The key political players were two parties in the Chuan government's ruling coalition: the Palang Dharma Party (PDP) which controlled the BMA, SRT, and Office of Land Transport System Management Office (LTMO); and the New Aspiration Party (NAP) with authority over the ETA and the MRTA. The BTSC project's links to Palang Dharma attracted opposition. Other parties were reluctant to see the party's de facto leader, Chamlong Srimuang, enhance his already considerable prestige by pushing the project forward. While the PDP held the BMA governor's post, the latter's limited independent powers[122] kept him dependent on support from the NAP, which held the Ministry of Interior portfolio.

The second Anand government set up the LTMO in 1992 to oversee the three mass transit and six highway projects, including the second and third-stage expressways and the Don Muang tollway. The new entity lacked decision authority, however, and had to coordinate with the BMA, the Bangkok Mass Transit Authority, the Department of Town and Country Planning, the Public Works Department, the ETA, the MRTA, and the NESDB.[123] In 1993 the LTMO began work preparing a new master plan, hiring consultants in January 1994 to begin work. Former Prime Minister Anand led a group of private interests trying to help in formulating the master plan. Their work led to a proposal that encompassed sixty-two measures put forward during a Traffic Crisis '94 gala dinner in late January. When reports circulated suggesting that at least some of the projects were not commercially feasible, anxieties deepened. A major new broadside came in April 1994 when the LTMO presented its report outlining three different options for the mass transit schemes and calling for all three projects to put below ground those portions that were within a central 25 square kilometer area. In May the Chuan government decided to implement this proposal and to shoulder the additional expense involved.[124] At first all three contractors accepted this stipulation, but BTSC and Hopewell soon decided for financial and technical reasons to resist the move; both had already signed contracts. In July the Cabinet gave its "final" approval to allow the Tanayong project to remain above ground. Hopewell also eventually gained permission to remain above ground. Two weeks after the July 1994 decision approving the Tanayong project, the Cabinet ordered construction delayed because of administrative technicalities.

In an August 1994 no-confidence debate, Opposition leaders called the Tanayong contract shameful and vowed to commence parliamentary and other hearings on the project.[125] In the 1995 elections the PDP lost control of the Bangkok governor's seat, raising worries about the impact this would have on the project. Nonetheless, officials insisted the project would be completed by 1998.[126]

Hopewell Holdings elevated rail and road project

The third part of the mass transit scheme was a plan by a subsidiary of Hopewell Holdings Ltd of Hong Kong to build 60 kilometers of elevated rail line and roadway at a cost of $3.2 billion. This project, like the others, was to proceed under a modified build-operate-transfer scheme, and officials slated completion of the first section for 1996, with the entire project to be completed by 2000. Hopewell signed a contract in November 1991 with the SRT. Early in 1992 the BoI denied Hopewell promotional privileges on the development of real estate, and the Cabinet refused a waiver of the withholding tax on foreign borrowing, but Hopewell determined to push forward. The Cabinet authorized preliminary work on the plan early in 1993[127] and in May the builders finally broke ground.[128] They did not get far.

Hopewell and the SRT fought each other throughout the implementation of the project. The Transport and Communications Ministry was sympathetic to Hopewell's concerns but was unable to budge the SRT.[129] Hopewell planned to pay for the project through the revenue it would realize by renting space at its stations. SRT resistance to Hopewell real estate plans endangered this element of the plan. The SRT also faced difficulties in gaining control over those of its lands that were occupied by squatters. The SRT, for its part, expressed concerns about the quality of the design Hopewell provided. By late 1993 Hopewell had secured SRT permission to build high-rise apartments along its routes. In May the SRT approved the Hopewell road design. As the property market in Bangkok began to stagnate in 1994, however, Hopewell's enthusiasm for the project diminished.[130]

By 1996 the Hopewell project was proceeding fairly smoothly, and firm directors tried to raise additional capital on the local equities market in an effort to increase their registered capital to $3 billion. Late that year Hopewell awarded a $1.3 billion contract to a British-German group for equipment. The firm expected to complete the project in the closing weeks of the century, three years behind schedule. Officials set a deadline for part of the project of December 1998, when Thailand would host the Asian Games athletic contests.

Urban Highways

By contrast with the mass transit systems, progress on building expressways in Bangkok went relatively smoothly. Kumagai Gumi

(Japan) led the Bangkok Expressway consortium that won the award of the right to build the second-stage expressway in 1988. The construction was dogged by delays resulting from slow progress in land purchasing. More important, however, were a series of contract disputes over toll prices, division of revenue, and toll management that broke into the open in 1993 and left a completed section of expressway closed to commuters (see page 140). Residents caught in interminable traffic delays had no access to the new route until a court order forced the consortium to open the expressway.[131] Concerned with the political reaction to any increases in existing tolls, politicians under the Chatichai, Anand, and Chuan governments had demurred from raising tolls to the levels stipulated in the contract.[132] In the last quarter of 1992 the Anand government raised tolls on the highway from ten to fifteen baht. The ETA was requesting twenty baht, as specified in the contract that the ETA, without adequate authority, had signed with Bangkok Expressway Co. Ltd (BECL).[133] The contract required a later toll rise to thirty baht (60 per cent to go to BECL, 40 per cent to ETA), but it remained at fifteen. Deputy Prime Minister Amnuay Virawan pushed a compromise of twenty baht for eighteen months, with a 25-baht toll to take effect in January 1995 and ETA receiving only two baht per car. The government would make a loan to ETA to enable it to function despite the shortfall.[134]

Those steps left the ETA with inadequate revenue to pursue its role as sponsor of new expressway construction schemes. Faced with this dilemma, the ETA began to reinterpret its contractual terms with the Bangkok Expressway group, in particular the date at which revenue-sharing between the consortium and ETA would begin and, more important, what entity would control the toll collection operations.[135] In February 1994 foreign bankers made clear to the MoF that they wanted to get out of the consortium. In March, as bankers froze their credit lines, Kumagai Gumi was forced to suspend interest payments on its loans. The result was not only delays, but skepticism among foreign investors. One Japanese banker noted that there is "excessive political risk when it comes to transportation projects in Bangkok."[136]

After imposition of the court order, a foreign banker insisted that "we will not negotiate with ETA, or the Interior Ministry, or the New Aspiration Party. We have to negotiate with the government." It was not immediately clear who or what agency he had in mind. After all, the court order apparently came at the initiative of Interior Minister Chavalit Yongchaiyut, leader of the New Aspiration Party. The banker might have been referring to Prime Minister Chuan and his top aides, who were out of the country at the time.[137]

These developments prompted Kumagai Gumi to seek a way out of the project. Later in 1994 Charoen Karnchang, a Thai consortium with links to the military, bought Kumagai Gumi's 65 per cent share in the second-stage expressway project. Twenty-three foreign banks also told the MoF that they wanted out.[138] Ironically, BECL had sought the participation of foreign banks in a time-honored effort to secure thereby political protection for the project. In this case the protection proved inadequate. A foreign banker suggested that "[t]here is an opinion emerging among international investors that Thailand has to be reclassified in the banana-republic category."[139]

Other expressway projects also faced delays and contractual tussles. The Don Muang tollway project, for example, slated for completion in May 1993, faced cost overruns and charges by foreign bankers of breach of contract. The Chatichai government awarded the contract in 1989 to a well-connected group despite opposition from state officials – the elevated scheme would require destruction of two existing bridges. Government officials, however, blocked those plans, which in turn made foreign creditors nervous. The project was years behind schedule and tens of millions of dollars over budget.[140] The third-stage expressway in the east of Bangkok also stalled, attracting few bids.[141] Eventually the Cabinet ordered the ETA to establish a subsidiary that would undertake the project, thereby avoiding such problems.

The obstacles that faced private operators of infrastructure schemes in Bangkok inspired awe. The limited results, accordingly, were predictable. In addition to a succession of governments (eight) between 1988 and 1996 (in 1993 one Hopewell executive noted that in the past three years he had been dealing with five different prime ministers, six transportation and commerce ministers, and two governors of the State Railways of Thailand),[142] firms had to work with dozens of government agencies under the authority of competing political parties.

Forging Agreements and Making Credible Commitments

A review of these cases reinforces the picture of a haphazard decision-making process shaping the Thai state's developmental roles. As noted at the outset, private sector input into early decisionmaking on the ESB projects was less than it was in many economic issues. Indeed broad input of any kind was generally inadequate. Poor project conception was a key factor in forcing subsequent adjustments, particularly in the case of the Bangkok transport plans. Private sector input was generally limited to those groups hoping to win contracts. Business associations representing Thai exporters eager to have access to improved transportation infrastructure, for example, were not prominent in the ESB plans. In both sets of projects, state agencies were unable to frame, defend, and adhere to a set of policy objectives. Instead, decisionmaking was plagued by delays, indecision, incoherence, and inconsistency.

Party spoils shaped the policy process and were the most important conduit through which private interests played policy roles. Party leaders had ample opportunities to block progress. In the absence of forceful, clear articulation of broad national needs, and without a prior inclusive deliberative process, political parties found it easy to exploit openings to delay and divert plans. Parties were particularly important when decisions took on zero-sum properties involving choice between competing projects. For example, the Chart Thai was committed to development of the Laem Chabang area.[143] While other factors were also at work, it seems likely that the Chart Thai's rejoining the ruling coalition after the July 1986 elections induced the government to assign unambiguous priority to the port at Laem Chabang.

The fragile nature of the state's authority may have resulted in part from the coalitional nature of the various Prem governments in the 1980s. At no time while he remained in power did any single party come close to holding a majority in parliament. This became increasingly important over the years as parties' powers increased. Muscat argues that to keep support of all coalition members, leaders avoided clear-cut decisions, opting instead for delays and obfuscation.[144]

It seems unlikely, however, that a dominant political coalition would have made a difference. Political parties were so weak and the centrifugal pull of factions within them so pronounced that even had a single party enjoyed a parliamentary majority, it is not clear that this would have affected the decision process significantly. A single party's solid parliamentary majority could make a difference in a country such as Malaysia, where the United Malay National Organization's dominance enabled it to dispense pork authoritatively.[145] In Thailand, however, no comparable party existed. The weakness of the parties and the nature of political competition in Thailand – over access to a limited number of ministerial portfolios – ensured the workings of the logic of minimum winning coalitions. One MoF official complained that in Korea bureaucrats can implement decisions because the opposition is fragmented; in Thailand the opposition is fragmented also, but so are the supporters.[146]

The principal obstacles to implementation of these infrastructure projects were their one-shot nature and, in most cases, the relatively indivisible benefits they afforded. While relatively few actors were involved, these obstacles proved insurmountable even by a limited number of players. The petrochemical projects differed in that they more nearly resembled a game of recurring and divisible benefits, so side payments were more feasible.

The Bangkok transportation projects differed from those on the ESB in that the need for action was crystal clear and, in the former cases, seemingly inevitable. In both cases, however, inadequate mechanisms for forging winning coalitions of support either within the state or among social groups frustrated progress in implementation. As a result, authoritative decisions lacked credibility. Here we get a sense of a crucial role that interest-articulating institutions, including state agencies, can play. By outlining a vision and making associated credible commitments, such institutions have the potential to align the expectations of both social and state actors. In Thailand such harmonization came neither from authoritative state actors nor from social institutions articulating a broad consensus. The absence of such institutions can be costly, as much of this chapter suggests. At the same time, however, benefits can also accrue as a result of the flexibility that follows from an absence of stable expectations.

The most striking element in these stories, however, is the limits of the coordinating capacities of Thai state agencies themselves. With limited expertise, these agencies frequently emphasized political criteria in their decisionmaking. The *ad hoc* links with private interests and broader social groups reduced the potential for officials to augment their capacities by drawing on the latter's expertise. And in the case of these massive projects, but unlike the textile industry, officials had no option of simply letting the market allocate resources. Authoritative decisionmaking was necessary to provide public goods, and officials could not simply wait for the market to reveal the relative merits of different actors and proposals.

The discussion above makes clear that there were many points of access to the decision-making process in Thailand. Easy access did not simply result in Thai decisionmakers having more data that they could use in weighing options. Rather, it tended at times to produce system overload and easy derailment of the decisionmaking process. In particular, the institutional context afforded multiple veto points and undermined the potential for sustained state action in the face of even minor private opposition.

Muscat provides the most generous interpretation of the Thai record on infrastructure provision. He emphasizes the ways in which the process provided ample opportunities for vetting projects and reevaluating prior decisions. Putting it less generously, an MoF official insisted that the Prem government's principal claim to fame was that it did nothing; it simply allowed things to happen.[147] This characterization captures both the strengths and weaknesses of the policy record.

PART THREE

Chapter 7

Growing Social Capital

This book has argued that low levels of social capital in Thailand help to explain the ways in which business and state institutions operate and, more broadly, the development strategy choices selected by Thai political leaders. A relatively weak impulse toward, or capacity for, spontaneous sociability leaves Thai firms and state officials confronting economic challenges with relatively few institutional tools at their disposal to facilitate cooperation. Several important results have flowed from this institutional landscape that, together with other factors, encouraged Thai officials' adoption of a market development strategy. Given the problems and advantages associated with particular Thai and Chinese endowments of social capital, how did firms and officials interact and with what impacts on those sectors? To account for different patterns of policy and private–public interaction in the three issue areas, the sectoral studies examined the number of public and private actors who interacted to shape policies, the duration and frequency of their interaction, the extent to which the prospect of future gains was salient, and the divisibility of benefits and costs at stake.

This chapter reviews the book's conclusions and goes on to address three issues not discussed at length earlier: the wider costs associated with the amalgam of Thai and Chinese social capital endowments; evidence that Thai sociability and social capital endowments are changing; and what the Thai case teaches us about the development prospects of poor countries. The following section begins by briefly recounting the rationale for using the concept of social capital to analyze Thailand's political economy.

What Does the Social Capital Concept Teach Us?

Part I offered an explanation of salient features of Thailand's economy, polity, and society through an examination of Thai social organization. By recognizing the embedded nature of Thai institutions, their rootedness in Thai society and attitudes, I was able to highlight, and offer plausible explanations for, distinctive features of Thailand's political economy. While it is often essential to isolate different economic, political, and social features of social reality for purposes of analysis, the costs can be considerable.

Paring down the complexity of the realities we study enables us to isolate key causal variables from relatively unimportant ones and makes comparative analysis possible. By looking at firms, consumers, interest-representing institutions, or state agencies divorced from the context of the society in which they operate, however, we ignore elements necessary to an understanding of how and why they operate as they do. Abstracting reality by framing it in the familiar terms of utilitarian analyses – numbers of actors, their potential gains and losses, the costs of monitoring compliance with agreements, and the formal character of institutions in a particular sector – may not be adequate for understanding the patterns of interaction we observe among those actors.

Sensitivity to variable levels of sociability helps us to understand why institutions do or do not exist, and how effectively they perform.[1] An analysis of the social context in which individuals, firms, and state officials operate can help us to understand their preferences and their cost-benefit calculations. Social capital can influence transaction costs that confront firms, the extent of agents' opportunism, and the prospects of using norms of reciprocity and trust to overcome a variety of market failures. If social capital varies across communities, then that variation ought to manifest itself in significant institutional and performance differences. In short, this approach demands that we take actors seriously as agents who interpret their social contexts rather than as ones always responding predictably to structures that can be defined by a few utilitarian variables. Hence an understanding of the obstacles to collective action requires that we observe not only formal features of institutions but underlying normative ones as well. Different actors diverge in their perceptions of collective action obstacles, the means they select for trying to overcome them, and the costs and benefits they assign to the behavioral changes that will be necessary to do so.

Chapter 2 suggested that to understand Thailand's political economy it is essential to look at the social assets of Thais and Chinese. Thais did not readily participate in continuing cooperative groups beyond the family. They were not quick to join groups, tended not to remain long if they did, and generally did not contribute to making groups effective in achieving the goals common to their members. To the extent that one of those goals was to be as autonomous as possible, this was certainly to be expected. As a result, Thais could not easily achieve ends that required sustained voluntary participation. Many Thais recognized this difficulty, as reflected in the assessment that while "a Thai can beat a Japanese, ten Japanese can beat ten Thais."

As noted in the discussion of the textile industry, foreign capital played an extremely important part in Thailand's economic development, particularly of its export-manufacturing sector. Thais were extremely successful in mobilizing foreign skills and savings on behalf of Thai officials' national development goals. Indeed Thais generally were quite successful in cooperating with foreigners, whether the immigrant Chinese the Thais so easily assimilated or multinational firms that established operations in Thailand. It is worthwhile recalling the point made in Chapter 2, that groups with a high degree of trust and cooperation tend to be ones that erect relatively high barriers to entry and have relatively closed social networks. Thais had neither and showed little trust or cooperation among themselves. They have compensated, in part, by the skill with which they harness foreigners' ambitions for their own purposes.

As a consequence of the social capital endowments specific to the Chinese and to the Thai, the Chinese owners of many small firms tended to extend their interests across different economic sectors rather than concentrating resources in a single sector. In this case, with a multiplicity of firms increasing collective action problems, firms were not apt to form effective business associations. Furthermore, because in the aggregate key business decisionmakers' assets were diversified, their incentives to invest in political support for any given activity were muted. (Clearly this was not the case when the promised economic rents were very large, as with many of the projects discussed in Chapter 6.) The status of the Chinese at least into the late 1960s as a pariah minority also worked to curb their potential political influence.

For two reasons we should expect to find ineffective state agencies stemming from modest endowments of sociability and social capital. Despite the possibility that authority relations among state officials might help them overcome this weak sociability, the tasks of coordinating individuals in large, complex organizations necessarily rest in large part on confidence in delegating authority and free flows of information. Where characteristics of social organization impede these, state agencies' effectiveness should be affected. The second ground for predicting low state capacity harked back to Riggs' notion that in the absence of interlocutors outside the state apparatus positioned to make

demands of state agencies, officials of the state are given to goal displacement – pursuing their self-interest with minimal reference to the
needs of their nominal clients in society.

A sparse network of social groups, labor unions, farmers' organizations, business interest associations, and so on, should reduce the
impediments officials typically face in committing themselves to market
development strategies. The same conditions, however, can also give
rise to a predatory state. Such a state is unlikely to produce growth,
enhanced international status, or, in the longer run, easily attract externally mobilized savings, whether through public or private channels.

Clearly social capital endowments alone do not predict the type of
development strategy officials will adopt. While the choice of a market
strategy was surely once the outcome of a complex mix of factors (by
the late 1980s officials everywhere perceived a narrowed range of
options), low social capital endowments offer conducive conditions for
such a choice for three reasons. First, low state capacities suggest that
alternative strategies will fail. Failure alone is clearly no guarantee that
officials will change strategies, but it must increase the odds in the long
run. Second, because neither producers nor popular groups are apt to
be well organized to press their perceived interests on state officials,
political factors that typically militate against adoption of market
strategies are less likely to be important. Third, if the response to market incentives on the part of firms is relatively rapid and robust, officials may be more likely to remain aloof from the goose that lays the
golden eggs. I can offer at least partial agreement with James Stewart's
observation in the eighteenth century that where "an opulent, bold,
and spirited people" have "the prince's wealth in their own hands . . .
[t]he consequence of this has been a more mild, and a more regular
plan of administration."[2] In Thailand the opulent, bold, and spirited
Chinese clearly did produce a rapid and robust response to market
policies, and the same appears to have been true in most of East Asia, a
region apparently strong in "civic market competence."[3] The relatively
abundant social capital among the Chinese helped produce positive
economic results and, therefore, assuming that officials' fears of the
Chinese did not get in the way, made the market alternative more
attractive than it might otherwise have been. In Thailand the fears
of the Chinese were relatively mild, and political competition for
resources, including those the Chinese made available, largely offset
those fears.

Concerning the nature of institutions mediating between individuals
and the state, low levels of social capital tend to induce *ad hoc*, diffuse,
clientelistic channels of representation, making policy deliberation
difficult. So the heart of politics tends to rest not in institutions that

represent interests such as political parties but in the implementation processes within state agencies as directly affected interests mobilize political resources in an *ad hoc* manner and through clientelist challenges to nudge specific elements of public policies of direct concern to them. The permeability of the Thai policy process is often explained as a product of weak state institutions. This discussion suggests, however, that it also serves politically to engage actors outside the state, albeit in haphazard manner, and administratively to offer an opportunity to vet decisions made within state agencies. To borrow a political metaphor, Thai economic policymaking is akin to elections taking place without political parties or electoral campaigns. Gramsci noted that "[t]he counting of votes is the final ceremony of a long process." It is preceded by competing efforts to craft shared identities, visions, and commitments in a diverse array of civic and political institutions. In Thailand, however, officials make policies ("elections") without benefit of these processes.[4]

The analysis of the consequences of limited social capital in Thailand provided the broad context against which subsequent chapters examined policymaking and firms' responses in three economic sectors. The impact of specific social capital endowments varied, both because of idiosyncratic factors and because, consistent with a utilitarian analysis, the obstacles to cooperation in different contexts differed. Where the obstacles were few, the importance of social networks receded. All else equal, however, cooperation was likely to be greater where a small number of players were involved, where they interacted over a long period, where cooperation offered the promise of recurring benefits, and where those benefits, and the costs, were divisible. Finally, the impact on economic outcomes did not depend entirely on levels of cooperation. In certain sectors where asset flexibility was high (sunk costs low), the need to cooperate was less. Indeed sparse networks of cooperation had the advantage of impeding the creation of distributional coalitions that inhibit flexibility and growth. The compatibility of limited cooperation with a vibrant market economy surely helps us to understand Thailand's tremendous economic success. Nonetheless, it is worth recalling the central role that the Chinese, with their higher social capital endowments, played in that achievement. And it is worth reflecting on some of the potential costs, and assessing the sustainability, of this model of political economy, an issue considered below.

Findings

Thai financial authorities and private financial institutions created a strong and relatively stable sector that provided strong support to the

Thai economy as a whole during the era of rapid growth. Over the postwar years the goals of both state officials and private bankers changed, as did the degree of cooperation between the two. The comparative success of Thai financial institutions and of cooperation between bankers and bureaucrats resulted from several factors, including the historical contingencies discussed in Chapter 4. The small number of powerful bankers and public officials in this sector also facilitated cooperation as they interacted regularly and learned to cooperate with each other. The BoT and the MoF on the one hand, and the Thai Bankers' Association on the other, developed enduring institutional links that they used in regular discussions of goals and policies.

Another factor, the financial sector's importance, was not incorporated in this book's explanatory framework. It also seems, however, to have contributed to higher levels of cooperation in the financial field. Since the nineteenth century, Thai officials saw financial probity as linked to the preservation of the country's sovereignty. Financial authorities enjoyed support from British financial advisors, and later from World Bank and IMF officials. These agencies supported technocratic orientations and values and thereby bolstered the representatives of those orientations and values in Thailand.

During the 1980s, when the financial system was threatened with systemic collapse, bankers and bureaucrats increasingly saw their interests as ineluctably intertwined. As financial institution failures spread, financial authorities rode in to the rescue of the system as a whole. To do so they had to claim stronger regulatory powers and increased access to information. Official policymakers in this sector benefited from the concentration of authority in a small number of agencies, regular deliberations with the affected financial institutions, and a certain *esprit de corps*. One result was that policy pronouncements routinely were fairly clearly articulated and coherent, which helped private financial institutions and state authorities to harmonize their expectations. In announcing policies, financial officials' interests matched fairly closely those of the larger and more powerful banks. Some of the smaller banks not only were the principal mischief-makers but had fewer hopes of competing successfully in providing financial services. Instead they used their banks mainly to boost their own and their cronies' interests in other non-financial businesses.

The alignment of preferences between financial officials and the larger banks was important, but it did not last. By the late 1980s finance officials launched a long-delayed set of financial reforms that introduced greater competition into the system, including new firms. At the same time, the financial industry became increasingly subject to oversight by politicians. Hence to some degree bankers' and bureaucrats' preferences diverged again as the regulatory framework which had been moving toward what Samuels described in Japan as "reciprocal consent"[5] moved back again toward arm's-length relations. The disastrous collapse of the baht in 1997 against a backdrop of a crumbling financial sector suggested that the institutions in the financial sector, both public and private, were not yet adequately developed to handle the complexities associated with a liberal, deregulatory state. The default policy option – do nothing – that may have worked effectively in agriculture and some industries, for example textiles, was inadequate in this instance as well as in the planning and implementation of infrastructure discussed in Chapter 6. In both cases the negative externalities of bad policymaking were simply too large.

The Thai textile industry was perhaps a more qualified success than the financial sector. The industry's development was uneven, and its weaknesses threatened its sustainability. By the mid-1990s the dynamic garment sector was facing increasingly stiff competition. It nonetheless became a major employer and foreign exchange earner. The industry's development, however, owed little to state promotion policies beyond the protection afforded by tariffs. Even these policies may have done as much damage to the industry as good. In the textile industry, networks rooted in social organization had less influence than in other sectors. The negative consequences flowing from these conditions were limited, however, because in most subsectors assets were relatively flexible and sunk costs comparatively low. These features made possible a fairly close approximation of a perfectly competitive market.

Low levels of cooperation among firms in the textile sector, or between firms and state officials, resulted from the many firms, politicians, and state agencies with interests at stake. Despite the ongoing interaction among them, the divisibility of benefits and their recurring nature, cooperation repeatedly proved elusive. We might expect that the default policy for state officials operating in such a context would be something close to laissez-faire, but in fact Thai officials regulated the industry closely. This might have damaged the industry severely had it been effective. It was not. The BoI, by regularly doling out promotional privileges in fairly indiscriminate fashion,[6] helped to offset the effects of the regulations of the Ministries of Industry and of Commerce. The industry ministry's occasional amnesties on firms that had previously violated capacity controls had a similar effect. Firms' ability to defy or elude state officials' edicts ensured that Thai textile firms continued to face strong competition. Despite contrary intent on the part of regulatory officials, the de facto regulatory environment was fairly liberal. In the absence of supportive state policies, furthermore, private institutions were relatively important in fostering cooperation.

While the textile associations enjoyed only limited (though increasing) effectiveness in fostering cooperation or supplying collective goods, the Bangkok Bank played a more important role, financing the industry, bailing it out during hard times, providing analyses of its weaknesses and needs, and compelling firms to cooperate at several critical junctures. Finally, foreign capital played an enormous part in the industry's development.

Thai state officials performed most poorly in providing transportation and heavy industrial infrastructure. Even here, however, officials and firms enjoyed some successes, including rapid development of the Thai petrochemical industry (an ambiguous success given its ongoing dependence on protection) and avoiding expensive errors of commission. Viewed with hindsight, the complex of projects on the ESB appeared as successes, particularly if we take into account the work private interests did in going where state agencies feared to tread. In contrast, policy chaos in implementing the mass transit projects in Bangkok was nearly disastrous. Weak outcomes in this sector resulted from divisions among and within state implementing agencies, and a lack of support from organized business interest associations. Without bargaining institutions within which dominant interests could debate policies before officials made decisions, conflicts were particularly sharp at the implementation stage. As a result the projects were subject to frequent reversals of fortune. The advantages of a limited number of players in this sector were more than offset by the problems that arose as a result of the indivisibility and non-recurring nature of the private benefits that were on offer.

The Costs of Low Social Capital Endowments

This book has argued that institutional weaknesses rooted in Thai social habits help to account for the poor record of Thai firms and state officials cooperating in pursuing shared goals. And yet, by most standards, Thailand was a remarkable economic success story after the adoption of a private sector–led development strategy in the late 1950s. The same weaknesses that inhibited cooperation in Thailand also tended to limit the extent and impact of distributional coalitions. Competition among firms, divisions between state agencies, and the many points of access to the policymaking process produced an approximation of a laissez-faire strategy ("laissez-faire by accident"). The strong social capital of the Chinese provided the necessary counterpart, ensuring a vigorous response to market incentives and the ability at times to build social bridges that enabled firms to overcome market failures and the absence of certain well-functioning market institutions.

And a key weakness in state administration – the inability to offer credible commitments – at times manifested itself as an advantageous source of policy flexibility.

If this strategy in many respects served Thai firms well in the past, nonetheless we cannot assume that Thai-style liberalism will fare as well in the future. Even more conventional forms of liberalism require a considerable degree of state competence (the "orthodox paradox"). This truth was borne home with the baht's collapse in 1997, a result due in considerable measure, and not only with the benefit of hindsight, to policy errors. And any observer of Thailand was acutely aware by the late 1980s of some of the more costly consequences of weak public administration. Traffic and pollution problems in Bangkok were severe. State officials' inability to provide public goods was evident in the lack of physical infrastructure, including energy, transportation, and telecommunications. More important were weaknesses in skill training. Shortages in labor skills had serious economic consequences, helped to explain worsening income disparities in the 1980s, and slowed economic growth in the mid-1990s.[7] The 1997 crisis, argued one analysis, showed the limits of a development strategy that depended on public monopolies, cheap labor, illegal businesses, asset inflation, and protection.[8] And Thais faced serious public health and environmental hazards as well. The king captured the frustration many Thais felt when floods hit Bangkok yet again in late 1995 and officials were unable to act: "They only talk, talk, talk, and argue, argue, argue."[9]

This book's account of Thailand's successful economic performance has pointed to a serendipitous match of Thai and Chinese social capital endowments. It is now appropriate, however, to consider more directly some of the major costs associated with that marriage. Any student of the country is as familiar with its anarchic, Wild West facet as with its economic successes.

The most striking feature of Thai law is its weakness. Thais habitually ignore regulations of all kinds, resulting in everything from pollution to catastrophic fires. Rumors of a variety of assassination plots targeting the highest reaches of the state and society circulate for years without eliciting legal action of any kind. Political murder is not uncommon.[10] Development quickly destroys beautiful natural scenery, including at resorts that bring valuable foreign exchange. Illegal businesses including drug smuggling, prostitution, and logging are very lucrative and finance many Thai political parties and leading state officials. Corruption is widespread in the bureaucracy, as evidenced by a Pollwatch proposal to enhance police effectiveness by giving them four-fifths of the take from the arrest of political canvassers dispensing cash. The theft by a Thai of jewels from a Saudi in Saudi Arabia, their discovery by the

Thai police, and the return to the Saudis of fakes embroiled the country in years of diplomatic controversy that even the top-level Thai political leadership had difficulty resolving.[11]

One manifestation of the limited role that law plays in Thailand is the popularity of amnesties. Most observers praised the wisdom of amnesties that authorities used to sap insurgency movements in the 1980s. These showed once again that Thais' tolerance and lack of dogmatism enabled them to elude the worst consequences of seemingly intractable conflicts. As noted in Chapter 5, violations of capacity controls in the textile industry also enjoyed periodic amnesties. In still other cases, however, the wisdom of this tolerance-rooted approach to public policy is less evident. Military officers who plot coups enjoy amnesties, for example, even when unsuccessful.

One of the most blatant failures in public policy is evident in education policies. In the early 1990s well under a third of children of secondary school age were in school (in the Philippines the figure was 73 per cent, in China 44 per cent).[12] By the mid-1990s weak labor skills and rising costs were posing major problems for Thai firms producing tradable goods. While some firms were trying to improve the quality of their goods, scarcity of skilled labor and rapid turnover of workers often slowed their efforts. Many other firms simply continued using temporary workers to reduce costs, violated labor laws, employed larger numbers of illegal immigrants, or simply moved their production abroad to follow the cheap labor.

Perhaps the single most disastrous example of bad public policymaking concerned the spread of the AIDS virus in Thailand. In the late 1980s as the virus spread, authorities were at first very circumspect about tackling the problem head on, out of concern about the impact that publicity would have on the tourism industry, a key foreign exchange earner. With prodding from several particularly prominent individuals, policies eventually changed dramatically in the late 1980s. In this instance, after a painfully slow adjustment, Thai officials implemented more effective public health policies.

It is certainly very easy to make the case that for all the kudos due Thai state officials for their restraint in the area of macroeconomic policymaking, and the indirect benefits that accrued from the ineffective implementation of some other economic policies, public policies featured an array of serious failures of omission. These failures stemmed in part, this book has argued, from the limited degree to which social and economic groups were organized to make effective and enduring demands of state officials. Further improvements in public policy may depend on the strengthening of social capital in Thailand. While evolving political institutions will have profound effects on the development of Thai social capital endowments, the former will not entirely determine the latter.

The Mutability of Social Capital

It is not unusual to argue that prevailing Thai administrative practices will have to change if Thailand is to continue to succeed. The World Bank made the point in the late 1950s, arguing that the government had played only a minor role in stimulating growth up to that time, but that its role would become more important in sustaining future growth.[13] Wit argued in the 1960s that only the fundamental integrity of the idea of a Thai national community enabled the Thai economy and polity to survive the impact of weak public administration and politics. He suggested that in the future, however, improved administrative and political institutions would be required. While Thai administration did indeed improve after the late 1950s and state agencies made more effective contributions, the Thai economy's performance must be seen in part as belying these warnings.

Nonetheless, forty years later I offer the same warning. It is likely that Thais will increasingly need effective coordination among firms, and between firms and state authorities, as the industrial structure shifts toward more capital and technology-intensive production. Thai manufacturing has depended heavily on foreign capital, technology, management, and marketing. Attracting foreign capital in the future as wages rise will require more than stable macroeconomic policies, particularly as wage costs rise. As Lazonick observed of the United Kingdom, "market coordination," with small firms relying on markets to buy their inputs and distribute their output, was adequate until the late nineteenth century, after which relative decline set in as a result of firms' inability to coordinate the "specialized divisions of labor" that played key roles in the rise of German and US firms.[14] If Thai firms are going to make comparable transitions, they will increasingly need supportive public policies and a capacity to cooperate among themselves.

Chapter 5 suggested that institutional patterns that emerge with the development of a textile industry are likely to influence an economy's later institutional development. The weakness of patterns of cooperation in Thai agriculture or the textile industry may therefore lead us to be pessimistic about the prospects for cooperation either among firms or between firms and state officials. Nonetheless, there was some evidence in Thailand in the 1990s that new, more cooperative patterns were indeed emerging both in the private sector and the broader civil society. This evidence suggested that the accumulation of social capital may take place quite rapidly under some circumstances.

Thai officials over the 1980s and 1990s moved fairly rapidly to address some of the more glaring economic problems, and even environmental and social ones, that emerged during those years. After long delays, for example, officials implemented fairly effective campaigns designed to limit the spread of AIDS. To cope with shortages of skilled workers, politicians allocated more funds to education and authorities encouraged greater roles for private institutions in education and labor training. From 1996 compulsory education increased from six to nine years.[15]

Thailand's Eighth Five-Year Plan (1997–2001) was important both for the goals it emphasized (developing human resources, protecting the natural environment and resources) and the ways in which NESDB officials formulated it. The secretary-general of the NESDB, Sumet Tantiwechakun, elicited broad participation in the formulation of the plan's goals and details. With considerable publicity and frequent meetings, Sumet attracted the participation of politicians and NGOs in the process. While business leaders had worked with NESDB committees drafting parts of development plans since the early 1970s,[16] few Thais had previously taken part in the development of plan goals.[17]

Similar and startling changes were also evident in the processes through which Thais drafted and approved a new constitution in 1997. Groups rooted in civil society overcame strong opposition from political leaders and mobilized wide participation in the drafting process. The vision embodied in the new charter marked a striking change from accustomed administrative and political practices. Various provisions provided new protections of individuals' rights, called for the decentralization of state power to local levels, and elicited greater accountability and monitoring from both politicians and state officials.

Changing policy formulation processes also emerged in the 1990s as Thai firms confronted a succession of new trade arrangements (the Uruguay Round of the GATT talks and the subsequent GATS talks; AFTA; and APEC). While former Deputy Prime Minister Supachai Panichpakdi worried that Thailand lacked a "tradition of having state involvement in pursuing trade objectives overseas,"[18] business groups made explicit their determination to participate in trade policy formulation in order to anticipate implementation problems that might arise in the absence of prior discussions. The Business Economics Department within the Ministry of Commerce set up a joint working group with the Board of Trade, the Federation of Thai Industries, and the Thai Bankers Association for such purposes.[19]

The private sector also grew more vocal about the need for a national policy to develop the smaller firms necessary to support assembly industries in Thailand. Perhaps in part as a result of assistance provided by

Japanese firms and the Japanese government,[20] Thai firms urged a national plan to support the development of smaller firms. The BoI, for its part, established an office in Osaka seeking to attract Japanese firms and set up a Unit for Industrial Linkage Development that was to match assemblers and supporting industries. The Ministry of Industry also hoped to issue a plan for promoting smaller firms in 1996, and the Small Industrial Finance Corporation of Thailand aimed to promote smaller firms.[21] Even in rural development, agencies such as the Ministry of Industry showed unaccustomed innovation and flexibility, for example drawing on ideas introduced by NGOs to promote the footwear industry in villages.[22]

In an interesting new development noted in Chapter 4, financial authorities began to be more active in industrial policy issues outside the financial industry. Financial officials' engagement with these issues resulted from their efforts to sort out the diverse concerns of different upstream and downstream firms within sectors affected in opposite ways by proposed tariff reductions.[23] An editorial that appeared in *The Nation* in late 1994 summarized the context for these developments:

> [A] laissez-faire and hands-off approach might have worked in the past but with trade dependency and dismantling of tariff barriers worldwide, Thailand ought to . . . [adopt] a comprehensive sectoral approach to man-power development, product research and development, conditions for the transfer of technology, and other legal and policy support measures . . . Such a comprehensive approach to strengthening Thai industry is still very much lacking, especially at the implementation level.[24]

In short, Thai officials increasingly faced pressures to extend their competence from macroeconomic policies to sectoral issues. In the past the former policy areas were the preserves of Thai technocrats, while the latter presented opportunities for Thai party leaders to dispense largesse. New economic challenges, however, raised business demands for the extension of technocratic policymaking criteria to the sectoral policymaking agencies. This suggested the possibility that efforts to create cooperation-inducing institutions would receive further impetus.

The prospects for the development of more institutions fostering cooperation also increased as a result of the shrinking social space between bureaucrats and private interests. By the 1990s the ethnic divide between Chinese and Thais was all but gone from the conscious-ness of Thais in Bangkok. Indeed the situation was relaxed enough to allow space for the ethnic Chinese to indulge in back-to-our-roots sentiments as more Chinese started studying Mandarin and learning about Chinese culture (see page 55). State employment no longer bestowed status greater than private sector jobs, particularly given the much higher salaries available in the latter. At the same time the level of skills in both public and private sectors continued to grow rapidly (though far more rapidly in the latter) as the ever larger middle class was able to give its children better education. As Deyo noted of social change in general, concentrated employment in factories, the emergence of class-homogeneous communities, and the growth of the middle class were all likely to stimulate popular organization.[25] Finally, a further factor emphasized by Phongpaichit and Baker that may assume major significance is the disappearance of the Thai "frontier." Thai labor in the 1990s was becoming decreasingly seasonal, its links to villages frayed so that the latter no longer acted as often as a buffer against economic shocks. With Thais less able than in the past to simply exit from onerous conditions, pressures for voice in the shaping of the polity might intensify.[26]

The Eeyore Complex[27]

What does the Thai case tell us about the prospects for development in poor countries? We might conclude, with Adam Smith, that administrative and political development is not a precondition for the rapid creation of wealth.[28] And, as often argued, precisely because of Thailand's less than formidable institutional assets, as compared to the East Asian capitalist developmental states, it offers a hopeful model for other countries similarly endowed. Nonetheless, the political capacity to implement a liberal model, this book has suggested, depended in part on particular characteristics of Thai social organization. Furthermore, the astonishing results that stemmed from liberal policies required the complement of the particular social capital endowments of the immigrant Chinese.

Perhaps, however, we do not need so much to emphasize that any particular path is necessary and sufficient to induce wealth creation (establishing only necessary preconditions is easier, and to some extent academics have already done so). Many social scientists – political scientists and sociologists more than economists – believe that economic growth is an almost insuperable task not likely to be achieved except under narrowly constrained circumstances. Certainly this conclusion seems sensible when we consider the appalling extent of material misery around us. This suffering persists despite decades of efforts by legions of individuals, including officials and academics, to say nothing of efforts by those affected most directly, to alleviate it. Until about thirty years ago, the pessimistic conclusion that the bettering of the material conditions of life was, and was likely to remain, a rare achievement was bolstered by the fact that only European economies, and those of European settlement, and Japan, had managed to sustain rapid economic growth.

Today, however, the picture looks different, and particularly if we think in a longer historical perspective. Viewed this way, it has taken a remarkably short time for the habits of wealth creation to spread around the world. The habit has been so pervasive that even in many countries with rapidly increasing populations, per capita income has been increasing. With the depressing exception of Sub-Saharan Africa, it seems possible that by the middle of the next century the most extreme material poverty will be restricted to relatively small pockets, rather than pervading entire continents. The point is not to celebrate the depressingly limited reduction of poverty already achieved but rather to cast doubt on the notion that wealth creation is an unusual process sharply circumscribed culturally, geographically, temporally, or structurally. If in fact a considerable diversity of economic, political, and social arrangements are compatible with wealth creation, this book's frequent reference to *levels* of social capital might better be modified to refer to *types* of social capital.

Our assumptions, whether explicit or implicit, about the formidableness of the task of getting rich influence both policy prescriptions and analysis. Some policy professionals and academics, particularly economists, believe we understand the requisites of economic growth well enough to refer, for example, to a "Washington Consensus"[29] on the legal framework, institutions, and public policies necessary for economic growth. For this group, the chief obstacles to growth lie in political arrangements that preclude the adoption of appropriate policies, but for other observers, getting the prices right is either not a necessary step or is necessary but not sufficient in the face of pervasive market failures. For this latter group, institutional arrangements, including, but not restricted to, the creation of state capacities are required to overcome these market failures and to shift industrial structures and create new comparative advantages.[30]

The habit of pessimism about the prospects for prosperity appears deeply rooted. A number of scholars, for example, argued in the 1980s that the East Asian NIEs, all of them difficult-to-deny successes, benefitted from unusual circumstances unlikely to recur. Hence these scholars held that other developing countries, without the same propitious opportunities, were unlikely to achieve sustained and rapid economic growth.[31] These analyses, however, confused historically specific conditions with structural necessities, thereby precluding developmental possibilities prematurely. The facilitative external circumstances enjoyed by the East Asian NIEs when they launched their export-led industrialization strategies in the 1960s were indeed unique. Perhaps, however, they were not uniquely supportive, and later developing countries will face new facilitative circumstances, as well as new obstacles. The increasing globalization of production, the development of the information industry, the expansion of new investment vehicles that funnel savings from capital-rich to capital-poor economies, and the strength of global distribution networks all constitute facilitative circumstances more in evidence today than during the late 1960s when the NIEs launched their extraordinary economic performances.

If we look back into the past, we also can find widely divergent examples of successful economic adaptation in the face of similar external constraints and opportunities. On the Italian peninsula, Genoa and Venice were among the city-states that helped to usher in the modern era of more or less uninterrupted wealth creation. The two city-states differed sharply. While Venice was rich, Venetians were not, at least as compared to the most wealthy Florentines or Genoese of the same era. Indeed the celebrated cooperation between state and society constituted part of the "'myth' of Venice."[32] Venice was unusual for its day and its place in its combination of an egalitarian social structure, political stability, extensive and effective regulation of commerce and industry, and resource poverty. Looking at oligarchical domination in Venice, Rousseau saw a "city of 3,000 tyrants." Others, however, were impressed more by the rule of law, impersonal administration, and extensive cooperation between private and public sectors. In short, Venice Inc. foreshadowed modern Singapore.[33]

On the other side of Italy the Genoese handled economic, political and social matters in altogether different fashion. Governments were weak and changed frequently. In one five-year period the doge changed ten times; in at least one case his tenure was counted in hours. Polarization between the Guelphs and the Ghibellines (followers, respectively, of the Roman Church and the Holy Roman Empire) and factionalism within each group afflicted Genoa. Ultimately the Genoese ceded sovereignty to external rulers, including the Viscontis of Milan and the King of France,[34] in order to maintain a modicum of order. Meanwhile the Genoese prospered. Riven by faction, for centuries Genoa was able to dominate trade in the western Mediterranean and compete successfully with the Venetians as a principal conduit for trade between Europe and the Near East. A despondent Spaniard noted that "our Spain is the Indies of the Genoese."[35] If Singapore approximates a latter-day Venice, Thailand is East Asia's Genoa.

If trading states as disparate as Genoa and Venice both could have been successful, what can we learn from their experiences about the causes of economic growth? Part of the answer, surely, is that for all their differences, both republics shared crucial innovations not evident elsewhere at the time. The republics were without the feudal tethers that restrained economic activity elsewhere, and individuals were free to pursue their fortunes. The city-states' key institutional break-through, however, was the *compania*, which enabled them to cooperate in risky economic undertakings. As Putnam noted, elsewhere in Europe "force and family" were the means employed to overcome collective action obstacles. The Italian city-states invented new ways of doing so.[36]

This book attempts to make sense of Thailand's extraordinary economic record over the last forty years. Thailand is one of the most successful cases of economic development in the postwar era. Its growth has been very rapid, and arguably its economy was more stable over the last forty years (until 1997) than that of any other industrializing economy. This book argues that we cannot easily recognize Thailand in any of the pictures academics typically sketch of successful economic development models. Paradoxically, the nature of social organization in Thailand explained the economy's principal weaknesses while also accounting in considerable part for its success over the last forty years. Thailand's institutional stock, its social capital, lent itself better to the achievement of some economic and social tasks than others.

Notes

Introduction

1 IBRD, *A Public Development Program for Thailand*.
2 World Bank, *Atlas, 1996*.
3 *FEER*, August 15, 1996, pp. 44, 46.
4 Interview with MoF official, 1987.
5 Phongpaichit and Baker, *Thailand's Boom!*
6 Siamwalla, "Stability, Growth and Distribution," p. 30.
7 Samuels, *"Rich Nation Strong Army,"* p. 332; Pye, *Asian Power and Politics*, pp. 19–21.
8 Kobkua Suwannathat-Pian, *Thailand's Durable Premier*, p. 131.
9 Ingram, *Economic Change in Thailand*; Feeny, "Paddy, Princes, and Productivity," pp.132–50; idem, "Infrastructure Linkages and Trade Performance."
10 Warr, "The Thai Economy," p. 1.
11 Pei, "The Puzzle of East Asian Exceptionalism," pp. 116–17. Presumably civic market competence varies even where microeconomic policy frameworks do not.
12 Schumpeter, *The Theory of Economic Development*.
13 For example, Olson, *The Rise and Decline of Nations*, pp. 9–10, 82–5.
14 One notable exception is Hewison in *Bankers and Bureaucrats*.
15 Doner, "Approaches to the Politics of Economic Growth," pp. 832–4.
16 Yoshihara, *The Rise of Ersatz Capitalism*.
17 Bernard and Ravenhill, "Beyond Product Cycles and Flying Geese."
18 On this point, see Samuels, *"Rich Nation, Stong Army,"* pp. 16–17, 332.

1 The Stock of Social Capital in Thailand

1 For a discussion of this issue see Granovetter, "Economic action and social structure," pp. 53–6.
2 This point appears in the Introduction to Migdal et al., *State Power and Social Forces*, pp. 1–4.
3 See Crone, "States, social elites, and government capacity," pp. 254–6.
4 Emmerson applies this argument to Indonesia: "The bureaucracy in political context."
5 Seth, *A Suitable Boy*, pp. 540–3.

6 Jackson, *Quasi-States*.
7 Tarrow levels this charge against Putnam in the latter's work on Italian democracy: Tarrow, "Making social science work," p. 395.
8 See Introduction to Migdal et al., *State Power and Social Forces*.
9 See Clark and Roy, *Comparing Development Patterns in Asia*.
10 Migdal et al., *State Power and Social Forces*.
11 Granovetter, "Economic action and social structure," pp. 54–5.
12 Gerschenkron, *Economic Backwardness*, pp. 16–21.
13 Emile Durkheim, quoted in Fukuyama, *Trust*, p. v.
14 Kohli, "Centralization and powerlessness," p. 89.
15 Emmerson, "The bureaucracy in political context," pp. 122, 136.
16 Shue, "State power and social organization in China."
17 Jumbala pointed to this characteristic of Thai policymaking when he suggested that Montri Chenvidyakarn's conclusion that Thai business associations had little policy influence might have been in error because Montri had ignored their influence in policy implementation: Jumbala, "Towards a Theory of Group Formation," p. 538. In Thailand the hidden face of power concerns not only control over the formation of policy agendas but also influence in the policy implementation process. This power is particularly important in Thailand because the policy content of legislation is generally vague, leaving wide leeway for administrative policymaking in implementation. See Christensen, "Democracy Without Equity?" p. 22.
18 From Landau, "Linkage, Coding, and Intermediacy."
19 Putnam, *Making Democracy Work*, pp. 173–4.
20 Ibid. p. 129.
21 Ibid. p. 90.
22 Ibid. p. 170.
23 Yoshihara, "Culture, Institutions, and Economic Growth."
24 Quigley, PhD thesis.
25 Solow in "But Verify" and Wolf in "The Limits of Trust" complain that Fukuyama's use of the concept "trust" does not allow for its measurement.
26 Fukuyama defines culture as "inherited ethical habit": *Trust*, pp. 34–40.
27 Often in the context of the debates stirred by Putnam's *Making Democracy Work* and Fukuyama's *Trust*. Both authors themselves make this point.
28 Granovetter, "Economic Action and Social Structure," pp. 61–3.
29 Ibid. p. 60.
30 Coleman, "Social Capital in the Creation of Human Capital."
31 Putnam makes this argument: where solidarity and self-discipline are lacking, "hierarchy and force provide the only alternative to anarchy": *Making Democracy Work*, pp. 112–13, 147. Fukuyama makes a similar point: where low levels of trust prevent private firms from achieving the scale economies necessary to compete in certain sectors, states may take on the burden: *Trust*, pp. 23–32.
32 Tarrow, "Making Social Science Work," p. 396.
33 Fukuyama, *Trust*, pp. 23–32.
34 This inference seems to flow from Williamson's analysis in *The Economic Institutions of Capitalism*.
35 Other factors could have this same effect, such as a combination of family-owned firms and the need to divide assets equally among offspring. While limited trust may play a role in preventing firms from taking on talented outsiders in high positions, the need to provide for each son also helps to explain the tendency of firms to fissure.
36 Olson, *The Rise and Decline of Nations*.

37 Riggs, *Thailand*.
38 These amounted to nearly half the population in the 1950s and about a third as late as 1970: Mabry, *The Development of Labor Institutions*.
39 Jacobs, *Modernization Without Development*, pp. 75–76, 84.
40 Shor, "The Public Service," p. 67.
41 Siffin, "Economic Development," p. 144.
42 Sutton, "Political and Administrative Leadership," p. 19.
43 Anderson suggested such a description for the Thai state up to the late 1960s in "Studies of the Thai State."
44 Huntington, *Political Order*, Hutchcroft's description of politics and administration in the Philippines is consistent with Huntington's description: "Booty Capitalism," p. 217.
45 Quoted in Phongpaichit and Baker, *Thailand's Boom!*, p. 201.
46 Williamson, "The Economics of Organization." See also Shafer, *Winners and Losers*.
47 Olson, *The Rise and Decline*, pp. 38–41.
48 Fukuyama, *Trust*, p. 31.
49 Wolf, "The Limits of Trust," p. 20.
50 Fukuyama, *Trust*, p. 30.
51 For a statement of this argument, see Milner, "Trade Policy."
52 Bowie and Unger, *The Politics of Open Economies*, p. 187.
53 Alternatively, these coordination problems might be balanced by the gains resulting in performance that flowed from competition between agencies. This may be the case, for example, between Japan's ministries.
54 For a discussion of battles over localization policy in the auto industry suggestive of less-than-credible commitments, see Doner, *Driving a Bargain*, p. 203.
55 Doner makes this point in ibid. p. 190.
56 Muscat sees the multiple checks in this process and the resulting cautious policy approach as largely advantageous: *The Fifth Tiger*, pp. 6, 179–80, 221–2.
57 Doner, "Limits of State Strength," p. 430.
58 Cited in Putnam, *Making Democracy Work*, p. 91.

2   Sociability and Social Capital

1 Swedberg and Granovetter emphasize the importance of such a perspective in the Introduction to *The Sociology of Economic Life*.
2 Granovetter, "Economic Action and Social Structure," p. 53.
3 Ayal, "Value Systems," p. 35.
4 On the distributional consequences of social institutions, see Knight, *Institutions and Social Conflict*.
5 Pye, *Asian Power and Politics*, p. vii.
6 Ibid. p. 27; Bowie and Unger, *The Politics of Open Economies*, pp. 14–15.
7 Skinner, *Chinese Society in Thailand*, p. 92.
8 Mulder, *Everyday Life in Thailand*, pp. 64, 190, 199–200.
9 Cited in Girling, *Interpreting Development*, p. 73, fn. 79.
10 Ayal, "Value Systems," p. 48.
11 See, for example, Mulder, "Origin, Development," pp. 57–60, 87–9.
12 Jack and Sulamith Potter, for example, insisted that Thai villages were characterized by predictable structural features, widespread and durable associations based on regular patterns of reciprocity, and corporate village

ownership of property: *Thai Peasant Social Structure* and *Family Life in a Northern Thai Village*. For the purposes of this study, it is possible by and large to ignore this debate among cultural anthropologists (though not some of the differences in observed behavior among Thai villagers). As the discussion below makes clear, a review of the secondary literature can support the positions of those scholars who were struck by the relatively low levels of sociability and social capital in traditional Thai society. Patterns of trust and reciprocity, of course, change over time. In particular, the profound changes that accompany urbanization are likely to have important effects on those patterns. Hence it is important to remain alert to indicators of fundamental changes in Thai social organization over time.

13 Mabry, *The Development of Labor Institutions*, p. 17.

14 This depended crucially, however, on ending systems of slave or obligatory labor. For contrary views of the extent to which capitalist relations of production had penetrated and transformed the Thai countryside, see Lysa, *Thailand in the 19th Century*; Bowie, "Unraveling the Myth of the Subsistence Economy."

15 Brennan, "Class, politics and race in modern Malaysia," p. 93; Case, "Malaysia, Aspects and Audience of Legitimacy," pp. 82–3; Yin, *Class and Communalism in Malaysia*, pp. 11–14, 34, 38–9.

16 Yin, *Class and Communalism*, pp. 12–14, 24.

17 Hong Lysa and Bowie also take exception to the notion that rural life in Thailand was noteworthy for comparatively little misery and oppression. They react, at least in part, to the obviously misleading and romantic accounts or village life in Thailand. That conditions were far from universally pleasant is clear: *Thailand in the 19th Century*; "Unraveling the Myth of the Subsistence Economy."

18 Phillips, *Thai Peasant Personality*, pp. 41–2.

19 Benedict, *Thai Culture and Behavior*, pp. 9, 26.

20 Phongpaichit and Baker emphasize the ongoing importance, at least into the 1980s, of the capacity of rural Thailand to absorb the adjustment shocks of a market economy: *Thailand's Boom!*, pp. 72, 90, 162–3, 206.

21 Ingram, *Economic Change in Thailand*, p. 210.

22 Feeny, "Paddy, Princes, and Productivity"; Feeny, "Infrastructure Linkages and Trade Performance."

23 Geertz, *Agricultural Involution*.

24 Wilson, *Politics in Thailand*, pp. 38, 277–8.

25 Wars in Southeast Asia were generally fought over labor rather than land. Where an economic factor enjoys such scarcity, this is likely to condition the nature of its exploitation and encourage sound management of a scarce resource.

26 Faced with unendurable exploitation, labor would have the theoretical option of exit.

27 While a landlord class began to emerge in the nineteenth century, it was crushed by the centralizing reign of Rama V. See Rabibhadana, *The Organization of Thai Society*.

28 Sutton, "Politics and Administrative Leadership," p. 15.

29 Ingram, *Economic Change in Thailand*. David Feeny (pers. comm.) noted that later research has raised questions about Ingram's conclusions. Sompop Manarungsan argues that in fact economic growth in Thailand was greater than Ingram suggested: Manarungsan "Economic Development of

Thailand, 1850–1950." I am indebted to David Feeny for bringing this later work to my attention.

30 Nairn, *International Aid to Thailand*, p. 99.
31 Skinner, *Chinese Society in Thailand*, p. 121.
32 Ibid.
33 See, for example, Young, "The Northeastern Thai Village," p. 261.
34 Putnam, *Making Democracy Work*, p. 139.
35 Piker, "The Relationship of Belief Systems to Behavior."
36 Mulder, *Everyday Life in Thailand*, pp. 46–7.
37 Wijeyewardene, "Some Aspects of Rural Life in Thailand," pp. 65–71.
38 Wichiencharoen, "Social Values in Thailand."
39 Somvichian, "The Thai Political Culture and Political Development," p. 163.
40 Klausner, *Reflections on Thai Culture*, p. 321.
41 Wit, *Thailand: Another Vietnam?*, pp. 72–3.
42 Jacobs, *Modernization Without Development*, pp. 85–91.
43 Cited in Sutton, *Problems of Politics*, p. 7.
44 Cited in Shor, "The Public Service," p. 66.
45 Phongpaichit and Baker, *Thailand's Boom!*, pp. 142–3.
46 Lengel, "Markets in Thailand," pp. 222–3.
47 Koichi Mizuno, "Thai Patterns of Social Organization," p. 15.
48 Ibid. pp. 16–21.
49 Coleman, "Social Capital."
50 Mackie and MacIntyre, "Politics," pp. 6–7; Wurfel, *Filipino Politics*, p. 35; Case, "Malaysia," p. 79; Sidel, "The Philippines," pp. 149–50; Jackson, "Political Implications," p. 35.
51 Wurfel, *Filipino Politics*, p. 34.
52 Sidel, "The Philippines," pp. 156–7.
53 For example, Liddle, "Participation and the Political Parties," p. 193.
54 Jumbala, "Towards a Theory of Group Formation," p. 533.
55 Van Roy, "Industrial Organization," pp. 19–27.
56 Siffin, "Economic Development," pp. 129–30.
57 Ibid. p. 139.
58 Graziano, cited in Putnam, *Making Democracy Work*, p. 144.
59 Gohlert, cited in Girling, *Interpreting Development*, p. 56.
60 Girling, *Interpreting Development*, pp. 56–67.
61 Pye, *Asian Power*, pp. 80–1.
62 In Thailand, as in the United States, racism and other forms of discrimination modify this assertion.
63 Fukuyama, *Trust*, pp. 153–4.
64 Gramsci, in Putnam, *Making Democracy Work*, p. 146.
65 Thailand does not seem to convey the bleak tone evident in the picture of Calabria painted in a 1863 report: there are "no associations, no mutual aid; everything in isolation. Society is held up by the natural civil and religious bonds alone; but of economic bonds there is nothing, no solidarity between families or between individuals or between them and the government": Putnam, *Making Democracy Work*, p. 143.
66 Bunnag, "Loose Structure," p. 150.
67 Riggs emphasized the roles of the extended royal family and clientage networks in addition to the Buddhist *sangha*: "Interest and Clientele Groups." See also Sutton, *Problems of Politics*, p. 158.
68 Sutton, *Problems of Politics*, p. 19.
69 Barme makes this argument in *Luang Wichit Wathakan*, pp. 6–7.

70 Jacobs, *Modernization Without Development*, pp. 262–3.
71 Wit, *Thailand*, p. 89.
72 Wijeyewardene, "Some Aspects of Rural Life," p. 73. He does note that villages provided the labor to maintain temples, as well as giving alms and participating actively in festivals.
73 Embree, "Thailand," p. 13.
74 An anonymous reviewer brought this point to my attention.
75 See Chapman, "Ministerial Patron–Client Networks." This debate has an analogue in the development administration literature. See, for example, Landau, "Linkage, Coding, and Intermediacy," pp. 91–109.
76 De Tocqueville, quoted in Fukuyama, *Trust*, pp. 39, 119–23; Putnam, *Making Democracy Work*, pp. 130–48.
77 Siffin, *The Thai Bureaucracy*, p. 27.
78 Cited in Evers, Korff, and Pas-Ong, "Peasants, Traders and the State."
79 The subsequent discussion in this paragraph draws on Hong Lysa, *Thailand in the 19th Century*; Rabibhadana, *The Organization of Thai Society*; Reynolds, *Thai Radical Discourse*.
80 The first of the Chakri kings worked to gain the support of the traditional nobility from the old Ayuddya-based monarchy: Steinberg, *In Search of Southeast Asia*, pp. 108–9.
81 Siffin, *The Thai Bureaucracy*, p. 126.
82 Sutton, "Political and Administrative Leadership," p. 12.
83 Piriyarangsan, *Thai Bureaucratic Capitalism*, pp. 21–2.
84 Riggs, "Interest and Clientele Groups," p. 161.
85 Siffin, *The Thai Bureaucracy*, pp. 73–5.
86 Barme, *Luang Wichit Wathakan*, p. 7.
87 Anderson, "Studies of the Thai State," pp. 13–14.
88 Shor, "The Public Service," p. 66.
89 Suwannathat-Pian, *Thailand's Durable Premier*, p. 103.
90 Evers and Silcock, "Elites and Selection," pp. 89–93.
91 Sukatipan emphasizes this point: "Thailand, The Evolution of Legitimacy," p. 199.
92 Shor, "The Public Service," p. 67.
93 Girling, *Interpreting Development*, pp. 28, 37.
94 Chenvidyakarn, "Political Control and Economic Influence," p. 92; Samudavanija, "State Identity Creation, p. 77.
95 *Bangkok Post Weekly Review*, September 6, 1996, pp. 8–9.
96 Anek Laothamatas, quoted in *Bangkok Post*, May 17, 1997, pp. 8–9.
97 Girling, *Interpreting Development*, p. 26.
98 Chenvidyakarn, "Political Control," pp. 8–9.
99 Boone, "States and Ruling Classes in Postcolonial Africa," pp. 131–2.
100 Phongpaichit and Piriyarangsan, *Corruption*, p. 77.
101 Skinner, *Chinese Society in Thailand*, pp. 165–6.
102 Interview with Board of Trade official, Bangkok, 1987.
103 Riggs, "Interest and Clientele Groups," pp. 161–7.
104 Phongpaichit and Baker, *Thailand's Boom!*, p. 114.
105 Mabry, *The Development of Labor*, pp. 44–5.
106 Riggs, "Interest and Clientele Groups," pp. 161–7.
107 Doner, *Driving a Bargain*, pp. 192–208.
108 Christensen et al., *The Lessons of East Asia*, p. 24.
109 See Chenvidyakarn, "Political Control and Economic Influence"; Laothamatas, *Business Associations in Thailand*, pp. 32–5.
110 Samudavanija, "State Identity Creation," p. 75.

111 Laothamatas, *Business Associations in Thailand*.
112 See ibid., Ch. 6.
113 Phongpaichit, "The Thai Middle Class and the Military," p. 32; Christensen and Siamwalla, "Beyond Patronage," p. 26.
114 Quigley, "Towards Consolidating Democracy," pp. 133–4.
115 For a discussion of Thailand's labor movement, see Mabry, *Development of Labor*.
116 Jumbala, "Towards a Theory of Group Formation," p. 542.
117 Chandravithun, "Consolidating Democracy." In the early 1990s the secondary school enrolment rate in Thailand was 29 per cent, compared to 59 per cent in Malaysia, 73 per cent in the Philippines, and 86 per cent in South Korea: *FEER*, February 4, 1993, p. 25.
118 Often, however, they have been the tools of politicians, particularly those with bases in the military.
119 *FEER*, July 27, 1989, p. 23.
120 Quigley, "Towards consolidating democracy," p. 265.
121 Quigley, PhD thesis.
122 *Economist*, January 26, 1995, p. 64.
123 *FEER*, October 19, 1995, p. 19.
124 Ibid. pp. 19–20.
125 Dhiravegin, "Tokugawa Japan," pp. 1.11–1.13.
126 Chenvidyakarn, "Political Control," pp. 66–7.
127 *Nation*, January 19, 1997, pp. B1, B3.
128 Jumbala, "Towards a Theory of Group Formation," pp. 538–9.
129 Chenvidyakarn, "Political Control," pp. 118–19.
130 Skinner, *Chinese Society*, p. 354.
131 Chenvidyakarn, "Political Control," p. 154.
132 Hirsch, "What is *the* Thai Village?" p. 323.
133 Laothamatas, quoted in Girling, *Interpreting Development*, p. 59.
134 Chenvidyakarn, "Political Control," p. 178.
135 *Nation*, January 19, 1997, pp. B1, B3.
136 Phongpaichit and Baker, *Thailand's Boom!*, p. 145; Lin and Esposito, "Agrarian Reform in Thailand," p. 437.
137 Turton, "Thailand," pp. 66, 88, 92.
138 See Ramsay, "The Political Economy of Sugar," pp. 248–70.
139 See, for example, Landon, *The Chinese in Thailand*, pp. 79–80.
140 *FEER*, October 19, 1995, p. 19.
141 Several leaders were murdered: *FEER*, October 19, 1995, p. 19.
142 *Nation*, April 23, 1997, p. A5; Hirsch, "What is *the* Thai Village?" p. 335.
143 *Bangkok Post Weekly Review*, November 29, 1996, p. 8.
144 Jacobs, *Modernization Without Development*, p. 265.
145 Swearer, *The Buddhist World*, p. 102.
146 Ibid. p. 103.
147 Somjee and Somjee refer to NGOs as "modern day progeny of the Buddhists": *Development Success in Asia Pacific*, p. 155.
148 *FEER*, July 4, 1991, pp. 21–2. Somjee and Somjee put the number of monks at 350 000: Development Success, p. 131.
149 *FEER*, May 4, 1995, pp. 54–6.
150 Discussed in Fukuyama, *Trust*, pp. 50–1.
151 Phongpaichit and Baker, *Thailand's Boom!*, p. 177.
152 *Bangkok Post Weekly Review*, September 6, 1996, pp. 8–9.
153 Samudavanija, "State Identity Creation," p. 80.

154 Ibid. p. 77.
155 *Far Eastern Economic Review*, June 29, 1995, pp. 14–19.
156 Phongpaichit and Piriyarangsan refer to data showing a growing gulf in attitude between this new middle class and bureaucrats, farmers, and the poor: *Corruption and Democracy in Thailand*, p. 149.
157 *FEER*, February 4, 1993, pp. 25–6.
158 Phongpaichit and Baker, *Thailand's Boom!*, pp. 127–33.
159 Interview with official in the Crown Property Bureau, Bangkok, 1993.
160 Suehiro, *Capital Accumulation in Thailand*, p. 71.
161 Phongpaichit and Baker, *Thailand's Boom!*, pp. 10–12.
162 Van Roy, "Industrial organization," p. 24.
163 Lengel, "Markets in Thailand," p. 202.
164 The literature on the Chinese in Southeast Asia is extensive. Among those works that include the Chinese in Thailand are Skinner, *Chinese Society in Thailand*; idem, *Leadership and Power*; idem, "Change and persistence in Chinese culture overseas"; Kenjiro, "Leadership and Strategy"; Prasartsert, *Thai Business Leaders*; *Journal of Southeast Asian Studies* issue on "Ethnic Chinese in Southeast Asia"; Suryadinata, *'Overseas Chinese'*; Coughlin, *Double Identity*; Lim and Gosling, *The Chinese in Southeast Asia*; Landon, *The Chinese in Thailand*; Shozo, *Kakkyo Keizai Ron*; Yu, *Kakkyo Keizai no Kenkyu*; Suehiro, *Capital Accumulation and Industrial Development*; Phipatseritham and Yoshihara, *Business Groups in Thailand*.
165 Ingram, *Economic Change in Thailand*, pp. 204–5.
166 Suehiro, *Tai no Kogyoka*, p. 87.
167 Skinner, *Chinese Society*, pp. 52, 212.
168 The lack of agreement on who is Chinese and who is Thai helps to account for considerable variation, say from 6 to 15 per cent, in estimates of the Chinese presence in Thailand.
169 Skinner, *Chinese Society*. Chinese not only were disproportionately represented in all lines of business, including exporting and finance, but also in the leading universities and among public officials and politicians: Wu and Wu, *Economic Development in Southeast Asia*, p. 31.
170 *RIM Pacific Business and Industries*, 2, 1992, p. 4.
171 Skinner, *Chinese Society*, pp. 109–10.
172 Suehiro, *Capital Accumulation and Industrial Development*, pp. 2-25–2-29.
173 Ichikawa, *Tonan Ajia in Okeru*, pp. 40–4.
174 Suehiro, *Capital Accumulation in Thailand*, p. 234.
175 Ichikawa, *Tonan Ajia in Okeru*, pp. 40–4.
176 Bonacich and Modell, *The Economic Basis of Ethnic Solidarity*, pp. 4–17.
177 Ibid. pp. 20–1.
178 Landon, *The Chinese in Thailand*, pp. 80, 136, 145.
179 Doner, *Driving a Bargain*, pp. 210–11.
180 Skinner, *Chinese Society*, pp. 118, 255.
181 Suehiro, "Bangkok Bank," p. 110; Suehiro, *Capital Accumulation in Thailand*, p. 156; Robert Muscat, pers. comm., 1987.
182 Suehiro, *Capital Accumulation in Thailand*, pp. 156–7.
183 *FEER*, August 31, 1995, pp. 61–2.
184 Pye, *Asian Power*, pp. 62–3.
185 Skinner, *Chinese Society*, pp. 93, 97.
186 Jumbala, "Towards a Theory of Group Formation," p. 537.
187 Chenvidyakarn, "Political Control," pp. 62–4.
188 Skinner, *Chinese Society*, p. 135.

189 Yoshihara, "Oei Tiong Ham Concern," p. 142.
190 Skinner, *Chinese Society*, pp. 139–43.
191 Yin, *Class and Communalism*, pp. 47–8.
192 Coughlin, *Double Identity*, pp. 33–4, 50.
193 Skinner, *Chinese Society*, pp. 289–90.
194 Coughlin, *Double Identity*, pp. 121–2.
195 Suehiro, *Capital Accumulation in Thailand*, p. 78.
196 Yoshihara, *The Rise of Ersatz Capitalism*, pp. 41, 44, 53–4; Lengel, "Markets in Thailand," pp. 200–1.
197 Barton, "Trust and Credit," pp. 49–61; Deyo, "Chinese Management Practices," p. 228.
198 Cited in Landa, "The Political Economy," p. 87; Lengel, "Markets in Thailand," pp. 223–5.
199 Landa, "The Political Economy," p. 101.
200 Ibid. p. 90; *Nation*, February 1, 1997, p. C1.
201 Yoshihara identified two exceptions (Boon Rawd and Italian-Thai Development Corporation) outside Siam Cement and the Siam Commercial Bank, both controlled by the Crown Property Bureau: *Ersatz Capitalism*, p. 50.
202 Quoted in Landon, *The Chinese in Thailand*, p. 145.
203 To some degree, assimilation varied by social class, progressing more slowly in the middle class than in the lower or upper classes: Taikuo, *Tonan Ajia Kajin*, pp. 96–7.
204 Suryadinata, "Ethnic Chinese," p. 144.
205 Skinner, *Chinese Society*, pp. 253, 256; Chenvidyakarn, "Political Control," pp. 114–21; Samudavanija, "State Identity Creation," p. 69; Chamarik, "Problems of Development," p. 11; Anderson, "Studies of the Thai State," p. 29, fn. 41.
206 Skinner, *Chinese Society*, p. 157.
207 Ibid.
208 Mabry, *The Development of Labor*, p. 38.
209 Skinner, *Chinese Society*, p. 158.
210 Wu and Wu, *Economic Development*, p. 71.
211 Thanamai, "Patterns of Industrial Policymaking," p. 16.
212 IBRD, *A Public Development Program for Thailand*, p. 95.
213 Yoshihara makes this point in "Indigenous entrepreneurs in the Asean countries," *Singapore Economic Review*, 29(2) October 1984, p. 147.
214 Phongpaichit and Baker, *Thailand's Boom!*, p. 15.
215 Jacobs, *Modernization Without Development*, p. 122.
216 Doner and Ramsay, "An Institutional Explanation."
217 Scott, "Corruption in Thailand," pp. 313–14.
218 Thanamai, "Patterns of Industrial Policymaking," p. 46.
219 Phongpaichit and Piriyarangsan, *Corruption*, p. 13.
220 Muscat, *Development Strategy in Thailand*, p. 276.
221 Yoshihara, *The Nation and Economic Growth*, pp. 28–40; Bowie and Unger, *The Politics of Open Economies*, pp. 188–9.
222 Doner, *Driving a Bargain*, p. 190.
223 Ayal, "Private Enterprise and Economic Progress."
224 Muscat, *Development Strategy in Thailand*, pp. 235–42, 276.
225 Tanaka et al., "Overseas Chinese Business Communities," p. 8. Siam Cement is owned by the Crown Property Bureau.
226 Skinner, *Chinese Society*, p. 112.

227 Suehiro, "Bangkok Bank," p. 106; Lengel, "Markets in Thailand," p. 202.
228 The impact of these factors is discussed at greater length in Bowie and Unger, *The Politics of Open Economies*, pp. 186–7, and Doner and Unger, "The Politics of Finance." See also Milner, *Resisting Protectionism*; Frieden, *Debt, Development, and Democracy*; Rogowski, *Commerce and Coalitions*.
229 *FEER*, January 11, 1996, pp. 22–4; Phongpaichit and Baker, *Thailand's Boom!*, p. 134.
230 Hamilton and Biggart, "Market, Culture, and Authority," p. 206.
231 Hongladarom, "Unemployment in Thailand," p. 171.
232 See Suehiro, "Family Business Reassessed."
233 Riggs, "Interest and Clientele Groups," p. 162.
234 Jacobs, *Modernization Without Development*, p. 74.
235 Phongpaichit and Baker, *Thailand's Boom!*, pp. 25–6.
236 Bonacich and Modell, *The Economic Basis*, pp. 20–1.
237 See Ockey, "Business Leaders," pp. 55–64.
238 Other factors include the impact of the turnover tax (until 1991), protection of poor-quality producers, export promotion (the BoI favored large firms), and the lack of policy coherence: Mukoyama, "Development of Supporting Industries in ASEAN," p. 70.
239 Tanaka et al., "Overseas Chinese Business Communities."
240 Skinner, *Chinese Society*, pp. 139, 165–71.
241 Siow, "The Problems of Ethnic Cohesion," p. 185.
242 See Yoshihara, "Indigenous entrepreneurs," p. 147; Suehiro makes the same point about the Bangkok Bank: "Bangkok Bank," p. 112.
243 Lim, "Chinese Business," pp. 245, 269–70.

3   Thailand's Political Economy

1 For a discussion of social support for state initiatives, see Evans, "The State as Problem and Solution," p. 179.
2 Van Roy, " Industrial Organization," p. 22.
3 Christensen, "Democracy Without Equity?" p. 22.
4 For the classic discussion of Thailand's traditional bureaucratic polity, see Riggs, *Thailand*.
5 Robison, "Class, Capital and the State in New Order Indonesia," pp. 302–3.
6 See Jackson, "Bureaucratic Polity."
7 Samudavanija, "Politics and Administration," p. 151; idem, "Thailand: A Stable Semi-democracy," p. 7.
8 For an interesting study of Sarit, see Chalermnatarana, *Thailand*.
9 Anderson offers an endorsement of the latter view in "Studies of the Thai State."
10 Muscat, *The Fifth Tiger*, pp. 90–2.
11 For a discussion of traditional Thai bureaucratic values, see Siffin, *The Thai Bureaucracy*.
12 Muscat, *The Fifth Tiger*, p. 61.
13 Ibid. p. 39.
14 Phongpaichit and Piriyarangsan, *Corruption and Democracy*, p. 37.
15 Silcock, "Outline of Economic Development," p. 20; Muscat, *The Fifth Tiger*, pp. 90–2.
16 Thanamai, "Patterns of Industrial Policymaking," p. 42.
17 Siamwalla, "Stability, Growth and Distribution," p. 36.

18 Suehiro, *Capital Accumulation and Industrial Development*, p. 4-1-17.
19 Stubbs, "Geopolitics," pp. 526–7.
20 Wu and Wu, *Economic Development*, p. 15.
21 ESCAP/UNCTC Joint Unit, *Transnational Corporations*, p. 468.
22 Bowie and Unger, *The Politics of Open Economies*, pp. 73–6.
23 Doner and Ramsay suggest, however, that those surpluses were intentional results of BoI policies. Officials apparently hoped that surpluses would induce exports – and they did. For a discussion of Thai state policies supporting the textile industry and eventually helping to induce exports, see Doner and Ramsay "Competitive Clientelism and Economic Governance," p. 253.
24 Siamwalla, "Stability, Growth and Distribution," pp. 27–30.
25 Girling, *Interpreting Development*, p. 19.
26 Ibid.
27 Phongpaichit and Piriyarangsan, *Corruption and Democracy*, pp. 11, 18, 55–73, 80–6, 176–8.
28 Ganjanapan, "Conflict over the Deployment and Control of Labor," pp. 101–2.
29 Suksamran, *Buddhism and Politics in Thailand*, pp. 64–6.
30 Girling, *Thailand, Society and Politics*, p. 133.
31 Muscat, *The Fifth Tiger*, p. 143.
32 Interviews with Boonchu Rojanasathien, Bangkok, 1991.
33 Overholt, "Thailand: a Moving Equilibrium," p. 179.
34 Interview with BoI official, Bangkok, 1987.
35 The IMF provided stand-by facilities in 1981, 1983, and 1985: Muscat, *The Fifth Tiger*, p. 176.
36 Ibid.
37 *BBMR*, November 1986.
38 Muscat, *The Fifth Tiger*, pp. 220–2; Suehiro, *Tai Hatten to Minshushugi*, pp. 117–19.
39 Samudavanija, "Thailand: A Stable Semi-democracy," p. 13.
40 Ibid. p. 42.
41 Ibid. p. 131.
42 Ibid.
43 Christensen, "Democracy Without Equity?" p. 4.
44 On the limited parliamentary role in law-making, see ibid. pp. 22–3; Christensen and Siamwalla, "Beyond Patronage," p. 15.
45 *FEER*, July 13, 1995, pp. 17–18.
46 *FEER*, June 29, 1995, pp. 14–19.
47 *Bangkok Post Weekly Review*, November 29, 1996, p. 5.
48 *Bangkok Post Weekly Review*, September 6, 1996, pp. 8–9.
49 *FEER*, September 26, 1996, pp. 16–17.
50 Phongpaichit and Baker, *Thailand's Boom!*, pp. 148, 156, 162–3, 204–9.
51 Quigley, PhD thesis, Chs 4 and 5.
52 See Xuto, "The Bureaucracy"; Siffin, *The Thai Bureaucracy*.
53 Jacobs, *Modernization Without Development*, p. 138.
54 Quarterly report No. 5 to the NEDB, October 1, 1962.
55 Wade, *Governing Markets*, p. 6.
56 Muscat, *Development Strategy in Thailand*, p. 280; idem, *The Fifth Tiger*, pp. 90–2.
57 Bowie, *Crossing the Industrial Divide*, pp. 136–7.
58 Prasith-rathsint, *Thailand's National Development*, p. 44.

59 Samudavanija and Paribatra, "Thailand: Liberalization Without Democracy," p. 136.
60 Christensen et al., *The Lessons of East Asia*, p. 24.
61 Maxfield points out that the central bank's informal influence is greater than its formal powers would suggest: "Financial Incentives and Central Bank Authority," pp. 560–2.
62 Phongpaichit and Baker, *Thailand's Boom!*, p. 90.
63 Industrial Survey Group, report for the Industrial Economics and Planning Division, Office of the Under-secretary of State for Industry, July 16, 1963, pp. 6–14.
64 Christensen et al., *The Lessons of East Asia*, p. 11.
65 Phongpaichit and Baker, *Thailand's Boom!*, p. 88.
66 Ibid. p. 33.
67 Ibid. p. 22.
68 Turton, "Thailand," p. 62; Christensen, "Between the Farmer and the State," pp. 26–31.
69 Ramsay, "Thai Domestic Politics."
70 The Asian Strategies Co. report for Monsanto Singapore Co., PTE Limited, "Thai Overview Study: Political, Economic, and Operational Climate," vol. 1.
71 Akrasanee, "Trade and Industry Reforms," p. 16.
72 *Nation*, July 13, 1981.
73 *Bangkok Post*, December 21, 1996, p. 15; *Nation*, May 2, 1997, p. A4.
74 Policymaking and, to a lesser extent, implementation under the military-backed Anand governments were exceptions to this rule.
75 Riedel, "Economic Development in East Asia," p. 32.
76 Ibid. pp. 1–38.
77 "Stability, Growth and Distribution," pp. 1–13; see also Dixon, "Origins, Sustainability," p. 43.
78 Jacobs, *Modernization Without Development*, pp. 122–3.
79 Ibid. p. 137.
80 Ibid. Ch. 4.
81 Scott, "Corruption in Thailand," p. 305.
82 Emmerson, "The Bureaucracy in Political Context," p. 89.
83 From *The End of Laissez-Faire*, quoted in *ASEAN Investor*, 4(3) August 1985, p. 35.
84 William Overholt makes a similar point, noting the difficulty that any group in Thailand has had in asserting its dominance. The point's significance is developed by Doner and Ramsay in "Competitive Clientelism."
85 Silcock, *Thailand*, p. 294.
86 Interview with Anand Panyarachun, Bangkok, 1987.
87 *International Herald Tribune*, July 20, 1989.
88 Interview with advisor to the prime minister (No. 49).
89 Naya, "The Role of Trade Policies," p. 89.
90 Riedel, "Economic Development in East Asia," p. 32.
91 Akrasanee, "Trade and Industry Reforms," p. 15.
92 *FEER*, June 25, 1987, p. 73.
93 See Lal, "The political economy of industrialization," p. 9. On Thailand as one of three successful cases (Malaysia and the Ivory Coast are the others) of forced industrialization in economies with a comparative advantage in primary exports, see Chenery, "Industrialization and Growth," pp. 57–8.
94 Girling, *Interpreting Development*, p. 47.

95 *Bangkok Post*, December 2, 1994, p. 22.
96 *Bangkok Post Weekly Review*, August 30, 1996, p. 13.
97 *Bangkok Post*, August 30, 1993, p. 21.
98 For example, Amsden, "The State and Taiwan's Economic Development"; Chan, "Developing Strength from Weakness"; various contributions in Deyo, *The Political Economy of the New Asian Industrialism*; Haggard, "The Newly Industrializing Countries"; idem, "The Politics of Industrialization"; Johnson, *MITI and the Japanese Miracle*; Wade, "The Role of Government."
99 Dower, "E. H. Norman," p. 19.
100 Phongpaichit and Baker, *Thailand's Boom!*, pp. 56–64, 69, 228–9, 235.
101 Laothamatas argues that state–business cooperation is further developed than is suggested here: Business Associations.
102 Olson, *The Rise and Decline of Nations*, pp. 43–7.
103 Overholt, "Thailand."
104 For a broad discussion of Southeast Asian economies' integration within regional networks, see Bernard and Ravenhill, "Beyond Product Cycles and Flying Geese"; Bowie and Unger, *The Politics of Open Economies*, pp. 185–6.

4 Bargains Between Bankers and Bureaucrats

1 This chapter draws on various previous incarnations, including Danny Unger, PhD thesis, U.C. Berkeley, 1989; and Doner and Unger, "The Politics of Finance in Thai Economic Development." My apologies to Kevin Hewison. In my predictable search for alliteration in this chapter's title, I inadvertently borrowed, without permission, from his book title, cited below.
2 Cited in Cameron, *Banking and Economic Development*, pp. 6–11.
3 World Bank, *Trade and Industrial Policies*, p. 113.
4 Johnson, *MITI and the Japanese Miracle*.
5 For further discussion of this see Amsden, *Asia's Next Giant*; Wade, *Governing the Market*; Haggard et al., *The Politics of Finance*; Fry, *Money, Interest, and Banking*.
6 Doner, *Driving a Bargain*, p. 211.
7 Doner and Unger, "The Politics of Finance," pp. 106–7.
8 Louis Pauly made this point in informal comments, noting the sophistication of some financial systems, including Thailand's, in East Asia.
9 Suehiro, *Tai no Kogyoka*, p. 168.
10 Feeny, "Paddy, Princes, and Productivity"; idem, "Infrastructure Linkages and Trade Performance"; Silcock, *The Economic Development of Thai Agriculture*, p. 173; Viseskul, "Public Investment Policy."
11 Sanittanont, "Exchange Rate Experience," p. 32.
12 Ibid. p. 39.
13 Ibid. pp. 39–40.
14 Vongvipanond, *Finance in Thailand's Industrial Development Context*, p. 26.
15 Suehiro, *Capital Accumulation in Thailand*, p. 221.
16 Silcock, *Thailand*, p. 174.
17 Harris et al., *Area Handbook for Thailand*, p. 447.
18 *Asia Week*, January 15, 1988, pp. 50–2.
19 Skully, *Asean Regional Cooperation*, p. 37.

20 *Asia Week*, January 15, 1988, pp. 50–2.
21 Simon, "The Thai manufacturing sector," pp. 83–4.
22 See Nartsupha, *Foreign Trade*.
23 See Muscat, *The Fifth Tiger*; Doner and Unger, "Thailand," p. 109.
24 Suehiro, *Capital Accumulation and Industrial Development*, pp. 4-66–4-70.
25 Viksnins, *Financial Deepening*, pp. 59–66.
26 Silcock, "Money and Banking," p. 178.
27 Suehiro, *Capital Accumulation and Industrial Development*, p. 5-40.
28 Silcock, *The Economic Development of Thai Agriculture*, p. 171.
29 Skully, *Financial Institutions*, p. 370; interview with foreign advisor to the Thai government (No. 23).
30 *FEER*, May 16, 1985, p. 101.
31 *FEER*, March 29, 1984, p. 86.
32 *FEER*, March 1, 1984, p. 44.
33 *FEER*, April 26, 1984, p. 114; September 6, 1984, pp. 96–7.
34 *FEER*, January 24, 1985, pp. 67–8.
35 The Japanese government aided an ineffective Capital Market Development Fund in 1979: Suehiro, *Tai no Kogyoka*, p. 187.
36 "The new opportunities," *Asian Finance*, August 15, 1984.
37 *Bangkok Post*, June 11, 1987.
38 *FEER*, November 28, 1985, pp. 70–1.
39 Phongpaichit and Baker, *Thailand's Boom!*, p. 38.
40 Quoted in Robert Heilbroner, *The Worldly Philosophers* 4th edn (New York: Simon & Schuster, 1972), p. 260.
41 *Bangkok Post Weekly Review*, October 20, 1995, p. 13.
42 Phongpaichit and Baker, *Thailand's Boom!*, pp. 82–3.
43 Interview with Bangkok Bank official, Bangkok, 1987.
44 See Takayasu, "A Study of Economic Development."
45 Bank of Thailand, *50 Years of the Bank of Thailand*, pp. 321–2.
46 *Bangkok Post Weekly Review*, January 21, 1994, p. 11; January 28, 1994, p. 12.
47 *Nation Year in Review 1992*, pp. 48–9.
48 *Economist Intelligence Unit*, 2nd quarter 1992, p. 32.
49 *Economist*, February 5, 1994, pp. 81–2.
50 *FEER*, January 12, 1992, pp. 34–5.
51 *Economist Intelligence Unit*, 3rd quarter 1992, p. 24; *Manager*, May 1994, pp. 34–40.
52 *FEER*, December 24–31, 1992, pp. 73–4.
53 *Bangkok Post Weekly Review*, August 13, 1993, p. 12.
54 *Bangkok Post Weekly Review*, January 28, 1994, p. 12.
55 *Economist Intelligence Unit*, 2nd quarter 1994, p. 31.
56 See, for example, *Bangkok Post Weekly Review*, May 13, 1994, p. 17; *Bangkok Post Economic Review, Mid-year*, 1994, pp. 21–2.
57 *Bangkok Post Weekly Review*, July 22, 1994, p. 17.
58 *Bangkok Post*, February 8, 1995.
59 *Nation*, February 7, 1995.
60 *Economist Intelligence Unit*, 2nd quarter 1992, p. 32.
61 *Bangkok Post Weekly Review*, June 10, 1994, p. 13.
62 *Matichon*, September 28, 1994, p. 9.
63 *FEER*, September 28, 1995, pp. 98–100.
64 *FEER*, July 27, 1995, p. 16.
65 *Nation*, November 12, 1997, p. A5.

66 *FEER*, September 26, 1996, pp. 16–17.
67 *Bangkok Post Weekly Review*, January 17, 1997, p. 16.
68 *FEER*, September 26, 1996, pp. 16–17.
69 *FEER*, August 15, 1996, p. 44.
70 Ibid. p. 47.
71 *Bangkok Post Year-end Review, 1996*, pp. 18–20.
72 *FEER*, March 21, 1996, pp. 61–2.
73 *FEER*, August 17, 1995, p. 51.
74 *Economist*, February 1, 1997, p. 78; May 24, 1997, pp. 69–71; *FEER*, March 6, 1997, pp. 48–50.
75 *FEER*, March 6, 1997, pp. 48–50.
76 *FEER*, June 12, 1997, pp. 70–1; *Economist*, June 21, 1997, p. 45; June 28, 1997, p. 48; *Bangkok Post Year-end Review, 1996*, pp. 18–20.
77 *Bangkok Post Year-end Review, 1996*, pp. 18–20.
78 *FEER*, January 11, 1996, p. 79; *Economist*, October 12, 1996, p. 80.
79 *Bangkok Post Weekly Review*, December 6, 1996, p. 12.
80 *BBMR*, 37(10) October 1996, p. 38; *FEER*, August 17, 1995, p. 44.
81 *Economist*, February 22, 1997, pp. 80–5.
82 *Nation*, November 12, 1997, p. A5.
83 *Bangkok Post Weekly Review*, January 7, 1994, p. 2; November 8, 1996, p. 17.
84 *Bangkok Post Weekly Review*, January 21, 1994, p. 11.
85 *Economist Intelligence Unit*, 1st quarter 1995, p. 24.
86 *Economist*, January 28, 1995, pp. 67–8.
87 *Economist Intelligence Unit*, 1st quarter 1995, p. 24.
88 *Business Day*, March 13, 1996, p. 3.
89 *FEER*, August 17, 1995, p. 44–5.
90 *FEER*, January 23, 1997, p. 18.
91 *South East Asia Monitor*, 8(5) May 1997, pp. 6–7.
92 *Nation*, November 12, 1997, p. A5.
93 *FEER*, March 6, 1997, pp. 48–50.
94 *Economist*, May 24, 1997, pp. 69–71.
95 *Economist*, February 22, 1997, pp. 80–5.
96 *Economist*, May 24, 1997, p. 15; *FEER*, June 12, 1997, p. 71. A near twofold rise in Thailand's incremental capital-output ratio between 1988 and 1991 supported the notion that investors were pursuing rapidly falling profits: *FEER*, March 6, 1997, pp. 48–50.
97 *Economist*, May 17, 1997, p. 82.
98 *FEER*, June 12, 1997, p. 70. Sachs et al. emphasize the role of domestic financial deregulation in the currency crises in Mexico and Argentina late in 1994 and early in 1995: "Financial Crises in Emerging Markets," pp. 8, 54–6.
99 *Economist*, May 24, 1997, pp. 69–71.
100 Ibid.
101 *FEER*, May 29, 1997, pp. 14–15.
102 *Economist*, June 21, 1997, p. 45.
103 *Washington Post*, June 24, 1997, p. 1.
104 This ratio is emphasized in Sachs et al., "Financial Crises in Emerging Markets." Ratios after the peso crisis calculated using IMF, International Financial Statistics, various issues.
105 *FEER*, July 17, 1997, p. 74.
106 *Washington Post*, July 22, 1997, pp. D1, D8.

107 *Washington Post*, July 29, 1997, p. A11.
108 *Bangkok Post Year-end 1993*, pp. 9–10.
109 *Bangkok Post Mid-Year 1993*, p. 15.
110 *Manager, August 1993*, pp. 26–9.
111 *Bangkok Post Weekly Review*, July 23, 1993, p. 12.
112 *Economist*, February 5, 1994, pp. 81–2.
113 *Bangkok Post*, August 30, 1993, p. 21.
114 *Manager*, August 1993, pp. 26–9.
115 *Economist Intelligence Unit*, 2nd quarter 1994, p. 32.
116 *Bangkok Post Weekly Review*, March 18, 1994, p. 11; *Economist Intelligence Unit*, 2nd quarter 1994, p. 33.
117 *Bangkok Post Weekly Review*, July 30, 1993, p. 13.
118 *Economist*, February 5, 1994, pp. 81–2; *FEER*, April 14, 1994, p. 71.

5   Controls and Contestation: the Thai Textile Industry

1 Depending on the context, the word "textile" will be used to refer to both textiles (cloth) and garments, or only to textiles (cloth) as distinct from garments.
2 In Thailand these services first developed in association with agricultural exports.
3 Santikarn, *Technology Transfer*, p. 206.
4 "Upstream" sectors include raw materials such as cotton and synthetic fibers; "midstream" ones refer to spinning, weaving, and knitting of those materials; while "downstream" activities encompass dyeing, finishing, cutting, and sewing fabrics.
5 Shafer, *Winners and Losers*, pp. 1–21.
6 In Thailand, moving from upstream to downstream subsectors of the industry, production becomes less capital-intensive, oligopolistic, and more export-oriented.
7 On the difficulties firms faced in Japan, see Fletcher, *The Japanese Business Community*, pp. 5–96; McNamara, *Textiles and Industrial Transition*, pp. 9–12.
8 *Thai Textile Statistics*.
9 *FEER*, August 3, 1995, p. 47.
10 *Thai Textile Statistics*.
11 World Bank, *World Development Report*, 1994, p. 173; *Bangkok Post Economic Review, Year-End 1994*, pp. 31–2.
12 *Thai Textile Statistics*.
13 Gerschenkron, *Economic Backwardness*, pp. 16–21.
14 Shafer, *Winners and Losers*, pp.1–21.
15 *Bangkok Post*, April 2, 1987, p. 28.
16 For a discussion of his ties to Japanese firms, see Girling, *Thailand*, pp. 98, 181.
17 Ito, *Tonan Ajia*, pp. 61–82; *Siam Rath*, December 7, 1986, p. 11.
18 Information from Toray executive, Bangkok, 1987.
19 Tambunlertchai and Yamazawa, *Manufactured Exports*, p. 7.
20 Hewison, *Bankers and Bureaucrats*, p. 70.
21 Santikarn, *Technology Transfer*, p. 150.
22 Yoshihara, *Japanese Investment in Thailand*, p. 91.
23 Senshishitsu, *Shittan-Meigo sakusen*, p. 689.
24 Tambunlertchai and Yamazawa, *Manufactured Exports*, p. 7.

25 Ito, *Tonan Ajia*, p. 63.
26 Hewison, *Bankers and Bureaucrats*, p. 169; idem, "The Development of Capital," pp. 305, 308.
27 Hewison, "The Development of Capital," p. 306.
28 Hewison, *Bankers and Bureaucrats*, p. 170.
29 Suehiro, *Development and Structure*, p. 4.
30 Santikarn, *Technology Transfer*, p. 151.
31 Tambunlertchai and Yamazawa, *Manufactured Exports*, pp. 24–34.
32 Ito, *Tonan Ajia*, p. 66.
33 Yoshihara, *Japanese Investment*, p. 105.
34 Suehiro, *Development and Structure*, pp. 7–9.
35 Ibid. p. 6.
36 Ito, *Tonan Ajia*, p. 64.
37 Suehiro, *Development and Structure*, p. 23.
38 Yoshihara, *Japanese Investment*, p. 112.
39 Yoshino, *Japan's Multinational Enterprises*, p. 72.
40 Yoshihara, *Japanese Investment*, p. 104.
41 Ibid. p. 105.
42 Santikarn, *Technology Transfer*, p. 153.
43 Yoshino, *Japan's Multinational Enterprises*, pp. 68–9.
44 Santikarn, *Technology Transfer*, pp. 162–3.
45 Suphachalasai, "Thailand's Growth," p. 54.
46 Santikarn, *Technology Transfer*, pp. 41–2.
47 Tambunlertchai and Yamazawa, *Manufactured Exports*, p. 81.
48 Suphachalasai, "Thailand's Growth," p. 59.
49 JETRO, *Saikin no Toshi*, 1989.
50 Ibid., 1987, p. 10.
51 *Thai Textile Statistics*, p. 19.
52 Author interview with researcher at the Institute for Developing Economies, Tokyo, 1986; and with executives at Seibu in Tokyo and Daimaru in Osaka, 1986.
53 *BIT*, October 1986, pp. 32–42.
54 *Bangkok Post*, October 11, 1996, p. 2.
55 Author interview with TTMA official, Bangkok, 1987.
56 Chenvidyakarn, "Political Control," p. 376.
57 Tambunlertchai and Yamazawa, Manufactured Exports, p. 5.
58 Mukoyama, "Development of Supporting Industries in ASEAN," p. 66.
59 Santikarn, *Technology Transfer*, pp. 156–7.
60 Suehiro, *Development and Structure*, pp. 33–5.
61 *China Economic News Service*, January 18, 1996.
62 See Bowie and Unger, *The Politics of Open Economies*, pp. 185–6.
63 *BBMR*, January 1985, pp. 24–5.
64 Tambunlertchai and Yamazawa, *Manufactured Exports*, p. 25.
65 Ibid.
66 *BIT*, August 1976, pp. 33–41.
67 Suehiro, *Development and Structure*, p. 10.
68 Yoshioka, "Overseas Investment," pp. 8–10.
69 Ibid. pp. 7–11.
70 Ibid. pp. 11–12.
71 *BIT*, May 1983, pp. 30–2.
72 Ibid. pp. 18–23.
73 *BBMR*, January 1985, pp. 24–6.
74 Suphachalasai, "Thailand's Growth," pp. 59–60.

75 Phongpaichit and Baker, *Thailand's Boom!*, p. 32.
76 Ibid. p. 159.
77 *Bangkok Post Weekly Review*, September 13, 1996, p. 13; US Embassy, Bangkok, "Market Reports," March 21, 1995.
78 *Thai Textile Statistics*, p. 3.
79 *FEER*, August 15, 1996, p. 38; August 3, 1995, p. 47; US Embassy, Bangkok, "Market Reports"; Simon, "The Thai manufacturing sector," p. 87; *Bangkok Post*, October 11, 1996, p. 2.
80 UNIDO, *Thailand*, pp. 94–9.
81 In the early and mid-1990s, Thai officials began to implement a variety of tax changes, including lower and simpler tariff codes. Maximum tariffs dropped from 60 to 20 per cent: *Nation*, December 23, 1994, p. A6.
82 *Bangkok Post Economic Review Year-End 1994*, pp. 31–2; *Bangkok Post*, September 10, 1996, p. 2; *FEER*, October 31, 1996, pp. 59–60.
83 *Bangkok Post Weekly Review*, September 13, 1996, p. 13; *Bangkok Post*, May 28, 1996.
84 Suphachalasai, *The Structure of the Textile Industry*, p. 19; Simon, "New patterns," p. 92.
85 *Bangkok Post*, October 11, 1996, p. 2.
86 *Thai Textile Statistics*.
87 US Embassy Bangkok, "Market Reports." Different figures, amounting to a total of under 5000 factories, appear in *Bangkok Post Economic Review Year-End 1994*, pp. 31–2.
88 The material used in this section is drawn almost entirely from the Gherzi Textile Organization's report prepared for United Nations Industrial Development Organization and the Government of Thailand, September 1986.
89 Author interview with official in the Textile Division, Department of Industrial Promotion, Ministry of Industry.
90 Deyo, "Human Resource Strategies," p. 34.
91 Stifel, *The Textile Industry*.
92 Interview with Anand Panyarachun.
93 Doner and Ramsay, "Competitive Clientelism and Economic Governance," p. 252.
94 For an extended contrast of these two economies, see Yoshihara, *The Nation and Economic Growth*.
95 Interviews with executives at Thai Toray and Luckytex. Simon notes the particular weakness of the Ministry of Industry: "The Thai manufacturing sector," p. 95.
96 Interview with former minister of industry, Bangkok, 1993.
97 Sibunruang and Tambunlertchai, "Foreign Direct Investment."
98 *BIT*, May 1983, pp. 25–8.
99 Some observers contended that the extent of competition could be gauged by the timing of retailers' approaches to monks leaving the monasteries. Monks returning to a lay existence were regarded as reliable customers for new clothing purchases, and the greater the competition, the earlier retailers would approach the monks: *ASEAN Investor*, July, 1984, p. 24.
100 *BIT*, May 1983, p. 27.
101 Praiphol Koomsup, unpublished master's thesis, Thailand Information Center #24520, Chulalongkorn University, p. 43. Suphachalasai suggests that mean Thai tariff protection in the industry was about average among developing countries, at over 50 per cent: "Thailand's Growth," p. 24.
102 *BBMR*, January 1985.

103 The BoI sponsored agreements among the principal yarn and fabric producers in the TTMA for production cutbacks and minimum prices, but
these were short-lived and largely ineffective. The board also attempted to
require that new capacity be for export only; this effort also failed. See
BIT, June 1983, pp. 19–25; August 1976, pp. 33–41.

104 *BIT*, August 1976, p. 34.

105 *BBMR*, January 1985.

106 *BBMR*, January 1985, p. 27. Interview with TTMA official (interview
no. 75).

107 *Nation*, June 12, 1987.

108 Ibid.

109 Doner and Ramsay, "Competitive Clientelism," p. 270.

110 Interviews with executives at Thai Toray and Luckytex.

111 Koomsup, unpublished master's thesis, pp.44–55.

112 Annual Textile Report, Department of State, 1991, 1993; *Bangkok Post*,
May 28, 1996.

113 *BBMR*, January 1985, p. 29.

114 Yoshihara, *Japanese Investment in Thailand*, p. 105.

115 Interview with NESDB official, Bangkok, 1993.

116 UNIDO, *Thailand*, p. 99.

117 US Embassy Bangkok, "Market Reports."

118 *Manager*, October 1993, pp. 44–8.

119 *BIT*, June 1983, pp. 19–25.

120 Interview with official at the NESDB, Bangkok, 1993.

121 *Textile Textile Statistics*.

122 Interview with official at the NESDB (interview no. 64).

123 Ibid.

124 Ibid.

125 Interview with former minister of industry, Bangkok, 1993.

126 Textile Industry Division document.

127 *BIT*, January 1985, p. 36.

128 *Manager*, October 1993, pp. 44–48.

129 Deyo, "Human Resource Strategies," p. 34.

130 *Bangkok Post*, October 14, 1995; February 15, 1996.

131 *BIT*, August 1976, pp. 74–76.

132 Interviews with officials at Toray Nylon Thai and Marubeni, Bangkok,
1987.

133 Interview with textile executive, Bangkok, 1987.

134 Interview with official at Thai Toray Textile Mills, Bangkok, 1987.

135 *BIT*, June 1983, p. 24.

136 Richard Doner first pointed this development out to me.

137 *Bangkok Post Economic Review Mid-Year, 1995*, pp. 62–3.

138 Interview with TTMA official, Bangkok, 1987; *Bangkok Post*, October 14,
1995; February 15, 1996.

139 *Bangkok Post Economic Review Year-End, 1994*, pp. 31–2.

140 Ibid.; *Bangkok Post Weekly Review*, January 3, 1997, p. 12.

141 Phongpaichit and Baker, *Thailand's Boom!*, p. 20.

142 *BIT*, May 1983, p. 32.

143 *Business in Thailand*, pp. 30–2.

144 Interview with Bangkok Bank official, Bangkok, 1993.

145 Interview with official at Bangkok Weaving Mills, Bangkok, 1987.
146 Hewison, *Bankers and Bureaucrats*, p. 171.
147 Phongpaichit and Baker, *Thailand's Boom!*, p. 136.
148 Laothamatas, *Business Associations*, pp. 110–12.
149 Interviews with executives at Luckytex and Thai Teijin Polyester, Bangkok, 1987.
150 Ito, *Tonan Ajia*, p. 77.
151 *Bangkok Post*, September 7–8, 1989; *Nation*, January 6, 1989.
152 US Department of Labor, *Labor Law and Practice in Thailand*, p. 11; *Nation*, January 21, 1997, p. A3.
153 *Financial Times*, Survey, December 5, 1996, p. I.
154 *FEER*, July 22, 1993, p. 18.
155 *FEER*, July 27, 1989, p. 23.
156 *Bangkok Post Weekly Review* December 27, 1996, p. 1; January 10, 1997, p. 13.
157 *Bangkok Post Economic Review Year-End*, 1994, pp. 31–2; *Bangkok Post Weekly Review*, January 3, 1997, p. 12.
158 UNIDO, *Thailand*, pp. 100–1.
159 Ito, *Tonan Ajia*, pp. 61–82; Doner and Ramsay, "Competitive Clientelism," p. 252.
160 See Christensen and Siamwalla, "Beyond Patronage," p. 5.
161 An anonymous reviewer of an earlier draft of this book made this point.
162 Interview with Thai Teijin official, Bangkok, 1987.
163 *Economist Intelligence Unit*, 3rd Quarter 1993, 17–19; 4th Quarter 1994.
164 *Financial Times*, Survey, December 5, 1996, p. I.

6   Incredible Commitments and Policy Chaos

1 *Nation*, November 14, 1985.
2 *Nation*, November 21, 1985.
3 *Bangkok Post*, November 11, 1985.
4 *Bangkok Post Weekly Review*, October 20, 1995, p. 10.
5 To the extent that heavy industries have large positive externalities, they are partial public goods. In the case of the ESB plan, the heavy industry and infrastructure projects were so entangled that separating them out would in any case be difficult.
6 World Bank, *World Development Report*, 1994.
7 Christensen and Siamwalla, "Beyond Patronage," p. 11.
8 *Financial Times Survey*, "Asia-Pacific Telecommunications," April 9, 1996, p. 3.
9 Phongpaichit and Piriyarangsan, *Corruption and Democracy*, pp. 14, 40.
10 Chinese public investment there amounted to over $3 billion in the first half of the 1990s, with plans for huge new investments for an international airport and deep-water port to come. Foreigners also poured in money, and the result was an astonishingly rapid transformation of the area. A look around the area at a huge number of unoccupied buildings and idle industrial sites suggested that this was a case of demand-anticipating investment. See The Economic and Trade Bureau, PNA, *Shanghai Pudong*, promotional brochure.
11 *FEER*, October 12, 1995, pp. 137–8; July 18, 1996, p. 73.

12 Interview with PTT official, Bangkok, 1987.
13 The proposed plant would have been one of the Japanese-financed ASEAN industrial projects.
14 Interview with official in the Prime Minister's Office, Bangkok, 1987; *FEER*, July 31, 1986, p. 71.
15 Hewison, *Bankers and Bureaucrats*, p. 121.
16 Interview with official at the NESDB, Bangkok, 1987.
17 Phongpaichit and Baker, *Thailand's Boom!*, pp. 84–8.
18 Thailand has received about $200 million in external assistance, mostly from Japan and the World Bank, to support Bangkok's transportation: Midgley, *Urban Transport in Asia*, p. 16–17, 44. A separate World Bank study reportedly estimated the 1992 traffic costs at $1.3 to $3.1 billion a year, about 10 per cent of the city's gross product, and suggested that traffic was causing between 500 and 2000 deaths a year: *Bangkok Post Weekly Review*, December 24, 1993, p. 1.
19 *FEER*, August 17, 1995, p. 45.
20 *FEER*, November 29, 1990, pp. 52–3; February 15, 1996.
21 In fact, to comply with Thai regulations, generally these assumed build-transfer-operate lines: Siroros and Haller, "'Thai-Style' Contractual Relationships," p. 329.
22 Bankoku Nihonjin Shookoo Kaigisho (Japanese Chamber of Commerce in Bangkok), "Toobu rinkai kaihatsu keikaku." In *Taikoku keizai gaikyoo* ("Eastern Seaboard Development Projects." In *General Outlook for the Thai Economy*), 1986–87 edn, 1987; Hongladarom, "Gas utilisation policies"; interview with Metro Group executive, Bangkok, 1987.
23 Muscat puts the total cost at about $4.5 billion, one-fifth for infrastructure and about two-thirds for heavy industry: *The Fifth Tiger*, p. 206.
24 *Bangkok Post*, August 7, 1982.
25 *Nation*, August 20, 1982.
26 *World Development Report*, p. 126.
27 *Bangkok Post*, November 25, 1983.
28 Arase, *Buying Power*.
29 JICA, *Final Report*, pp. 307–19.
30 *Nation*, August 7, 1982.
31 One foreign consultant referred to Savit, the center's energetic head, as "the Colonel North of the NESDB": Interview with foreign consultant in Thailand, Bangkok, 1987.
32 *Bangkok Post*, August 7, 1982.
33 *Nation*, April 30, 1993, p. 13.
34 *Nation*, August 5, 1982.
35 *Bangkok Post*, March 24, 1985.
36 "Natural gas and related industries in the ESB development project," *BBMR*, November 1982.
37 *Nation*, August 7, 1982.
38 *Bangkok Post*, November 25, 1982.
39 *Bangkok Post*, October 16, 1986.
40 *Bangkok Post*, July 21, 1983.
41 Ibid. More plausibly, he hoped to serve his naval backers who favored development of the port at Sattahip over which they exercised jurisdiction. He may also have been expressing pique at a client's failure to win a share of the contracts associated with another Japanese-funded project: Interviews.

42 *Bangkok Post*, December 23, 1983.

43 *Bangkok Post*, January 26, 1984.

44 *Bangkok Post*, June 2, 1984.

45 Interview with advisor to the prime minister, Bangkok, 1987.

46 *Bangkok Post*, May 16, 1984.

47 Muscat, *The Fifth Tiger*, p. 208.

48 *Nation*, April 2, 1985.

49 *Nation*, September 19, 1985.

50 *Nation*, October 25, 1985.

51 The World Bank later hailed the government's "cautious approach": *World Development Report*, 1988, p. 126.

52 Proponents of the plan, of course, used such arguments to win support for the projects.

53 *Nation* and *Bangkok Post*, December 25, 1985.

54 *Nation*, August 7, 1986.

55 *Bangkok Post*, October 16, 1986.

56 *Bangkok Post*, February 26, 1987.

57 *Bangkok Post*, June 10, 1987.

58 World Bank, *World Development Report*, 1988, p. 126.

59 Pers. comm., Bangkok, 1987.

60 Muscat, *The Fifth Tiger*, p. 177.

61 World Bank, *World Development Report*, 1988, p. 126.

62 *Bangkok Post*, December 26, 1989.

63 *Economist Intelligence Unit*, 1993(2) June 1, 1993.

64 *Japan Digest*, December 16, 1996, p. 5.

65 Parnwell, *Uneven Development in Thailand*, p. 9.

66 *FEER*, April 28, 1988.

67 *FEER*, November 23, 1989, p. 77.

68 *Financial Times*, Survey, December 5, 1996, p. III.

69 Fertilizer Advisory, Development and Information Network for Asia and the Pacific, *Marketing, Distribution and Use of Fertilizer in Thailand* (Bangkok, 1984). Even after more than doubling their use of fertilizers between 1980 and 1992, Thai farmers used far less fertilizer than almost any other Asian country, about two-thirds the level in the Philippines and far less than Bangladesh, China, India, Indonesia, Malaysia, Pakistan, or South Korea: World Bank, *World Development Report*, 1994, p. 169; *Bangkok Post*, November 18, 1996, p. 7.

70 *Nation*, July 8, 1991.

71 *BBMR*, December, 1985, pp. 549–51; interview with Metro Group executive, Bangkok, 1987.

72 *Nation*, July 8, 1991.

73 With a very long pipeline to shore, the natural gas was much more expensive than that available elsewhere, prompting some critics to charge that the PTT should be more flexible in its pricing of the gas, a concern also voiced by industries reluctant to follow government requests that they convert their energy use from oil to natural gas: Interview with National Fertilizer Corporation official in Bangkok; *FEER*, April 28, 1988, p. 88.

74 *BBMR*, December 1985, pp. 554–5; interviews with officials in Ministry of Finance and Prime Minister's Office, Bangkok, 1987.

75 Interviews with officials in the Finance Ministry and the Prime Minister's Office, Bangkok, 1987.

76 Interview with Metro Group executive, Bangkok, 1987.

77 The Thai Farmers Bank, linked with Loxley Construction which stood to win contracts in the region, including on the fertilizer project, stood behind the projects: Interviews with Coopers & Lybrand executive, Bangkok, 1987.

78 Interviews with Metro Group and NFC executives, Bangkok, 1987.

79 See *BBMR*, December, 1985, pp. 546–7.

80 Interview with MoF official, Bangkok, 1987.

81 Interview with MoF official, Bangkok, 1987.

82 Yoshihara, *Japanese Investment in Southeast Asia*, pp. 81–2.

83 *BIT*, March 1973, pp. 75–8; *Bangkok Post*, December 5, 1970, p. 47.

84 *Bangkok Post*, December 7, 1973.

85 *Chemical and Engineering*, July 20, 1970, p. 17.

86 Interview with NPC executive, Bangkok, 1987.

87 With the sharp rise in demand for these products into the early 1990s, the government rescinded the eight-year monopoly grants: Friel, "The International Competitiveness," p. 18.

88 *Nation*, September 14, 1987.

89 *FEER*, July 21, 1988.

90 *Nation*, December 17, 1992, p. B1.

91 Ibid.

92 *Bangkok Post Weekly Review*, June 9, 1995, p. 11; November 3, 1995, p. 11.

93 See, for example, World Bank, *Thailand, Managing Public Resources*, pp. 190–9.

94 *BBMR*, May, 1985, p. 235. A study of various potential uses of Thailand's natural gas deposits found petrochemical production one of the most efficient: Interview with NPC executive, Bangkok, 1987.

95 *Bangkok Post Weekly Review*, December 27, 1996, p. 16.

96 *Bangkok Post Weekly Review*, September 10, 1993, p. 12.

97 *Bangkok Post Weekly Review*, February 11, 1994, p. 11.

98 Among middle-income countries, only Burundi, the Congo, Guinea, and Mauritania had higher rates of urban concentration. World Bank, *World Development Report*, 1994, p. 223.

99 Nontapunthawat puts the average rush-hour speed at between 6.5 and 10 miles per hour, with considerable slowing expected in coming years: "Development and Financing," p. 63.

100 *FEER*, April 6, 1995, pp. 38–55.

101 World Bank, *Urban Transport in Asia*, World Bank Technical Paper No. 224, pp. 11, 16–17; Nimit, "Development and Financing," p. 62.

102 *Economist*, January 25, 1996, p. 6.

103 *Bangkok Post Weekly Review*, August 20, 1993, p. 20; September 24, 1993, pp. 1, 20.

104 *FEER*, August 17, 1995, p. 42.

105 *Bangkok Post Weekly Review*, October 1, 1993, p. 7.

106 Nontapunthawat, "Development and Finance," p. 74. Other estimates suggest a total of $57 billion on transportation infrastructure between 1995 and 2004, about 2.8 per cent of GDP: *Economist*, May 25, 1996, p. 66.

107 *Nation Year in Review 1992*, December 31, 1992, pp. 56–8.

108 *Economist Intelligence Unit*, 1992(1).

109 *Economist Intelligence Unit*, 1992(3) August 19, 1992.

110 *Bangkok Post Weekly Review*, January 14, 1994, p. 3.

111 *Bangkok Post Weekly Review*, October 22, 1993, p. 11.

112 *FEER*, February 15, 1996.

113 *FEER*, October 5, 1995, p. 84.
114 *Japan Digest*, September 23, 1996, p. 17.
115 *Japan Digest*, September 30, 1996, p. 9.
116 *FEER*, September 26, 1996, p. 17.
117 See, for example, *Bangkok Post Weekly Review*, August 30, 1996, p. 13; *FEER*, October 5, 1995, p. 84.
118 *Economist Intelligence Unit*, 1992(2) June 5, 1992.
119 *Economist Intelligence Unit*, 1992(3) August 19, 1992.
120 *Economist Intelligence Unit*, 1993(3) June 1, 1993.
121 *Economist Intelligence Unit*, 1992(3) August 19, 1992.
122 *FEER*, November 29, 1990, pp. 52–3.
123 *Nation Year in Review 1992*, pp. 56–8.
124 *Bangkok Post Weekly Review*, January 21, 1994, p. 1; May 6, 1994, p. 11; May 27, 1994, pp. 11, 20
125 *Bangkok Post Weekly Review*, August 19, 1994, p. 8.
126 Nimit, "Development and Finance," p. 76.
127 *Wall Street Journal*, February 11, 1993, p. A10.
128 *Economist Intelligence Unit*, 1992(3) August 19, 1992.
129 *Economist Intelligence Unit*, 1993(23) June 1, 1993.
130 This point was made by an anonymous reviewer.
131 Police had informed BECL that they were anticipating a public riot to try to force open the expressway. This threat, whatever its source, may have prompted the ETA to seek the court injunction: *Manager*, October 1993, pp. 40–3.
132 With the crisis coming to a head, Chavalit eventually did raise the toll fares to the full thirty baht stipulated in the original agreement. BECL management remained concerned, however, about how the tolls would be collected and divided: *Manager*, October 1993, pp. 40–3.
133 *Economist Intelligence Unit*, 1992(3) August 19, 1992.
134 *Economist Intelligence Unit*, 1993(23) June 1, 1993.
135 Interview with journalist, Bangkok, 1993.
136 *FEER*, March 24, 1994, p. 55.
137 *FEER*, September 16, 1993, pp. 18–19.
138 *Manager*, April 1994, p. 29.
139 *Manager*, October 1993, pp. 40–3.
140 *FEER*, June 10, 1993, p. 68.
141 Ibid.
142 *Bangkok Post Weekly Review*, December 31, 1993, p. 1.
143 Bowornwathana, "Public policies"; Interview with official in Prime Minister's Office (interview no. 9).
144 Muscat, *The Fifth Tiger*, p. 179.
145 *Economist*, October 22, 1994, pp. 81–2.
146 Interview with MoF official, 1987.
147 Interview with MoF official, Bangkok, 1987.

7 Growing Social Capital

1 Doner, "Approaches," p. 835.
2 Quoted in Hirschman, *The Passions and the Interests*, p. 83.
3 Pei, "The Puzzle of East Asian Exceptionalism," pp. 116–17.
4 Adam Przeworski and John Sprague, cited in Edward Gibson, "Conservative Electoral Movements," pp. 18–19.

5 Samuels, *The Business of the Japanese State*.
6 Doner and Ramsay, "Competitive Clientelism."
7 According to the World Bank, Thailand, unlike most other East Asian economies, made little progress in reducing the incidence of poverty during the 1980s: Mukoyama, "Development of Supporting Industries," p. 63.
8 *Financial Times Survey*, December 5, 1996, p. I.
9 *FEER*, October 19, 1995, p. 19.
10 *FEER*, February 27, 1992, p. 20.
11 *FEER*, September 29, 1994, pp. 14–15.
12 *FEER*, February 4, 1993, p. 25.
13 IBRD, *A Public Development Program for Thailand*.
14 Lazonick, *Business Organization*, pp. 6–13.
15 *FEER*, April 27, 1995, p. 30.
16 Laothamatas, *Business Associations*.
17 *Daily News* (in Thai); Foreign Broadcast Information Service (East Asia) 95-025, February 7, 1995.
18 *FEER*, August 17, 1995, p. 48.
19 *Bangkok Post*, December 2, 1994, p. 22.
20 See Mukoyama, "Development of Supporting Industries," RIM, p. 66.
21 Ibid.; *Bangkok Post Weekly Review*, November 3, 1995, pp. 18–19.
22 Satit Sirirangkamanont, Dept Industrial Promotion, in Manila, December 1997, pers. comm.
23 See, for example, *Nation*, December 23, 1994, p. A6. Richard Doner first pointed out this development to me.
24 Ibid.
25 Deyo, "Economic Policy and the Popular Sector," p. 200.
26 Phongpaichit and Baker, *Thailand's Boom!*, p. 163. Christensen and Siamwalla also make this point in "Beyond Patronage," p. 29.
27 Eeyore is the lugubrious donkey in A. A. Milne's *Winnie the Pooh*.
28 Hirschman, *The Passions and the Interests*, pp. 103–4.
29 See Williamson, "Washington Consensus."
30 Three excellent studies of the Northeast Asian cases are Johnson, *MITI and the Japanese Miracle*; Amsden, *Asia's Next Giant*, and Wade, *Governing the Market*.
31 Cumings, "Origins and Development," p. 81; Haggard, *Pathways from the Periphery*, pp. 363, 369; Chan, "Developing Strength from Weakness," p. 46; Stubbs, "Geopolitics," p. 540.
32 Hale, *The Civilization of Europe*, pp. 141–2.
33 Frederick II's explanation of his military foray against the Italian communes in the thirteenth century – "to punish those who 'preferred the luxury of a certain imprecise freedom to stable peace'" – suggests, however, a certain kinship with Singapore as well: John Larner, quoted in Putnam, *Making Democracy Work*, p. 123.
34 This was the fate in the end of all the northern Italian communes.
35 Hale, *The Civilization of Europe*, p. 150.
36 Putnam, *Making Democracy Work*, p. 127.

Bibliography

Abbreviations

BBMR   *Bangkok Bank Monthly Review*
BIT   *Business in Thailand*
FEER   *Far Eastern Economic Review*
RIM   *RIM, Pacific Business and Industry*

Akrasanee, Narongchai, "Trade and Industry Reforms in Thailand: the Role of Policy Research," *TDRI Quarterly Newsletter*, Thailand Development Research Institute Foundation, 4(2) June 1989
Alagappa, Muthiah (ed.), *Political Legitimacy in Southeast Asia: The Quest for Moral Authority* (Stanford University Press, 1995)
Amsden, Alice, "The State and Taiwan's Economic Development." In Evans et al., *Bringing the State Back In*, pp. 78–106
——, *Asia's Next Giant: South Korea and Late Industrialization* (New York: Oxford University Press, 1989)
Anderson, Benedict, "Studies of the Thai State." Paper presented at "The State of Thai Studies" conference, Chicago, March 30, 1978
Arase, David, *Buying Power: The Political Economy of Japan's Foreign Aid* (Boulder: Lynne Rienner Publishers, 1995)
Ayal, Eliezer B., "Private Enterprise and Economic Progress in Thailand," *Journal of Asian Studies*, 26(1) November 1966, pp. 5–14
——, "Value Systems and Economic Development in Japan and Thailand," *Journal of Social Issues*, 19, January 1963, pp. 35–51
Bank of Thailand, *50 Years of the Bank of Thailand*, 1942–1992 (Bangkok: Bank of Thailand, 1992)
Barme, Scot, *Luang Wichit Wathakan and the Creation of a Thai Identity* (Singapore: Institute of Southeast Asian Studies, 1993)
Barton, Clifton A., "Trust and Credit: Some Observations Regarding Business Strategies of Overseas Chinese Traders in South Vietnam." In Lim and Gosling, *The Chinese in Southeast Asia*, vol. 1, pp. 46–64
Benedict, Ruth, *Thai Culture and Behavior: An Unpublished War-time Study* (Ithaca:

Southeast Asia Program, Department of Far Eastern Studies, Cornell University, 1952)

Bentley, Arthur F., *The Process of Government: A Study of Social Pressures* (Evanston, Ill.: The Principia Press of Illinois, 1935)

Bernard, Mitchell, and John Ravenhill, "Beyond Product Cycles and Flying Geese: Regionalization, Hierarchy, and the Industrialization of East Asia," *World Politics* 47, 1995, pp. 171–209

Bhattacharya, Amar, and Johannes Lin, *Trade and Industrial Policies in the Developing Countries of East Asia* (Washington, DC: World Bank, 1988)

Bonacich, Edna, and John Modell, *The Economic Basis of Ethnic Solidarity: Small Business in the Japanese American Community* (Berkeley: University of California Press, 1980)

Boone, Catherine, "States and Ruling Classes in Postcolonial Africa: the Enduring Contradictions of Power." In Migdal, *State Power and Social Forces*, pp. 108–40

Bowie, Alasdair, *Crossing the Industrial Divide: State, Society, and the Politics of Economic Transformation in Malaysia* (New York: Columbia University Press, 1991)

Bowie, Alasdair, and Danny Unger, *The Politics of Open Economies: Indonesia, Malaysia, the Philippines and Thailand* (Cambridge University Press, 1997)

Bowie, Katherine A., "Unraveling the Myth of the Subsistence Economy: Textile Production in 19th-Century Northern Thailand," *Journal of Asian Studies*, 15(4) November 1992, pp. 797–823

Bowornwathana, Bidhya, "Public Policies in a Bureaucratic Polity." Paper presented at International Political Science Association meeting, Washington, DC, 1988

Brennan, Martin, "Class, Politics and Race in Modern Malaysia." In Higgott and Robison (eds), *Southeast Asia*, pp. 93–127

Bunnag, Jane, "Loose Structure: Fact or Fancy? Thai Society Re-examined." In Neher, *Modern Thai Politics*, pp. 133–52

Cameron, Rondo, *Banking and Economic Development* (New York: Oxford University Press, 1972)

——, *Banking in the Early Stages of Industrialization* (New York: Oxford University Press, 1967)

Case, William, "Malaysia, Aspects and Audience of Legitimacy." In Alagappa, *Political Legitimacy*, pp. 69–107

Chalermnatarana, Thak, *Thailand: The Politics of Despotic Paternalism* (Bangkok: Social Science Association of Thailand, Thai Khadi Institute, Thammasat University, 1979)

Chamarik, Saneh, "Problems of Development in Thai Political Setting." Paper No. 14 (Thai Khadi Research Insitute: Thammasat University, 1983)

Chan, Steve, "Developing strength from weakness: the state in Taiwan," *Journal of Developing Societies*, 4, 1988

Chandravithun, Nikom, "Report on Thailand: The Social Costs of Becoming the Fifth Tiger," Woodrow Wilson International Center for Scholars, 1995

Chapman, Sara E., "Ministerial Patron–Client Networks During the Reign of Louis XIV: The Phelypeau de Pontchartrain, 1675–1715," PhD, Georgetown University, 1997

Chenery, Hollis, "Industrialization and growth: alternative views of East Asia." In Hughes, *Achieving Industrialization in East Asia*, pp. 39–63

Chenvidyakarn, Montri, "Political Control and Economic Influence: A Study of Trade Associations in Thailand." PhD, University of Chicago, 1979

Christensen, Scott R., "Democracy Without Equity? The Institutions and Policy Consequences of Bangkok-based Development." Paper presented at Thailand Development Research Institute, 1993 Year-End Conference, December 10–11, 1993, Chon Buri, Thailand

Christensen, Scott R., and Ammar Siamwalla, "Beyond Patronage: Tasks for the Thai State." Paper presented at Thailand Development Research Institute 1993 Year-End Conference, December 10–11, 1993, Chon Buri, Thailand

Christensen, Scott R., David Dollar, Ammar Siamwalla, and Pakorn Vichyanond, *The Lessons of East Asia: Thailand – The Institutional and Political Underpinnings of Growth* (Washington, DC: World Bank, 1993)

Clark, Cal, and Kartik C. Roy, *Comparing Development Patterns in Asia* (Boulder: Lynne Rienner Publishers, 1997)

Coleman, James S., "Social Capital in the Creation of Human Capital," *American Journal of Sociology*, 1994 Supplement, pp. S105–8

Coughlin, Richard J., *Double Identity: The Chinese in Modern Thailand* (Hong Kong University Press, 1960)

Crone, Donald K., "States, Social Elites, and Government Capacity in Southeast Asia," *World Politics*, 40(2) January 1988, pp. 252–68

Cumings, Bruce, "The Origins and Development of the Northeast Asian Political Economy: Industrial Sectors, Product Cycles, and Political Consequences." In Deyo, *The Political Economy of the New Asian Industrialism*

Deyo, Frederic C., "Chinese Management Practices and Work Commitment in Comparative Perspective." In Lim and Gosling, *The Chinese in Southeast Asia*, vol. 2, pp. 15–30

—— (ed.), *The Political Economy of the New Asian Industrialism* (Ithaca: Cornell University Press, 1987)

——, "Human Resource Strategies and Industrial Restructuring in Thailand." In Stephen Frenkel and Jeffrey Harrod (eds), *Industrialization and Labor Relations: Contemporary Research in Seven Countries*. Cornell International Industrial and Labor Relations Report No. 27 (Ithaca: Cornell University Press, 1995), pp. 237–76

Dhiravegin, Likhit, "Tokugawa Japan and pre-Chulalongkorn Siam: Preconditions and Potential for Rural Development." Economic Research Unit, Proceedings of the Conference on Comparative Study of the History of Rural Development in Japan and Thailand

Diamond, Larry, J. Linz, and Seymour Martin Lipset (eds), *Democracy in Developing Countries: Asia* (Boulder: Lynne Rienner Publishers, 1989)

Dixon, Chris, "Origins, Sustainability," *Contemporary Southeast Asia*, 17(1) June 1995, pp. 38–52

Doner, Richard F., "Approaches to the Politics of Economic Growth in Southeast Asia," *The Journal of Asian Studies*, 50(4) November 1991, pp. 818–49

——, *Driving a Bargain, Automobile Industrialization and Japanese Firms in Southeast Asia* (Berkeley: University of California Press, 1991)

——, "Limits of State Strength," *World Politics*, 44(3) 1992, pp. 398–431

Doner, Richard F., and Ansil Ramsay, "Competitive Clientelism and Economic Governance: The Case of Thailand." In Maxfield and Schneider, *Business and the State*, pp. 237–76

Doner, Richard F., and Danny Unger, "The Politics of Finance in Thai Economic Development." In Haggard et al., *The Politics of Finance*, pp. 93–122

Dower, John W., "E. H. Norman, Japan, and the Uses of History." In Dower, *Origins of the Modern Japanese State*, pp. 3–17

—— (ed.), *Origins of the Modern Japanese State: Selected Writings of E.H. Norman* (New York: Random House, 1975)

Embree, John F., "Thailand – a Loosely Structured Social System," *American Anthropologist*, 52, 1950, pp. 181–93

Emmerson, Donald K., "The Bureaucracy in Political Context: Weakness in Strength." In Jackson and Pye, *Political Power and Communications in Indonesia*, pp. 82–136

ESCAP/UNTC, Joint Unit on Transnational Corporations, *Transnational Corporations From Developing Asian Economies: Host Country Perspectives* (Bangkok: Economic and Social Commission for Asia and the Pacific, 1988)

Evans, Peter, "The State as Problem and Solution: Predation, Embedded Autonomy, and Structural Change." In Haggard and Kaufman, *The Politics of Economic Adjustment*, pp.139–81

Evans, Peter B., Dietrich Rueschemeyer, and Theda Skocpol, *Bringing the State Back In* (Cambridge University Press, 1985)

Evers, Hans-Dieter (ed.), *Loosely Structured Social Systems: Thailand in Comparative Perspective* (New Haven: Yale University, Southeast Asian Studies, 1969)

Evers, Hans-Dieter, and T. H. Silcock, "Elites and Selection." In Silcock, *Thailand, Social and Economic Studies in Development*

Evers, Hans-Dieter, Rudiger Korff, and Suparb Pas-Ong, "Peasants, Traders and the State." Paper presented at Thai Khadi Research Institute, Thammasat University. Third Thai–European Seminar on "Village and State in Thai Studies," Hua Hin, Thailand, April 1985

Feeny, David, "Paddy, Princes, and Productivity: Irrigation and Thai Agricultural Development, 1900–1940," *Explorations in Economic History*, 1979, pp. 132–50

——, "Infrastructure Linkages and Trade Performance: Thailand, 1900–1940," *Explorations in Economic History*, 19, 1982, pp. 1–27

Fletcher, William Miles III, *The Japanese Business Community and National Trade Policy, 1920–1942* (Chapel Hill: University of North Carolina Press, 1989)

Fox, James, et al. (eds), *Indonesia: Australian Perspectives* (Canberra: Research School of Pacific Studies, Australian National University)

Frieden, Jeffrey, *Debt, Development, and Democracy* (Princeton University Press, 1991)

Friel, Patrick C., "The International Competitiveness of Thailand's Petrochemical Industry," *Journal of Southeast Asia Business* 7(1) Winter 1991, pp. 1–37

Fry, Maxwell J., *Money, Interest, and Banking in Economic Development* (Baltimore: The Johns Hopkins University Press, 1988)

Fuei Taikuo (ed.), *Tonan Ajia Kajin Shakai no Kenkyu* (Study of Southeast Asian Chinese Society) (Tokyo: Institute for Developing Economies, 1974)

Fukuyama, Francis, *Trust: The Social Virtues and the Creation of Prosperity* (New York: The Free Press, 1995)

Ganjanapan, Anan, "Conflict over the Deployment and Control of Labor in a Northern Thai Village." In Hart et al., *Agrarian Transformations*, pp. 98–122

Geertz, Clifford, *Agricultural Involution* (Berkeley: University of California Press, 1963)

Gereffi, Gary, and Donald L. Wyman (eds), *Manufacturing Miracles: Paths of Industrialization in Latin America and East Asia* (Princeton University Press, 1990)

Gerschenkron, Alexander, *Economic Backwardness in Historical Perspective* (Cambridge, Mass.: The Belknap Press of Harvard University Press, 1962)

Gibson, Edward, "Conservative Electoral Movements and Democratic Politics: Core Constituencies, Coalition Building, and the Latin American Electoral Right." In Douglas A. Chalmers, Maria do Carmo Campbello de Souze, and Atilio A. Boron (eds), *The Right and Democracy in Latin America* (New York: Praeger, 1992), pp. 13–42

Girling, John, *Thailand, Society and Politics* (Ithaca: Cornell University Press, 1981)

——, *Interpreting Development: Capitalism, Democracy, and the Middle Class in Thailand* (Ithaca: Southeast Asia Program, Cornell University Press, 1996)

Granovetter, Mark, "Economic Action and Social Structure: The Problem of Embeddedness." In Granovetter and Swedberg, *The Sociology of Economic Life*, pp. 53–81

Granovetter, Mark, and Richard Swedberg (eds), *The Sociology of Economic Life* (Boulder: Westview Press, 1992)

Haggard, Stephan, "The Newly Industrializing Countries in the International System," *World Politics* 38(2) January 1986, pp. 343–70

——, "The Politics of Industrialization in the Republic of Korea and Taiwan." In Hughes, *Achieving Industrialization in East Asia*, pp. 260–82

——, *Pathways From the Periphery: The Politics of Growth in the Newly Industrializing Countries* (Ithaca: Cornell University Press, 1990)

Haggard, Stephan, and Robert Kaufman (eds), *The Politics of Economic Adjustment: International Constraints, Distributive Conflicts, and the State* (Princeton University Press, 1992)

Haggard, Stephan, Chung H. Lee, and Sylvia Maxfield (eds), *The Politics of Finance in Developing Countries* (Ithaca and New York: Cornell University Press, 1993)

Hale, John, *The Civilization of Europe in the Renaissance* (New York: Atheneum, 1994)

Hamilton, Gary G., and Nicole Woolsey Biggart, "Market, Culture, and Authority: A Comparative Analysis of Management and Organization in the Far East." In Granovetter and Swedberg, *The Sociology of Economic Life*, pp. 181–221

Harris, George I., et al., *Area Handbook for Thailand* (US Government Printing Office, 1963)

Hart, Gillian, Andrew Turton, and Benjamin White, *Agrarian Transformations, Local Processes and the State in Southeast Asia* (Berkeley: University of California Press, 1989)

Hewison, Kevin, "The Development of Capital, Public Policy and the Role of the State in Thailand." PhD, Murdoch University, 1983

——, *Bankers and Bureaucrats: Capital and the Role of the State in Thailand.* Monograph Series 34 (New Haven: Yale University Southeast Asian Studies, 1989)

Higgott, R., and R. Robison (eds), *Southeast Asia: Essays in the Political Economy of Structural Change* (London: Routledge & Kegan Paul, 1985)

Hill, Hal (ed.), *Indonesia's New Order: The Dynamics of Socio-economic Transformation* (Honolulu: University of Hawaii Press, 1994)

Hirsch, Philip, "What is the Thai Village?" In Reynolds, *National Identity and Its Defenders*, pp. 323–49

Hirschman, Albert O., *The Passions and the Interests: Political Arguments for Capitalism before Its Triumph* (Princeton University Press, 1977)

Hong Lysa, *Thailand in the 19th Century: Evolution of the Economy and Society* (Singapore: Institute of Southeast Asian Studies, 1984)

Hongladarom, Chira, "Unemployment in Thailand." In Prasith-rathsint, *Thailand on the Move*, pp. 133–65

Hongladarom, Tongchat, "Gas Utilisation Policies: Some Observations on the Thai Experience." Paper presented to the Petroleum Institute of Thailand's symposium on "Gas Utilisation Policies: An International Perspective," Pattaya, October, 1987

Hughes, Helen (ed.), *Achieving Industrialization in Southeast Asia* (Cambridge University Press, 1988)

Huntington, Samuel P., *Political Order in Changing Societies* (New Haven: Yale University Press, 1968)

Hutchcroft, Paul, "Booty Capitalism: Business–Government Relations in the Philippines." In Andrew MacIntyre (ed.), *Business and Government in Industrialising Asia* (Ithaca: Cornell University Press, 1994)

IBRD, *A Public Development Program for Thailand* (Baltimore: The Johns Hopkins University Press, 1959)

Ichikawa, Kenjiro, "Leadership and Strategy of Chinese Enterprises: A Case Study of Siam Motors." In Ito, *Tonan Ajia ni Okeru*, pp. 29–57

Ingram, James C., *Economic Change in Thailand, 1800–1970* (Stanford University Press, 1971)

International Criminal Police Organization, *International Crime Statistics*, various years (International Criminal Police Organization)

Ito, Tadaichi (ed.), *Tonan Ajia ni Okeru, Keieisha no Kindaika* (Management Modernization in Southeast Asia) (Tokyo: Institute for Developing Economies, 1979)

Jacobs, Norman, *Modernization Without Development: Thailand as an Asian Case Study* (New York: Praeger Publishers, 1971)

Jackson, Karl D., "Bureaucratic Polity: a Theoretical Framework for the Analysis of Power and Communications in Indonesia." In Jackson and Pye, *Political Power*, pp. 3–22

——, "The Political Implications of Structure and Culture in Indonesia." In Jackson and Pye, *Political Power*

Jackson, Karl D., and Lucian W. Pye, *Political Power and Communications in Indonesia* (Berkeley: University of California Press, 1978)

Jackson, Peter A. (ed.), *The May 1992 Crisis in Thailand: Background and Aftermath*, National Thai Studies Centre, Australian National University, No. 2, June 1993

Jackson, Robert H., *Quasi-states: Sovereignty, International Relations and the Third World* (Cambridge University Press, 1990)

JETRO, "Recent Trends of Trade Between Thailand and Japan," August, 1987

——, *Saikin no Toshi* (Recent Investment Trends) (1989)

JICA, *Final Report for the Study on the Development Project of Laem Chabang Coastal Area*. Report for the Industrial Estate Authority of Thailand (1985)

Johnson, Chalmers, *MITI and the Japanese Miracle: The Growth of Industrial Policy, 1925–1975* (Stanford University Press, 1982)

Journal of Southeast Asian Studies 12(1) March 1981. Issue on "Ethnic Chinese in Southeast Asia" (Singapore University Press)

Jumbala, Prudhisan, "Towards a Theory of Group Formation in Thai Society and Pressure Groups in Thailand After the October 1973 Uprising," *Asian Survey*, 14(6) June 1974, pp. 530–45

Klausner, William J., *Reflections on Thai Culture*, 2nd edn (Bangkok: Siam Society, 1983)

Knight, Jack, *Institutions and Social Conflict* (Cambridge University Press, 1992)

Kohli, Atul, "Centralization and Powerlessness: India's Democracy in Comparative Perspective." In Migdal, *State Power*, pp. 89–107

Lal, Deepak, "The Political Economy of Industrialization in Primary Product Exporting Economies: Some Cautionary Tales." World Bank Report No. DRD215 (1983)

Landa, Janet T., "The Political Economy of the Ethnically Homogenous Chinese Middleman Group in Southeast Asia: Ethnicity and Entrepreneurship in a Plural Society." In Lim and Gosling, *The Chinese in Southeast Asia*, vol. 1, pp. 86–116

Landau, Martin, "Linkage, Coding, and Intermediacy: A Strategy for Institution Building." In Joseph W. Eaton (ed.), *Institution Building and Development* (New York: Sage Publications, 1972), pp. 91–109

Landon, Kenneth Parry, *The Chinese in Thailand* (New York: Russell & Russell, 1973)

Laothamatas, Anek, *Business Associations and the New Political Economy of Thailand: From Bureaucratic Polity to Liberal Corporatism* (Boulder: Westview Press, 1992)

Lazonick, William, *Business Organization and the Myth of the Market Economy* (Cambridge University Press, 1991)

Lee, S. Y., and Y. C. Jao, *Financial Structure and Monetary Policies in Southeast Asia* (New York: St Martin's Press, 1982)

Lengel, Francis K., "Markets in Thailand: An Analysis of the Interval between Socio-Cultural and Economic Factors," PhD, Columbia University, 1976

Liddle, R. William, "Participation and the Political Parties." In Jackson and Pye, *Political Power*, pp. 171–95

Lim, Linda Y. C., "Chinese Business, Multinationals and the State: Manufacturing for Export in Malaysia and Singapore." In Lim and Gosling, *The Chinese in Southeast Asia*, vol. 1, pp. 245–74

Lim, Linda Y. C., and Peter Gosling (eds), *The Chinese in Southeast Asia*, 2 vols (Singapore: Maruzen Asia, 1983)

Lin, Sein, and Bruce Esposito, "Agrarian Reform in Thailand: Problems and Prospects," *Pacific Affairs*, 49(3) Fall 1976, pp. 425–42

Mabry, Bevars D., *The Development of Labor Institutions in Thailand*. Data Paper No. 112 (Ithaca: Cornell University Department of Asian Studies, Cornell University Southeast Asia Program, 1979)

Mackie, James, and Andrew MacIntyre, "Politics." In Hill, *Indonesia's New Order*, pp. 1–53

Maxfield, Sylvia, "Financial Incentives and Central Bank Authority in Industrializing Nations," *World Politics* 46(4) 1994, pp. 556–88

Maxfield, Sylvia, and Ben Schneider (eds), *Business and the State in Developing Countries* (Ithaca: Cornell University Press, 1997)

McNamara, Dennis L., *Textile and Industrial Transition in Japan* (Ithaca: Cornell University Press, 1995)

Midgley, Peter, *Urban Transport in Asia: An Operational agenda for the 1990s*. World Bank Technical Paper No. 224 (Washington, DC: World Bank, 1988)

Migdal, Joel S., Atul Kohli, and Vivienne Shue, "Introduction: Developing a State-in-society Perspective." In Migdal (ed.), *State Power and Social Forces*

Migdal, Joel S. (ed.), *State Power and Social Forces* (Cambridge University Press, 1994)

Milner, Helen, "Trade Policy in France and the United States," *International Organization* 41(4) 1987, pp. 639–66

——, *Resisting Protectionism: Global Industries and the Politics of International Trade* (Princeton University Press, 1988)

Mizuno, Koichi, "Thai Patterns of Social Organization: Notes on a Comparative Study." In Shinichi Ichimura (ed.), *Southeast Asia: Nature, Society and Development* (Honolulu: University Press of Hawaii, 1976)

Morley, James (ed.), *Driven by Growth* (Armonk, New York: M. E. Sharpe, 1993)

Mukoyama, Hidehiko, "Development of Supporting Industries in ASEAN: A Case Study of Thailand," *RIM*, 4, 1993, pp. 58–72

Mulder, J. A. Niels, "Origin, Development, and the Use of the Concept of 'Loose Structure' in the Literature About Thailand: an Evaluation." In Evers, *Loosely Structured Social Systems*

——, *Everyday Life in Thailand: An Interpretation*, 2nd edn (Bangkok: Editions Duang Kamol, 1985)

Muscat, Robert J., *The Fifth Tiger: A Study of Thai Development Policy* (Armonk, New York: M.E. Sharpe, 1994)

——, *Development Strategy in Thailand: A Study of Economic Growth* (New York: Frederick A. Praeger, 1996)

Nairn, Ronald C., *International Aid to Thailand: the New Colonialism?* (New Haven: Yale University Press, 1966)

Nartsupha, Chatthip, *Foreign Trade, Foreign Finance and the Economic Development of Thailand 1956–1965* (Bangkok: Prae Pittaya Ltd, 1970)

Naya, Seiji, "The Role of Trade Policies in the Industrialization of Rapidly Growing Asian Developing Countries." In Hughes, *Achieving Industrialization in East Asia*, pp. 64–94

Neher, Clark D. (ed.), *Modern Thai Politics: From Village to Nation* (Cambridge, Mass.: Schenkman Publishing Co., 1979)

Nontapunthawat, Nimit, "Development and Financing of Infrastructure Improvements in ASEAN." In *The 21st ASEAN-Japanese Businessmen's Meeting, Meeting Report* (Tokyo: Keizai Doyukai, 1995)

Norville, Elizabeth Mary, "The Advantages of Backwardness: The Rise of Japanese Financial Power." PhD, University of California: Berkeley, 1992

Ockey, James Soren, "Business Leaders, Gangsters, and the Middle Class: Societal Groups and Civilian Rule in Thailand." PhD, Cornell University, 1992

Olson, Mancur, *The Rise and Decline of Nations: Economic Growth, Stagflation, and Social Rigidities* (New Haven: Yale University Press, 1982)

Overholt, William H., "Thailand: a moving equilibrium." In Ramsay and Mungkandi, *Thailand–U.S. Relations*, pp. 155–94

Parnwell, Michael J. G., *Uneven Development in Thailand* (Aldershot, England: Avebury Press, 1996)

Pei, Minxin, "The Puzzle of East Asian Exceptionalism." In Larry Diamond and Marc F. Plattner (eds), *Economic Reform and Democracy* (Baltimore: The Johns Hopkins University Press, 1995), pp. 112–25

Phillips, Herbert P., *Thai Peasant Personality: The Patterning of Interpersonal Behavior in the Village of Bang Chan* (Berkeley: University of California Press, 1965)

Phipatseritham, Krirkiat, and Kunio Yoshihara, *Business Groups in Thailand* (Singapore: Institute for Southeast Asian Studies, 1983)

Phongpaichit, Pasuk, "The Thai Middle Class and the Military: Social Perspectives in the Aftermath of May 1992." In Jackson, *The May 1992 Crisis in Thailand*, pp. 29–35

Phongpaichit, Pasuk, and Chris Baker, *Thailand's Boom!* (Chiang Mai, Thailand: Silkworm Books, 1996)

Phongpaichit, Pasuk, and Sungsidh Piriyarangsan, *Corruption and Democracy in Thailand* (Bangkok: The Political Economy Center, Faculty of Economics, Chulalongkorn University, 1994)

Piker, Steven, "The Relationship of Belief Systems to Behavior in Rural Thai Society." In Neher, *Modern Thai Politics*, pp. 114–32

Piriyarangsan, Sungsidh, *Thai Bureaucratic Capitalism, 1932–1960* (Bangkok: Chulalongkorn University Social Research Institute, October 1983)

Potter, Jack M., *Thai Peasant Social Structure* (University of Chicago Press, 1976)

Potter, Sulamith Heins, *Family Life in a Northern Thai Village* (Berkeley: University of California Press, 1977)

Prasartsert, Suthy, *Thai Business Leaders*. Joint Research Program Series No. 19 (Tokyo: Institute for Developing Economies, 1980)

Prasith-rathsint, Suchart (ed.), *Thailand's National Development: Policy Issues and Challenges* (Bangkok: Thai University Research Association and Canadian International Development Agency, 1987)

—— (ed.), *Thailand on the Move: Stumbling Blocks and Breakthroughs* (Bangkok: Thai University Research Association and Canadian International Development Agency, 1990)

Putnam, Robert D., *Making Democracy Work: The Civic Traditions in Modern Italy* (Princeton University Press, 1993)

Pye, Lucian, *Asian Power and Politics: The Cultural Dimensions of Authority* (Cambridge, Mass.: The Belknap Press of Harvard University Press, 1985)

Quigley, Kevin F. F., "Towards Consolidating Democracy: the Role of Civil Society Organizations in Thailand." PhD, Georgetown University, 1995

——, "Towards Consolidating Democracy: the Paradoxical Role of Democracy Groups in Thailand," *Democratization* 3(3) Autumn 1996

Rabibhadana, Akin, *The Organization of Thai Society in the Early Bangkok Period, 1782–1873*. Data Paper No. 74 (Ithaca: Southeast Asia Program, Department of Asian Studies, Cornell University, 1969)

Race, Jeffrey, "The Political Economy of New Order Indonesia in Comparative Perspective." In Fox et al., *Indonesia*

Ramsay, Ansil, "Thai Domestic Politics and Foreign Policy." Paper presented at the Third US-ASEAN Conference, Chiengmai, Thailand, January 1985

——, "The Political Economy of Sugar in Thailand," *Pacific Affairs*, 60(2) 1987, pp. 248–70

Ramsay, Ansil, and Wiwat Mungkandi, *Thailand–U.S. Relations: Changing Political, Strategic and Economic Factors* (Berkeley: Institute of East Asian Studies, University of California, Berkeley, 1988)

Reynolds, Craig J., *Thai Radical Discourse: The Real Face of Thai Feudalism Today* (Ithaca: Southeast Asia Program, Cornell University, 1987)

—— (ed.), *National Identity and Its Defenders* (Chiang Mai, Thailand: Silkworm Books, 1991)

Riedel, James, "Economic Development in East Asia: Doing What Comes Naturally?" In Hughes, *Achieving Industrialization in East Asia*, pp. 1–38

Riggs, Fred W., "Interest and Clientele Groups." In Sutton, *Problems of Politics*, pp. 153–92

——, *Thailand: the Modernization of a Bureaucratic Polity* (Honolulu: East-West Center Press, 1966)

Robison, Richard, "Class, Capital and the State in New Order Indonesia." In Higgott and Robison, *Southeast Asia*, pp. 295–335

Rogowski, Ronald, *Commerce and Coalitions: How Trade Affects Domestic Political Alignments* (Princeton University Press, 1989).

Rubin, Herbert J., *The Dynamics of Development in Rural Thailand Special Report*.

No. 8. De Kalb (Illinois: Center for Southeast Asian Studies, Northern Illinois University, 1974)

Sachs, Jeffrey, Aaron Tornell and Andres Velasco, "Financial Crises in Emerging Markets: The Lessons from 1995." Working Paper Series No. 97-1, Center for International Affairs: Harvard University, 1997

Samudavanija, Chai-anan, "The Politics and Administration of the Thai Budgetary Process." PhD, University of Wisconsin, 1971

——, "State Identity Creation, State Building and Civil Society, 1939–1989." In Reynolds, *National Identity*, pp. 59–81

——, "Thailand: a stable semi-democracy." In Diamond et al., *Democracy in Developing Countries*, pp. 305–46

Samudavanija, Chai-anan, and Sukhumbhand Paribatra, "Thailand: Liberalization Without Democracy." In Morley, *Driven by Growth*, pp. 119–41

Samuels, Richard J., *The Business of the Japanese State: Energy Markets in Comparative and Historical Perspective* (Ithaca: Cornell University Press, 1987)

——, "*Rich Nation, Strong Army": National Security and the Technological Transformation of Japan* (Ithaca: Cornell University Press, 1994)

Sanittanont, Sura, "Exchange Rate Experience and Policy in Thailand Since World War II." In Herbert G. Grubel and Theodore Morgan (eds), *Exchange Rate Policy in Southeast Asia* (Lexington, Mass.: Lexington Books, 1973)

Santikarn, Mingsarn, *Technology Transfer: A Case Study* (Singapore University Press, 1981)

Schumpeter, Joseph A., *The Theory of Economic Development*, translated by Redvers Opie (New York: Oxford University Press, 1961)

Scott, James C., "Corruption in Thailand." In Neher, *Modern Thai Politics*, pp. 294–316

Seth, Vikram, *A Suitable Boy* (New York: HarperCollins, 1993)

Shafer, D. Michael, *Winners and Losers: How Sectors Shape the Developmental Prospects of States* (Ithaca: Cornell University Press, 1994)

Shor, Edgar L., "The Public Service." In Sutton, *Problems of Politics*, pp. 23–40

Shozo, Fukuda, *Kakkyo Keizai Ron* (On the Overseas Chinese Economy) (Tokyo: Ganshodo, 1940)

Shue, Vivienne, "State Power and Social Organization in China." In Migdal, *State Power*, pp. 65–88

Siamwalla, Ammar, "Stability, Growth and Distribution in the Thai Economy." In Siamwalla (ed.), *Finance, Trade and Economic Development in Thailand* (Bangkok: Sompong Press for the Bank of Thailand, 1975), pp. 25–48

Sidel, John T., "The Philippines, The Languages of Legitimation." In Alagappa, *Political Legitimacy*, pp. 136–69

Siffin, William J., "Economic Development." In Sutton, *Problems of Politics*, pp. 125–52

——, *The Thai Bureaucracy: Institutional Change and Development* (Honolulu: East-West Center Press, 1966)

Silcock, Thomas Henry (ed.), *Thailand, Social and Economic Studies in Development* (Canberra: Australian National University in association with Duke University Press, 1967)

——, *The Economic Development of Thai Agriculture* (Ithaca and New York: Cornell University Press, 1970)

Simon, Jean-Christophe, "The Thai Manufacturing Sector: New Patterns of Expansion." In Parnwell, *Uneven Development in Thailand*, pp. 82–108

Siow, Moli, "The Problems of Ethnic Cohesion among the Chinese in Peninsular Malaysia: Intraethnic Divisions and Interethnic Accommodation." In Lim and Gosling, *The Chinese in Southeast Asia*, vol. 2, pp. 170–88

Siroros, Patcharee, and Kenneth J. Haller, "'Thai Style' Contractual Relationships: Two Case Studies," *Contemporary Southeast Asia* 16(3) December 1994, pp. 317–41

Skinner, William G., *Chinese Society in Thailand: An Anthropological History* (Ithaca: Cornell University Press, 1957)

——, *Leadership and Power in a Chinese Community in Thailand* (Ithaca: Cornell University Press, 1958)

——, "Change and Persistence in Chinese Culture Overseas: A Comparison of Thailand and Java." In John T. McAlister (ed.), *Southeast Asia: The Politics of National Integration* (Random House, New York, 1973), pp. 399–415

Skully, Michael T., *Asean Regional Cooperation: Developments in Banking and Finance*. Occasional Paper No. 56 (Singapore: Institute of East Asian Studies, 1979)

——, "Financial Institutions and Markets in Thailand." In Skully, *Financial Institutions and Markets in Southeast Asia* (Hong Kong: Macmillan, 1984), pp. 296–378

Solow, Robert M., "But Verify," *New Republic*, September 11, 1995, pp. 36–9

Somjee, A. H., and Geeta Somjee, *Development Success in Asia Pacific: An Exercise in Normative-Pragmatic Balance* (New York: St Martin's Press, 1995)

Somvichian, Kamol, "The Thai Political Culture and Political Development." In Neher, *Modern Thai Politics*, pp. 153–69

Steinberg, David Joel (ed.), *In Search of Southeast Asia* (New York: Praeger, 1971)

Stifel, Laurence David, *The Textile Industry: A Case Study of Industrial Development in the Philippines*. Data Paper No. 49, Southeast Asia Program, Department of Asian Studies: Cornell University, 1963

Stubbs, Richard, "Geopolitics and the Political Economy of Southeast Asia," *International Journal*, 44, 1989, pp. 517–40

Suehiro Akira, *Development and Structure of Textile Industry in Thailand: 1946–1980* (Bangkok: Social Research Institute, Chulalongkorn University, 1983)

——, *Capital Accumulation and Industrial Development in Thailand* (Bangkok: Chulalongkorn University Social Research Institute, 1985)

——, *Tai no Kogyoka – NAIC e no Chosen* (Thailand's Industrialization) (Tokyo: Institute for Developing Economies, 1987)

——, "Bangkok Bank: Management Reforms of a Thai Commercial Bank," *East Asian Culture Studies*, 28(1–4) March 1989, pp. 101–25

——, *Capital Accumulation in Thailand: 1855–1985* (Tokyo: Centre for East Asian Cultural Studies, 1989)

——, "Family Business Reassessed: Corporate Structure and Late-Starting Industrialization in Thailand," *The Developing Economies*, 22, 1993

——, *Tai Hatten to Minshushugi* (Thai Development and Democratization) (Tokyo: Iwanami, 1993)

Sukatipan, Saitip, "Thailand, The Evolution of Legitimacy," Alagappa, *Political Legitimacy in Southeast Asia*, pp. 193–223

Suksamran, Somboon, *Buddhism and Politics in Thailand* (Singapore: Institute of Southeast Asian Studies, 1982)

Suphachalasai, Suphat, "Thailand's Growth in Textile and Clothing Exports." In Kym Anderson (ed.), *New Silk Road* (Cambridge University Press, 1992)

Suryadinata, Leo, "Asia's Ethnic Chinese in Southeast Asia: Problems and Prospects," *Journal of International Affairs*, 41(1) Summer/Fall 1987, pp. 135–52
——, *"Overseas Chinese" in Southeast Asia and China's Foreign Policy* (Singapore: Institute of Southeast Asian Studies, 1978)
Sutton, Joseph L. (ed.), *Problems of Politics and Administration in Thailand* (Bloomington: Institute of Training for Public Service, Indiana University, 1962)
Suwannathat-Pian, Kobkua, *Thailand's Durable Premier: Phibun Through Three Decades, 1932–1957* (Kuala Lumpur: Oxford University Press, 1995)
Swan, William L., "Japanese Economic Relations with Siam: Aspects of Their Historical Development, 1894–1942," PhD, Australian National University, 1986
Swearer, Donald K., *The Buddhist World of Southeast Asia* (Albany, New York: State University of New York Press, 1995)
Takayasu, Kenichi, "A Study of Economic Development of the Asian NIEs and ASEAN Countries from a Financial Perspective," *RIM*, 1, 1994, pp. 2–15
Tambunlertchai, Somsak, and Atchaka Sibunruang "Foreign Direct Investment in Thailand: A Background Paper." Presented at seminar on "The role of TNCs in Thailand," August, 1986
Tambunlertchai, Somsak, and Ippei Yamazawa, *Manufactured Exports and DFI: A Case Study of the Textile Industry in Thailand* (Bangkok: Thammasat University, 1981)
Tanaka, Kozo, Minako Mori, and Yoko Mori, "Overseas Chinese Business Communities in Asia: Present Conditions and Future Prospects," *RIM*, 2, 1992, pp. 2–24
Tarrow, Sidney, "Making Social Science Work Across Space and Time: A Critical Reflection on Robert Putnam's *Making Democracy Work*," *American Political Science Review*, June 1996, pp. 389–97
Thai Textile Statistics, Textile Intelligence Unit, Textile Industry Division, Department of Industrial Promotion, Ministry of Industry, 1993
Thanamai, Patcharee, "Patterns of Industrial Policymaking in Thailand: Japanese Multinationals and Domestic Actors in the Automobile and Electrical Appliances Industries." PhD, University of Wisconsin, 1985
Turton, Andrew, "Thailand: Agrarian Bases of State Power." In Hart et al., *Agrarian Transformations*, pp. 53–69
——, "Local Powers and Rural Differentiation." In Hart et al., *Agrarian Transformations*, pp. 70–97
UNIDO, *Thailand: Coping With the Strains of Success* (Vienna: Blackwell Publishers, for UNIDO, 1992)
US Department of Labor, *Labor Law and Practice in Thailand*, Bureau of Labor Statistics Report 405 (Washington, DC: US Government Printing Office, 1972)
US Department of State, *Annual Textile Report*, 1991, 1993
US Embassy, Bangkok, "Market Reports"
Unger, Danny, "Japan, the Overseas Chinese, and Industrialization in Thailand," PhD, University of California, Berkeley, 1989
Van Roy, Edward, "The 'Industrial Organization' of a Pre-Industrial Economy and some Development Implications," *Journal of Development Studies*, April 1971, pp. 19–27
Viksnins, George J., *Financial Deepening in ASEAN Countries* (Honolulu: University of Hawaii Press for the Pacific Forum, 1980)

Viseskul, Chintala, "Public Investment Policy During the Reign of Rama VI, 1910–25." Masters thesis, Thammasat University, 1976

Vongvipanond, Pairoj, *Finance in Thailand's Industrial Development Context.* Research Report No. 1A (Bangkok: Thai University Research Association, 1980)

Wade, Robert, "The role of government in overcoming market failure: Taiwan, the Republic of Korea, and Japan." In Hughes, *Achieving Industrialization in East Asia*, pp. 129–63

——, *Governing the Market: Economic Theory and the Role of Government in East Asian Industrialization* (Princeton University Press, 1990)

Warr, Peter G. (ed.), *The Thai Economy in Transition* (Cambridge University Press, 1993)

. Wichiencharoen, Adul, "Social values in Thailand," *Journal of Social Science Review*, 1(1) March 1976, pp. 125–31

Wijeyewardene, G., "Some Aspects of Rural Life in Thailand." In Silcock, *Thailand: Social and Economic Studies in Development*, pp. 65–84

Williamson, John, "Washington Consensus," *The Political Economcy of Policy Reform* (Washington, DC: Institute for International Economics, 1994)

Williamson, Oliver E., "The Economics of Organization: The Transaction Cost Approach," *American Journal of Sociology*, 87(3) 1981, pp. 548–77.

——, *The Economic Institutions of Capitalism: Firms, Markets, Relational Contracting* (New York: The Free Press, 1985)

Wilson, David A., *Politics in Thailand* (Ithaca: Cornell University Press, 1962)

Wit, Daniel, *Thailand: Another Vietnam?* (New York: Charles Scribner's Sons, 1968)

Wolf, Charles Jr., "The Limits of Trust," *National Interest*, 41, Fall 1995, pp. 95–8

World Bank, *Thailand, Managing Public Resources for Structural Adjustment* (Washington, DC: World Bank, 1984)

——, *World Development Report* (New York: Oxford University Press, 1988)

——, *World Development Report* (Washington, DC: World Bank, 1994)

——, *Atlas, 1996* (Baltimore:The Johns Hopkins University Press, 1996)

Wu, Yuan-Li, and Chun-hsi Wu, *Economic Development in Southeast Asia: the Chinese Dimension* (Stanford: Hoover Institution Press, 1980)

Wurfel, David, *Filipino Politics: Development and Decay* (Ithaca: Cornell University Press, 1988)

Xuto, Somsakdi, "The Bureaucracy." In Xuto (ed.), *Government and Politics in Thailand* (Singapore: Oxford University Press, 1987)

Yin, Hua Wu, *Class and Communalism in Malaysia: Politics in a Dependent Capitalist State* (London: Zed Books, 1983)

Yoshihara Kunio, *Japanese Investment in Thailand* (Honolulu: University Press of Hawaii, 1978)

——, "Indigenous entrepreneurs in the ASEAN countries," *Singapore Economic Review*, 29(2) October 1984

——, *The Rise of Ersatz Capitalism in South-East Asia* (Singapore: Oxford University Press, 1988)

——, "Oei Tiong Ham Concern: The First Business Empire of Southeast Asia," *Southeast Asian Studies*, 27(2) September 1989

——, "Culture, Institutions, and Economic Growth: A Comparative Study of Korea and Thailand." In *Tonan Ajia Kenkyu* (Southeast Asian Studies), 33(3) 1995, pp. 379–426

Yoshino, Michael, *Japan's Multinational Enterprises* (Cambridge, Mass.: Harvard
    University Press, 1976)
Young, Stephen B., "The Northeastern Thai Village: A Non-Participatory
    Democracy." In Neher, *Modern Thai Politics*, pp. 251–67
Yu, Chung-hsun, *Kakkyo Keizai No Kenkyu* (Research on the Overseas Chinese
    Economy) (Tokyo: Institute for Developing Economies, 1969)

Newspapers and journals

Asean Investor
Asia Week
Asian Finance
Bangkok Post Weekly Review
Bangkok Bank Monthly Review
Bangkok Post Year-end Review
Business in Thailand
Business Day
China Economic News Service
Daily News (in Thai)
Economist
Economist Intelligence Unit
Far Eastern Economic Review
Financial Times
International Herald Tribune
Japan Digest
Manager
Matichon
Nation
Siam Rath
Singapore Economic Review
Social Issues
South East Asia Monitor
Thansetakit
Washington Post

Interviews cited in the notes were conducted by the author.

Index